André Malraux and the
Metamorphosis of Death

ANDRÉ MALRAUX AND THE METAMORPHOSIS OF DEATH

Thomas Jefferson Kline

COLUMBIA UNIVERSITY PRESS
NEW YORK AND LONDON 1973

This study, prepared under the Graduate Faculties of Columbia University, was selected by a committee of those faculties to receive one of the Clarke F. Ansley awards given annually by Columbia University Press.

LIBRARY OF CONGRESS CATALOGING IN PUBLICATION DATA

Kline, Thomas Jefferson, 1942–
André Malraux and the metamorphosis of death.

Bibliography: p. [195]–197
1. Malraux, André, 1901–   I.   Title.
PQ2625.A716Z6865   843'.9'12   72-10817
ISBN 0-231-03608-6

For Sue and Lee

ACKNOWLEDGMENTS

I would like to thank Leon S. Roudiez for his constant encouragement and invaluable comments during labor and my wife, Kate, for her patient editorial midwifery. Bert M-P. Leefmans, Jeanne M. Ragner, and Vinio Rossi were kind enough to inspect the first version and suggest remedies. Richard S. McKinley has never seen this book but nonetheless had a hand in its making.

My sincerest thanks go also to Columbia University and the Columbia Alumni in France for supporting a year of research in Paris; to the Ansley Award Committee for making possible this publication; and to the Roswell Park Foundation of Buffalo for assistance in the preparation of the manuscript.

Grateful acknowledgment is made to the following publishers for their kind permission to reprint from the copyrighted works of André Malraux: to Random House, Inc., for excerpts from *The Royal Way, Man's Fate, The Temptation of the West,* and *Days of Wrath;* to Holt, Rinehart and Winston, Inc., for excerpts from *Anti-Memoirs,* translated by Terence Kilmartin, copyright © 1968 by Holt, Rinehart and Winston, Inc., and Hamish Hamilton Ltd.; to Phaidon Press Ltd., for excerpts from *Saturn;* to John Lehmann Ltd., for excerpts from *The Walnut Trees of Altenburg;* to Hamish Hamilton Ltd., for excerpts from *Days of Hope,* copyright © 1968 by André Malraux; and to Doubleday and Co., for excerpts from *The Voices of Silence.*

Finally, my thanks are due to Horizon Press, New York, for permission to reprint from Irving Howe's *Politics and the Novel,* copyright 1957; to Penguin Books Ltd., for permission to quote from Pascal's *Pensées,* translated by A. J. Krailsheimer, copyright © A. J. Krailsheimer, 1966; to Bernard Grasset, Editeur, for permission to reprint from Roger Stéphane's *Portrait de l'aventurier,* copyright Roger Stéphane, 1965; and to Editions du Seuil, for permission to reprint from Gaëtan Picon's *Malraux par lui-même.*

THOMAS JEFFERSON KLINE

State University of New York at Buffalo
August, 1972

CONTENTS

André Malraux and the
Metamorphosis of Death

Abbreviations

In the interest of clarity and concision I have employed the following abbreviations to designate Malraux's works. For further details the bibliography should be consulted.

A	*Antimémoires*
C	*Les Conquérants*
CH	*La Condition humaine*
E	*L'Espoir*
JE	*D'une jeunesse européenne*
LP	*Lunes en papier*
MD	*La Métamorphose des dieux*
NA	*Les Noyers de l'Altenburg*
RF	*Royaume farfelu*
TM	*Le Temps du mépris*
TO	*La Tentation de l'Occident*
VR	*La Voie royale*
VS	*Les Voix du silence*

Also in the interest of consistency, I have maintained these titles throughout, despite the use of English translations.

Following each passage of material cited from Malraux's works are to be found two page references. The first refers to the translation (see bibliography), the second to the original French edition.

METAPHOR AS A
RECTIFICATION OF THE WORLD

Suggestion is the highest technical perfection in art.
—TO, p. 65:113

André Malraux has several times ridiculed the notion that a writer envisions his complete works from their inception. His belief that artistic creation implies a long, often painful elaboration of an idea, problem, or obsession is fully borne out by his own works. Each of his novels represents one step in the evolution of an answer to man's anguished alienation from an absurd society within a meaningless universe.

Because of the development in his thinking from the pessimistic activism which drove his early heroes from escapism to revolution, toward a more optimistic reflection upon man's possible harmony with nature, many of Malraux's philosophical pronouncements often appear confused or contradictory when juxtaposed from chronologically disparate writings. Even when sequential, his statements occasionally prove vague, and often indicate an intuitive rather than a coldly rational stance at a particular moment. If, therefore, we are truly to understand Malraux's work and his philosophical development, the key must be furnished by a careful analysis of the subterranean or imagistic levels, rather than the explicit manifestations of his thought.

Unfortunately, most of Malraux's critics have failed to appreciate the importance of his gradual development. Some, enthusiastically championing particular points of view, completely ignore questions of chronology, piecing together, for example, statements or images from *La Voie royale* and *Les Noyers de l'Altenburg.* This irresponsible patchwork implies that Malraux had envisioned his entire evolution from the first written word in one sweeping visionary outpouring. Conversely, most critics conscious of the necessity of respecting chronological order have rarely taken into account the vital significance of tensive language as a mirror and elucidation of his development.

Thus Malraux's style has been the subject of few adequate studies. Most of the short articles devoted to his style deal with one particular and limited aspect. More often critics simply characterize Malraux's style erroneously and incompletely as being so imprecise as to defy any hope of elucidation, or so obscure as to defy logical order.

The time has come for a serious analysis of Malraux's style throughout his novelistic development. The present study is limited to metaphor, since any general stylistic analysis of all of Malraux's works would prove too ambitious for the scope of one work. The analysis of a single novel, on the other hand, would not permit the demonstration of any evolution. An analysis of metaphor alone seemed not only manageable but appropriate, given the generally accepted opinion that Malraux seldom relies upon logical argumentation.

The present study proposes, by analyzing Malraux's major image patterns, to demonstrate an increasing sophistication in his novelistic technique from *Les Conquérants* to *Les Noyers de l'Altenburg,* and, in so doing, to reveal fundamental changes in his attitude toward the human condition.

The novel has always been the battleground of two conflicting tendencies: an attempt on the one hand to capture the real through the description of sensuous impressions which compose our perception of life, and, on the other, a tendency to relate that life to larger abstractions, whether social or metaphysical. Irving Howe concludes that this conflict is inescapable: "The novel tries to confront experience in its immediacy and closeness, while ideology is by its nature general and inclusive." [1]

In his *Théorie du roman,* Georg Lukaćs proposed a more organic explanation of this conflict. Lukaćs defined the novel as a work centered on a problematic character, born of the conflict between the novelist's desire for unity and community in the world, and the alterity of that world.[2] Thus the novelist becomes conscious in the creative act of the necessity of opposing destiny with a construct of the ideal.[3] Grounded in the distance between the chaos of the concrete world and the protagonist's interiorized desire for a utopic unity,[4] the novel paradoxically fuses the mimesis of the heterogeneous and discontinuous elements of the concrete world with an organic unity,[5] an abstract system which is the ultimate base of the novel but which cannot be visible,[6] a mobile equilibrium between being and becoming.[7]

If the novel is a mimesis of chaos, then the necessary organizing factor must be introduced on a nonexplicit level.[8] It is the very nature of language, argues I. A. Richards, to arrive at just such an organizing factor through a "completion" of intuitions and sensations: words serve as "the occasion and the means of that growth which is the mind's endless endeavor to order itself," and their true function is "to restore life itself to order." [9]

Metaphoric language can be considered a hyperbole of the ordering process of language. Metaphor's constructive potential cannot be underestimated, for it not only renews language usually taken for granted but also juxtaposes and relates ordinarily disconnected phenomena. The more apparently incongruous the two objects of comparison, the greater the fundamental system of correspondences postulated beneath everyday experience. One of imagery's primary functions, therefore, is the "perpetual discovery of new relationships . . . and the rediscovery and renovation of old ones." [10]

Imagery implies another level of fundamental order. To the degree that the novelist resorts to his most private visions and obsessions to increase the scope of man's experience through the revelation of some personal and private truth, he may dredge up images from his unconscious. Whereas on the concrete level, the world appears totally contingent, Jung postulates a fundamental cohesion in the unconscious image-making process in *Archetypes of the Collective Unconscious:* [11] "The psyche contains all the images that have ever given rise to myths and . . . our unconscious is an acting and suffering subject with an inner drama which primitive man rediscovers, by means of analogy, in the processes of nature, both great and small." In other words, recourse to certain fundamental images shared by all men implicitly postulates an element of the unified community which the problematic hero is seeking.

In *Style in the French Novel,*[12] Stephen Ullmann suggests that literature which introduces new philosophical concepts often embodies a corresponding originality in the imagery. He claims, for example, that existentialism "unquestionably endowed Sartre with a new view of life, an original way of looking at the world," and that this new approach is "fully reflected in his imagery. Indeed, the image is one of the most effective means through which this vision is communicated in a concrete and artistic form." Ullmann implies that the regular occurrence of certain images will construct a unity of meaning as powerful as any explicit level of the work.

In a discussion of Malraux's *Antimémoires,* Michael Riffaterre generalizes this notion:

> A structure will generate symbols and filter reality whenever the reality described lends itself ever so little to a reorganization along the lines of the structure. Then, every time, the words used to describe that reality will change into a special vocabulary whose meaning will be regulated by the structure, not by the things depicted.[13]

This distillation of diffuse, isolated images into a coherent fabric constitutes a potent restructuring of experience. Such patterns (series of images whose common vehicle can be related to a single theme) [14] serve to orient the text, since the novelist's selection of comparisons disposes the reader's set of attitudes toward the action or ideas explicitly expressed. More than being simply rhythmic or repetitive elements, image patterns that develop from a personal concrete impression serve to unify by relating the specific sense impression to larger abstract themes.

Though the novel does not basically alter man's position in the universe, it can provide a successful confrontation with it. As C. Day Lewis has observed, "The image is a drawing-back from the actual, the better to come to grips with it: so every successful image is the sign of a successful encounter with the real." [15]

We are thus at the core of Malraux's own aesthetic theories.[16] In *Les Noyers de l'Altenburg*, Berger observes:

> Man knows the world is not on the human scale, and he wishes it were. And when he rebuilds it, it's on that scale that he does so. . . . our art seems to be a rectification of the world, a means of escaping from man's estate. . . . The mere fact of being able to represent it [fatality], conceive it, release it from real fate, from the merciless divine scale, reduces it to the human scale. Fundamentally, our art is a humanisation of the world. (*NA*, pp. 96–97:128)

Imagery implements this rectification both by relating man and the world to each other via the terms of metaphor, and by establishing image patterns which imply an essential continuity of man's existence.

Questions of style in both visual and literary art have always been of paramount importance to Malraux. Although his own works have been primarily viewed as vehicles for philosophical or political thought, Malraux is as conscious of the form of a work as he is of the content:

> It is not emotion that destroys a work of art, but the desire to demonstrate something; the value of such a work depends neither upon its emotion nor its detachment, but upon the blending of its content with the method of its expression. (*TM*, p. 5:9–10)

Indeed, in his study of Laclos, Malraux seems primarily concerned with means rather than ends: "Almost all fiction consists only in making others believe that an old dream has come true; the problem lies in the means the artist uses to make us believe it." [17]

In a passage which resembles Lukács's theories on the novel, Malraux proposes that these means are oriented around a search for internal coherence:

> The modern artist . . . is searching through form for an interior schema which may or may not subsequently take the form of objects, but in which the objects are only the means of expression. The first desire of the modern artist is to be able to submit everything to his style.[18]

Malraux, then, defines style as "a series of creations couched in a language peculiar to itself" (*VS*, p. 121:119) constituting an interior pattern, subsequently externalized through objects or specific *mises en scène.* Conscious of the role of private experience in such choices, he wrote in the margin of Picon's study, "I am convinced that the creative process of the novelist is linked to the nature of the past which inhabits or escapes him." [19] The crucial word "escapes" indicates that Malraux, despite an early disdain for Freud and the revelations of psychology, clearly admits the existence of an area of experience or consciousness which evades the grasp of the novelist, and yet which haunts him.

In *Les Voix du silence,* Malraux discusses the presence of both the conscious and the subconscious in the artist's deliberating process:

> A reason why men understand their experience so little is that they usually apprehend it by way of logic; they rationalize it. Art sometimes has recourse to a symbolical rendering of emotions that we know (a method involving logic); but sometimes to an irrational, vividly compulsive expression of feelings that we all can recognize. (*VS*, p. 221:219)

He not only recognizes the subconscious and oneiric in man, but claims for them a major role in artistic creation:

> We all know that other worlds besides the real world exist, but nothing is gained by relegating them indiscriminately to a dream world, where the word "dream" expresses at once the vagaries of sleep and satisfaction of desire. The world of art is fantastic in the sense that its elements are not those of reality; but its fantasy is intrinsic and fundamental, quite other than the wayward imaginings of the daydream. (*VS*, p. 312:310)

A later passage of *Les Voix du silence* suggests the degree to which every artist is fascinated by those forms that express the subconscious:

In Goya as in Goethe, Nerval and Baudelaire . . . there now became apparent a curiously persistent affinity between the obscure side of certain great works of art and the dark places of man's heart. (A circumstance regarding which psychoanalysis legitimately for once, may find much to say). . . . Though a surrender to the dark powers may tempt the artist as a man, figures expressing that uncharted world of unknown powers fascinate him, as an artist, by reason of the domination which they require. (*VS*, p. 590:588)

Yet, despite his gradual acceptance of the significance of the subconscious, Malraux firmly insists that, however fascinated, the artist never completely surrenders his conscious reason:

Like other men, and no more than they, the artist is conscious of the human tide bearing him up, but he is also conscious of the control he exercises on it, even if that control be only of its forms and colors. When instinctive artists arise in any human group, it means that they had the creative instinct to begin with. (*VS*, p. 306:304)

Elsewhere he adds: "Artistic creation does not spring from a surrender to the unconscious but from an ability to tap and canalize it" (*VS*, p. 306:304). This distinction between submission to the unconscious and control over it constitutes the basis of artistic creation. "All psychology, all experience derives from man seen as mystery. All mythology is a victory over this mystery." [20] This "power over men's dreams" (*VS*, p. 620:618) is the most significant step in the humanization of the world for its reduction of mystery to the scale of man, a principle fundamental to art.

In addition to stressing the role of the subconscious in artistic creation, Malraux acknowledges a collective subconscious of cultural archetypes upon which the artist may, indeed must, draw. He has suggested the relation between the irrational and the collective in metaphor:

It is precisely the genius of the poet to discover metaphors which inspire in the listener feelings related to, but not rational expressions of, his civilization. What interests us is precisely this discovery. It operates within "conditioning" but escapes it precisely to the degree that it is art.[21]

The "conditioning" of the poet's choices by his particular civilization and culture has also been noted by Malraux. I cite the following important passage at length, since it indicates the extent to which Malraux appears to have accepted Jung's theory of the collective unconscious:

> All poetry implies the destruction of the relationships between things which seem evident to us, in favor of special relationships imposed by the poet. His means of imposing these particular relationships is evidently metaphor. Obviously the domain of metaphor available to the poet can be circumscribed. . . . The system of metaphors in which the poet [of a particular civilization] expresses himself blends feelings and sensations in which [his particular culture] plays a large and valuable role. The metaphors of military civilizations are not the "rational" expression of military values. . . . Under the particular forms of civilizations, whose vast domains of metaphor are, after all, classifiable, there are in man eternal feelings; those born of the night, of the seasons, of death, of blood (the entire cosmic and biological domains). It is their permanence that we discover so clearly . . . in the Chinese as well as in modern men the minute the latter express feelings.[22]

The importance of this passage lies in Malraux's recognition that all poetry, and by extension all literary art, includes metaphors selected from a combination of the eternal and the specifically cultural consciousness of man. Malraux's insistence on the subconscious and its collective archetypes implies a belief that the artist may reveal as much through his choice of metaphor as through his rational and philosophical language.

Whether the creative process be rational or irrational, however, Malraux insists on metaphor's fundamental role in that part of the creative process which involves the "humanisation of the world." "No doubt all true poetry is irrational in the sense that it substitutes a new system of relations between things for the established order" (*VS*, p. 63:61). The necessity for a re-creation of the apparent world system into a new and personal order recurs consistently throughout Malraux's thought. As early as *La Voie royale,* Claude muses on the rela-

tionship of the artist and the world: "How he longed to wrench his
dreams (*arracher ses propres images*) clear of the inert world that
shackled them!" (*VR,* p. 44:54–55). In his marginal notes to Picon's book, Malraux specifically relates this idea to the novel:

> I don't believe it's true that the novelist should create *characters:* he
> should create a coherent and particular world, like any other artist.
> Rather than competing with the civic archives, he should compete
> with the reality around him, with "life," sometimes seeming to sub-
> mit to it, sometimes transforming it, in order to rival it.[23]

His preoccupation with this power of transformation extends into
Les Voix du silence: "The artist [should] never let himself be mastered by the outside world; always he subdues it to something he puts
in its stead. Indeed, this will to transform is inherent in his artistic
personality" (*VS,* p. 324:322).[24] Given both Malraux's belief that
metaphor allows the poet to impose his particular relationships on the
world, and his thoughts on the role of the transformation of reality in
art, metaphor emerges as one of the most critical factors in the creative act.

In the process of transforming the chaos of apparent reality into
the manageable universe of the poet, metaphor, Malraux suggests,
may fulfill still another function. In addition to suggesting, through
the relating of things seemingly disparate, an underlying system or
order, the metaphor contributes stylistic coherence through its repeti-
tion in patterns or schemata.[25] In a discussion of the plastic arts, Malraux reasons as follows:

> Every art purporting to represent involves a process of *reduction.*
> The painter reduces form to the two dimensions of his canvas; the
> sculptor reduces every movement, potential or portrayed, to immobil-
> ity. This reduction is the beginning of art. (*VS,* p. 275:273)

When applied to literature, it becomes apparent that this problem of
reduction is most commonly solved through the creation of patterns
or schemata which knit elements from the chaos of apparent reality
into a cohesive whole. As aesthetician, Malraux seems almost obsessed
by this idea of pattern:

Far from studying the visible world with a view to subjecting himself
to it, the true artist studies the world with a view to "filtering" it.
His first filter, once he has got past the stage of the pastiche, is the
schema or preconceived system, which simultaneously, if rather
roughly, filters both the world of visual experience and the pastiche
itself. (*VS,* p. 348:346)

In literature such schemata may occasionally dominate the narrative:

The poet is haunted by a voice with which his words must harmonize; the novelist is so strongly ruled by certain initial conceptions
that they sometimes completely change his story (to which, however,
they have not given rise). . . . A poor poet would he be who never
heard that inner voice; a poor novelist for whom the novel was no
more than a tale. (*VS,* p. 335:333)

These dominating patterns may dictate most of the novelist's choices,
even those usually attributed to chance;

"Favored" almost always by an encounter, a "contact" of some kind
—for which chance is only responsible in part. . . . These encounters with a special subject, a special architecture or a special color are
invited by the artist's "schema" and by the very act of creation, and
may be due to a conscious quest, a flash of insight, or occasionally to
mere chance. (*VS,* pp. 458, 460:456, 458)

Metaphor's rich suggestiveness avoids obvious and explicit statements of fact in favor of an intuition appropriate to the mysterious
nature of the *correspondances* underlying reality. "Suggestion," according to Malraux, "is the highest technical perfection in art" (*TO,*
p. 65:113).

An examination of the structures of Malraux's imagery in six novels will illustrate the critical part that metaphor, suggestion, and intuitive schemata actually play in the development of his thought.

THE IMPASSE OF
LES CONQUÉRANTS

He is always comparing things to death now.
—*C, p. 157:219*

Malraux telegraphs his subject in the electrifying first sentence of *Les Conquérants;* this, the first novel of proletarian revolution in the twentieth century,[1] begins with the announcement of a general strike. And yet, in the light of the rest of the work, the opening sentences seem to lead nowhere. Although the revolution remains the general context of the work, the reader witnesses nothing of it for at least one-third of the work, and when he does, he is allowed a view which is at best limited, and at worst "corroded by the excesses of individualism and aesthetic caprice." [2]

It soon, in fact, becomes evident that the novel focuses primarily on a single problematical character, Garine, in search of an authentic value or values.[3] There is a general and understandable tendency, given the revolutionary milieu of the novel and Garine's militant activities, to see the work in Marxist terms and to equate those sought-after authentic values solely with the Communist ideology. Lucien Goldmann, for example, despite an otherwise perceptive analysis of the work, commits this error.[4] Any claim that Marxism is the authentic value for Garine overlooks the entire metaphorical level of the work. As frequently in his later work, Malraux uses recurring series or patterns of metaphor to develop or refute a particular point of view. Two important metaphoric themes of *Les Conquérants* undermine and finally rule out Garine's possible adherence to a Marxist doctrine.

Early in the novel, as the narrator peruses Garine's dossier, he recalls his friend's youthful statement: "I am a-social just as I am a-theist and in the same way" [5] (p. 56:67). This claim establishes two important themes in Garine's thought: an inability to identify with a social group, and an equation between social and religious beliefs. The addition of "in the same way" to an otherwise explicit comparison places more emphasis on the similarities between the two dogmas than on the fact of Garine's refusal to believe in them. This statement also establishes the first of many parallels between the beliefs and requirements of the Communist Party and those of the Catholic Church.[6] Garine, who renounces only with great difficulty his strong individualism in favor of imposed doctrine and obedience to central authority, assesses the Party as being "like all these powerful doctrines . . . a freemasonry" [7] (p. 223), and other people in terms of their faith or submission to official doctrine. Of Borodine he observes in a separately published chapter of the novel, "He believes himself a Marxist like thousands of Frenchmen believe themselves to be Christians. . . . He is haunted by a feeling to which he attaches no importance." [8] And later he relates with heavy irony Borodine's "profession of faith":

> To have faith is to be tied to principles. For him, it's precisely to the principles that he is no longer tied. One day he replied to a journalist who told him people were accusing him of spreading Soviet propaganda: "What are the Christian missionaries doing here? They are spreading a doctrine that they hold above all worldly things and for which they are ready to give their lives, right? Well then, so am I." [9]

However little Borodine himself accepts the faith, he nonetheless labels deviation from official thoughts as "sacrilege." [10] It is to prevent such sacrilege and to convert the ignorant "heathen" that the Party has sent its missionaries, of whom Borodine is one, according to Garine's characterization of him:

In all the old "Bolsheviks" there is something of the founders of religious orders. Those old men founded their monasteries, then converted their pagans: converting and organizing were linked for them; moreover, no organization seemed comparable to their own.[11]

Borodine's character contains an undeniable element of the missionary, but an even more powerful suggestion of the crusader. Years of struggle have substituted a Machiavellian dedication to efficacy for his faith in Marxist doctrine. "Didn't certain knights of the military orders end up by substituting for Christianity Christian combat?" muses Garine,[12] who concludes of Borodine:

He is living in an apocalypse. . . . I am thinking of the first Christians who saw in the Empire what should disappear but not what should reappear in the Church. Of course, that was their role, and apocalypses can be very effective: but still one must accept them as such.[13]

Given this mistrust of Party doctrine and organization, both Garine and the narrator see Party regulars in terms of their Catholic counterparts.[14] Nicolaieff's calm expression and "the unction of his attitude suggest some venerable priest" (p. 80:104). He is later again described as having "a pontifical manner (*Sa voix de prêtre*)" (p. 128:176).

At the meetings of representatives of the striking dock workers, the narrator notes that the cries of the crowd resound "like a refrain (*comme des repons de litanies*)" (p. 121:163).[15]

In addition to similarities between the faith and obedience of Party and Church, Garine detects resemblances in the gospel expounded by each:

All Asia is entering on a phase of individualism and discovering death. . . . When lepers ceased to believe in God they poisoned the wells. Any man who has cut himself adrift from the old Chinese life, from its rites and its vague beliefs, and who rebels against Christianity, is a good revolutionary. . . . Was it not in some such impulse as this, in a desire to attain to some distinct individual life in the eyes of God, that the strength of Christianity lay? (p. 91:120–21)

According to Garine, the gospel inculcated by both institutions aims to instill in the Oriental, so long accustomed to considering himself only part of a larger whole,[16] a sense of himself as an individual.[17] The original Christian missionaries, exploiting the extreme frustration of the poor, developed in them a new sense of self which was carefully diverted from potential revolt to humility. The Party deliberately and paradoxically built on this nascent sense of individuality, but directed the poor away from the abstract concept of sin to a concrete class consciousness.[18] The result is evidently the substitution of one dogma for another; in Garine's eyes, any rigid doctrine tends to stagnate and atrophy, producing nonthinking lip-service on the part of its communicants.

Through these many Party-Church comparisons Garine sketches a caustic and highly individualistic view of the Party.[19] Although he is unable as a member of the Canton Revolutionary Committee to attack the Party directly, his imagistic descriptions of Borodine reveal his underlying contempt for the Party's rigidity and authoritarian centralization. Garine's participation in social revolution results, then, not from a willingness to submit to the rigid ideology and discipline of the Party but from some other concern.

One might be tempted to conclude that Garine's energy and apparent devotion to his work, if not motivated by orthodox Communism, must arise instead from a genuine but unorthodox desire for social change. Again we must recall, however, Garine's equation of his social commitment and atheism. His social skepticism stems on the explicit level from his experience with "justice"; but the depth and permanence of his feeling are more convincingly conveyed through a pattern of images which conveys the farce of social behavior. This pattern is most clearly exposed in Garine's own recollections of his trial for subsidizing abortion.

The court inspires in Garine an almost macabre fascination: the judge, "an automaton, who was but a second-rate dialectician" (p. 54:65), distorts the facts into a "kind of judicial allegory" (p. 54:65).

The mechanical, automatic, and blind functioning of the tribunal renders the dispensation of justice wholly ritualistic:

> The idea that they might not be able to understand the case evidently did not trouble them. . . . all convinced Pierre that there was practically no connection between the actual facts and the ceremony going forward. . . . The attempts of the judge and the leading counsel to bring this succession of events home to the jury in the terms of an ordinary crime, seemed to him *so completely a parody that he could hardly help laughing.* (p. 55:65-66; italics mine)

Pierre concludes: "Any passing of judgment implies a failure to comprehend" (p. 55:66).

This disparity between the tribunal's fundamental ignorance and the camouflaging ritual impresses Garine with an overpowering sensation of absurdity: "Pierre fell into that state of exasperated powerlessness, contempt and disgust which any gathering of fanatics or any great demonstration of human foolishness (*absurdité*) will produce" (p. 55: 66).

Malraux had demonstrated in *La Tentation de l'Occident* that the experience of the absurd arises from a meditation on man's inability to judge his own acts.[20] Here the absurd springs from the realization that man cannot judge others, and that any attempt to do so can be founded only on ignorance. Yet, realizing that just such ignorance has placed his liberty at stake, Garine adopts a thoroughly anti-Marxist position of "social atheism": "I do not consider society bad, in the light of being capable of improvement; but I consider it futile (*absurde*). That is a very different matter" (p. 56:67).

The dimensions of such a farce can be transmitted only through a vocabulary derived from the theater. The reader's attitude toward the proceedings is deliberately manipulated by the phrase "the absurdity (*grotesque*) of bringing such matters into court amazed him" (p. 54:64). "He told me later," reports the narrator, "that the proceedings throughout seemed to him unreal (*un spectacle irréel*), with the unreality not of a dream but *of some strange comedy,* something rather ignoble and quite beside the point (*tout à fait lunaire*)" [21] (pp. 54–55:65). Explicitly reinforcing the novelist's recourse to the language of the theater, the narrator reflects: "Outside the theater, stage conventions are only to be found in law courts" (p.55:65). Garine can only view the trial as a "ceremony" in which "the conduct (*le jeu*) of the defense intrigued him" (p. 55:66).

The proceedings force Garine himself into a role:

> He [Garine] found his super's part (*son rôle de comparse*) extremely irritating. He seemed to be a lay figure acting some drama, utterly wrong psychologically, but appealing to a stupid house. Sick and jaded, with an impatience mingled with resignation, having lost even the wish to tell these people that they were mistaken, he awaited the end of the play, which would also end his ordeal. (p.55:66)

Yet the sinister dimensions of this play-acting had to be taken seriously; "this empty comedy might end in his being condemned to this vegetable life (*cette vie humiliante et larvaire*) for some indefinite period" (p. 56:67).

An earlier sadistic parody of social conventions had forced Garine to recognize the absurd. He had witnessed the mock marriage and subsequent rape of a young soldier while taking shelter in a church during the war. The sadists had carefully arranged all aspects of scenery, lighting, and costumes; the passage [22] (Ed. G. pp. 213–14) teems with words denoting a theatrical or carnival situation: "cortège," "killing game," "grotesques," "characters," "carnival ladies," etc. Garine conclueds:

> I have been obsessed by that for some time. . . . Not because of the outcome of the action, of course; but because of its absurd and parodied beginning. . . . It is not unrelated, moreover, to the impressions I felt during the trial. (Ed. G. p. 214; translation mine)

Both "wedding" and trial profoundly mark Garine; each shelters the basic inequality, ignorance, and cruelty in man behind the convenient screen of accepted conventions. Ignorant and sadistic, the soldiers can

cruelly violate an individual within the context of the rituals of the
marriage act. Equally ignorant and prejudiced, the judges can carry
out their hatred of Garine according to socially prescribed and acceptable rites.

The trial so convinces Garine of the ritualistic falsehood of all aspects of Western society that he is driven to equate war with a spectacle, its combatants with actors, and the noncombatants with mere
spectators (p. 56:68). In Canton, where his revolutionary commitment at first suggests a reversal of his earlier "social atheism," Garine
conceives instinctively of his position in the Chinese struggle as a
"leader's part that he was playing" (p. 63:78). The perceptive Gerard
considers Garine as one of those who came to China

> to take their chances and risk their lives (*jouer leur vie*) and who
> were adventurers. For them the evolution of China was a *drama*, in
> which they were more or less involved. They were people who had
> never been able to accept social conditions, who made great demands
> on life, who wanted to give a meaning to their existence. (pp.
> 17–18:22; italics mine)

Disillusioned by both Socialists and Anarchists in Canton, Garine
views their professed dedication to the betterment of mankind as a
mere "parody" (p. 52:62).

For "the others" power simply consists of a role assumed to gain
material advantage or consideration. Thus Garine, arriving in Canton, views the Propaganda Office he is to direct as "a caricature . . .
more or less of a comic opera" (p. 62:76) and Canton itself as a
"comic opera republic" (p. 171:241). Judging both friends and enemies for the extent that they engage in role-playing, Garine notes
that Tcheng-Dai had refused to assume the presidency of the young
republic because "the part (*rôle*) of arbitrator seemed to accord with
his character better than any other" (p. 76:98). Having become the
symbolic, if ineffective, leader of the oppressed Chinese, Tcheng "unconsciously, of course, arrived at the position of preferring that role to
the victory of those whom he is defending" (p. 76:98). Garine concludes, "A noble figure of a victim preparing his own biography" (p.

77:99). Tcheng-Dai's saintly "contempt for temporal things . . . becomes (*par une subtile comédie*) the center of his whole being" (p. 77:100). Rebecci is described as "a withered little man . . . a regular Guignol figure" [23] (p. 30:39). Even Borodine is characterized as one who "is playing at representing the proletariat here as best he can" [24](Ed. G. p. 226).

The pattern of concealment imagery, mask, and theater decisively evaluates Garine's social commitment. His two major disillusionments, the trial and mock marriage, as well as numerous other comparisons throughout the novel, present society as a complex ritual dedicated to disguising man's natural cruelty to man by formalizing his savagery into acceptable contexts.[25] Those like Borodine who justify their actions in terms of the necessities of their roles effectively abdicate human responsibility. Since Garine regards this masking of man's innate antisocial nature as the paradoxical premise on which society is erected, he posits its fundamental absurdity and exclaims:

> The possibility of reforming society is a question which does not interest me. It is not the absence of justice from society that strikes me, but something deeper; my incapacity for adhering to any social order whatever. I know I shall be up against society all my life, and that I shall never be able to enter it without being false to my inner self. (p. 56:67–68)

Such a rigorous statement—one which the theater imagery throughout carefully sustains—leaves little doubt that no socially prescribed value, certainly not Marxism, is authentic for Garine.

Garine's pessimistic indictment of society can condone only a philosophy based on the deliberate and calculated exercise of "power for its own sake" (p. 53:63). Unrelated to any desire for either wealth or prestige, this drive for power sustains Garine by constantly pitting him against the submissive ones and by obliging him to live every moment as if it were his last. Undeterred by dangers, "he determined to dedicate his whole life to it [power], accepting all the risks that it involved" (p. 53:63). This life style of considered risk aligns Garine with Perken (of *La Voie royale*); both gamble and frequently resort to gambling imagery. Having opted for the exercise of power, Garine "was prepared to risk everything (*se jouer*). He realized that death can put an end to any situation; and, being very young, he had no fear of death. As for anything that was to be won, he had no clear idea of that as yet" (p. 53:63). At this point in his life, Garine views his choices in Pascalian terms; not to gamble is passively to submit both to the control of an absurd society and to the inevitable process of aging. To gamble on a life of action, then, means to live; abstention signifies submission.

Given Garine's readiness to gamble his life on the successful exercise of power, one is not surprised that he gambles in the more limited sense of the word: "Loses his fortune in various financial speculations," reads his dossier; the narrator observes, "He was always a gambler" (p. 57:69).[26]

He had burned to participate in the Russian Revolution though the Party had ignored him. Anguished at the waste of his youth and energies, he exclaimed:

> If I say that I consider my youth is the card to play, then they seem to regard me as a poor visionary. But this is the game I am playing, believe me, just such a game as any poor wretch at Monte Carlo plays, a game, after which he will kill himself, if he loses. If I could cheat, I would. . . . In staking one's life one can make no mistake. That is clear, though to fix one's mind on one's own destiny might appear less wise than to center it on one's daily cares, one's dreams and one's hopes. (p. 58:70–71)

Once again Garine relies on gambling to suggest his willingness to die young for an active participation that will give his life meaning and furnish an escape from submission to social conformity. His every act is a calculated gamble whose stakes are death. Any situation unrelated to the exercise of this wager thus leaves Garine apathetic: "When what he regards as most important is not at stake (*en jeu*), Garine is rather flabby" (p. 129:176).

Garine's choice of the Orient throws significant light upon his gambling. The theater of revolution in Canton obviously offers high

stakes and few restrictions on Garine, who had abandoned Europe
since "it seemed absurd to stake his life on a card so sordid, so ridiculous, on a card that he himself had not chosen" (p. 54:65). We know,
however, that the voyage to the East in Malraux's universe signals a
quest for self-knowledge and self-definition: [27] "How can I find myself, except in an examination of your race?" (*TO,* pp. 39–40:70).

Garine's gamble on action, then, must be seen not merely as a refusal to submit, but rather as the only form of self-definition open to
him, the only possibility, in fact, of defining man.

Even when he finally realizes that he will have to abandon the
struggle in Canton, he maintains his will to gamble and insists on his
permanent willingness to accept the stakes:

> If I readily threw in my lot with the Revolution it was because its
> results are remote and uncertain. At bottom I am a gambler; and,
> like all gamblers, my whole mind is concentrated on my play. Today
> I am playing for bigger stakes than in the past; I have learned how
> to gamble; but it is still the same game. . . . Another thing I have
> learned is that though a life is worth nothing, there is nothing that is
> worth so much as a life. (p. 155:216)

Nowhere in Malraux's work do we find such a strong link between
the notion of action for its own sake (as suggested by the gambler
image) and the definition of life itself ("une vie ne vaut rien, mais
rien ne vaut une vie"). For Garine, then, the entire meaning of life
and the definition of man lie in *action as a process.* He senses, however, the impossibility of sustaining the active process indefinitely (i.e.,
beyond death) and recognizes the necessity of including in his definition of life-as-action the notion of results: "It is not so much the soul
of a man that makes a leader . . . but his achievements (*la conquête*)
. . . Unfortunately" (p. 53:63). The "unfortunately" admits that action cannot exist independently of results and that action leading to
defeat may vitiate the entire system. Garine translates this problem
into a gambling image: "When one gambles, one must run the risk of
losing" (p. 152:211). Ideally, then, a definition of man should remain
at the level of a potentiality which inspires Garine's favorite image:

If . . . he ever dreamed of power, it was in a manner almost physical . . . with a tension of his whole being, like that (*l'image ridicule*) of a beast preparing to pounce upon his prey; and this led him to regard the actual exercise of power as a kind of relief, a deliverance. (p. 53:63)

The possibility of action thus becomes preferable to action itself; a system whose sole value is action cannot embrace completed action. On the other hand, the mere possibility of action remains without real value (hence the adjective "ridicule"), so Garine is caught in a philosophical trap. We can understand much better, then, when Garine pessimistically notes: "Whether one lives in one absurd world or another . . . there can be no strength, there cannot even be any *real life* without the conviction, without the obsession of the futility of everything" (p. 162:229). And the narrator explains:

I know that for him the true meaning of life resides in that idea, that the strength of his personality lies in this profound conviction of the vanity of things; that if the world is not absurd, then his whole life has been wasted in vain gestures, vain not with that fundamental vanity which exalts, but with the vanity which drives one to despair. (pp. 162–63:229)

This impasse, although suggested explicitly, is fully developed only through a series of metaphors of sickness. Aware of the possibility of losing both the ability and the will to fight, Garine is compelled to acknowledge the insurmountable odds against aging and death, an integral part of life itself, a step toward an inevitable death: "Disease, old chap, ah! no one who is not ill can have any idea of it. They think it something that can be striven against, something outside oneself. They are wrong: disease becomes one's very self" (p. 119:161).

This awareness leads Garine gradually to relinquish his original total involvement in action. The narrator notes: "Ever since that evening when I saw him in the hospital, he has seemed to be something apart from his own conduct; his deeds are drifting away from him with his health and his hold on life. . . . He is always comparing things to death now" (p. 157:218–19). Garine's increasing preoccu-

pation with his sickness parallels the growing awareness that the end
of his active involvement in China will remove any real significance
from his life.[28] Garine's awareness of these destructive forces *within*
parallels a growing sense of absurdity, since sickness produces that inaction which, as Pascal saw, inevitably provokes despair about the
human condition.[29] In this light, sickness assumes a symbolic significance in the novel.[30] Garine's delirium provides a turning point in
both his physical deterioration and his metaphysical despair. Against
the droning of the insects swarming around the light bulbs, he cries
out:

> It is strange. But after my trial I was obsessed by the vanity of life
> and of humanity as a whole. It seemed a prey to *absurd* forces. Now
> this obsession recurs. . . . It is idiotic, of course, and comes from my
> illness. Yet it seems to me that in doing what I am doing here I am
> struggling against this vanity (*l'absurde*) of life. . . . And that it
> (*l'absurde*) is reasserting its rights. (p. 125:169)

Illness reevokes the absurdity of his trial. Whereas the meaningless
judicial rites had nearly stripped Garine of his liberty of action, sickness threatens his liberty both through physical incapacitation and
through the emotional paralysis accompanying an awareness of mortality.[31] In a moment of profound despair, Garine underscores the metaphysical weight of the sickness metaphor: "Suffering merely intensifies life's futility (*absurdité*), rendering it despicable" (p. 163:230).

Perceiving its symbolic value, Garine uses the metaphor of sickness to describe others who have made a futile leap to action in the
face of metaphysical despair.

Although he is forced ultimately to eliminate Hong, Garine senses
in the young terrorist a desperate imperative to action identical to,
although perhaps more furious than, his own. His resort to the
metaphor of sickness communicates the strength of their existential
bond: "Hong regards his life in much the same way as might a con-
sumptive who knows there is no hope and yet feels in full vigor"
(p. 115:156).

Aware of Borodine's involvement despite loss of principles, Garine understands his comrade's overriding and unorthodox quest for personal satisfaction as yet another parallel to his own malady:

> It is in order to be able to continue his action that he is gambling his life, not for any future result. He doesn't just want doctrine propagated, he wants to make sure that it will be propagated by himself. And when I say he wants to make sure, I am understating the case: he needs this, it is necessary, even indispensable for him. . . . He has it in his blood like a poison.[32]

As with Garine, Borodine's gamble on personal rather than collective achievement forces upon him an existential awareness and anguish. This impasse makes him metaphorically, then actually, sick, substantiating Garine's predictions.

Unable to subscribe to social values, forced to gamble on the value of pure action yet already disabled by the realization of the poverty of that wager, Garine remains a problematic character in search of an authentic value which does not exist in the form he desires. Malraux finalizes this pessimistic orientation through another system of images whose recurrence in scenes of tension constantly overshadows Garine's actions with doom.

The insect has from Malraux's earliest writing evoked the obsession with, and anguish of, death and the absurd. One has only to recall death described in *Lunes en papier* as "a huge insect" and, in *Royaume farfelu,* the lines of the damned stretching "like ants" across the desert or the deadly ultimate invasion of scorpions.[33] These early obsessive metaphors of death recur vividly in *Les Conquérants.* Indeed, the deeper the narrator penetrates into the Oriental world, the more often he encounters the sinister, emotionless insect.[34]

Malraux obliquely suggested the importance of insect imagery in an article written shortly after the publication of *Les Conquérants.* "The true life which animates the metempsychosis of the enormous insect of China is the battle of various ideas against dark forces." [35] A reference to the growing restlessness of the Chinese too long submissive to the "dark forces" of Western economic imperialism recurs imagistically with remarkable consistency in the novel.

Walking through a popular quarter in Hong Kong, the narrator senses the "passive resistance of three hundred thousand Chinese, who are determined that they will no longer submit" (p. 35:45). In the midst of such hostility, the shop signs hang ominously: " . . . in this kind of blind alley one is surrounded by Chinese characters of all sizes, black, red, gold, inscribed on tablets, or over doors or hanging out in squares against the sky; they seem to surround one like a swarm of insects" (p. 35:44).

In addition to suggesting the alien qualities of the Orient (e.g., "the cloud of locusts surrounding Tcheng-Dai" [p. 85:111]), insects invite analogies with the devaluation of human life in an overcrowded society which consistently denies individuality (e.g., "twenty cadets have descended like a cloud of flies upon our two motorcars" [p. 102:136]).

The insect's presence is communicated partly by a number of powerful metaphors but more often through the use of the objective correlative, a series of descriptions of insects which, owing to their presence in scenes saturated with the menace of death, take on the weight of symbols.

Leaving Hong Kong by night, the narrator contemplates the darkened city whose light has, significantly, been extinguished by the strikers. The city disappears into obscurity "as night approaches, . . . swarming with mosquitoes, just as it did three thousand years ago" (p. 47:55). The narrator later talks with Klein, whose hatred of the bourgeoisie is twice reinforced stylistically by the leitmotif of the insect. As the Belgian's tired voice drones on, enumerating the acts of terror committed by the ruling class, "his voice is flat, sounding almost hoarse through the buzz of mosquitoes" (p. 48:57). Haunted by the dead he had seen in Munich and Odessa, he falls silent and his body droops almost lifeless. "Denser and denser grow the clouds of mosquitoes and other insects, swarming round the veiled lights on deck" (p. 49:59). Every time Klein's rage at class inequality elicits memories of the dead, the novelist's camera focuses on insects, usually on their submissive and fatal attraction to light.[36]

Three other scenes interweave the disquieting presence of death with insects, which become more ominous with each reappearance. Borodine warns Garine, Klein, and the narrator that, in the face of growing terrorism, "We shall be among the first." As he leaves, the narrator notices that "there is a large black mark (*large tache noire*) on the wall, the reflection of a big moth which has flown on to the electric light bulb" (p. 118:160). Not only does this disquieting spectacle hauntingly suggest the shadow of death,[37] it also prefigures the crushed dark forms of the mutilated Klein and his co-workers "stiff already . . . leaning against the wall, like posts," with "great black splotches (*grandes taches noires*) of congealed blood . . . a large mark in the middle of the face: the mouth has been slit by a razor" (p. 148:204).[38] When Klein is discovered, flies carry the psychological impact of death to overpower the narrator:

> One of the flies, buzzing round, has alighted on my forehead; and I cannot raise my arm to brush it away (*je ne peux pas, je ne peux pas lever mon bras*). . . . His voice rouses me; and with an awkward, swift and violent movement I brush away the fly. . . . Flies buzzing round her head. Such a smell! (pp. 148–49:205)

The three references to flies depict a narrator involuntarily paralyzed by the presence of death, and whose maladroit attempt to shake off the hovering pests is powerless against the pervading aura of decay and futility.

Just as they appeared to devour Klein's corpse, "the eternal mosquitoes buzzing outside" threaten Garine, feverish and helpless in his hospital bed (p. 124:168). The hospital, like the battlefield, constitutes an appropriate backdrop for reflections on man's mortality: "The lamps in the room and passage, veiled by clouds of insects, burn, burn as if they would burn forever. . . . this hospital where the only living things seem to be the swarms of insects buzzing round the lamps" (p. 125:169). The insects supersede the patients, dehumanize the hospital, their furious hum around the lights insistently recalling man's submission to destiny.[39]

Insects play their most forceful symbolic role, however, during Garine's questioning of the suspected saboteurs. The aura of death hangs portentously over the entire scene.

Not only do hundreds of lives depend on the success of Garine's investigation, but both judge and spies are themselves already doomed: Garine by the tropical disease and political deviations which will signal the end of his career; the spies by Garine's short temper. The presence of May flies (significantly *éphémères* in the French) several times in the text reinforces the sense of immanent and inevitable death. As Garine obstinately confronts the mute defiance of the two suspects, "Nicolaieff, utterly worn out, gazes at the lamp round which clouds of insects (*éphémères*) are buzzing" (p. 167:235). After Garine executes the first spy, terrifying the second into confessing, "Nicolaieff blows the dead bodies of insects off the paper on which he is writing" (p. 168:236). The parallel between insects and spies is underscored by the second man's collapse "flapping his arms (*les bras en ailerons*)" (p. 168:237). Learning of the possibility of additional sabotage, Garine sets off to hunt down the third agent, leaving Nicolaieff "absorbed in brushing away the dead insects which are still falling on to the desk" (p. 169:238). This last reference to the dying insects suggests once again the futility of this acceleration of Garine's activity in the context of his imminent departure.

The frustration conveyed by the submissive clustering of the May flies is heightened by two other powerful images. The first compares Garine's frustrations to those of Lenin himself. Feverish from both the sickness destroying his body and the fury at being relieved of his duties, Garine tells the narrator:

> "Service is what I have always hated. . . . And yet who has served more and better than I? For years, many years, a craving for power has obsessed me; and yet I have not even been able to invest my own life with it. . . . You know that Lenin had written an article in defense of Trotsky, which was to appear in—*The Pravda,* I think.

. . . In the morning [his wife] brought him the newspapers: he could hardly move. 'Open it,' he said. His article was not there. His voice became so confused that no one could understand what he said. He was looking so intently that everyone followed the direction of his glance and it fixed on his left hand. It lay flat and open, like that, on the sheet. He wanted to take up the paper but could not. . . .

"Then he opened his right hand with a jerk, stretched out his fingers, and, while he was speaking, slowly bent his fingers and looked at them.

"While his right hand was still, the left began to close its fingers, like a spider folding its tentacles. . . .

"He died soon afterwards." (p. 151:208–9)

This critical image not only reiterates the previously postulated relationship between the insect and frustration but also reequates the spider with the advent of death. It expresses both the inevitable destiny of man ("He died soon afterwards") and the visceral experience of all that is the Other. In *La Voie royale*, Perken's hand, as he loses his hold on life, will become

. . . something apart, something quite independent of him. At rest now on his thigh, his hand was gazing up at him. . . . white thing . . . with its fingers higher than the heavy palm, its nails clawing the threads of the trouser-seam, somehow recalled the spiders hooked to their webs in the warm leafage; like the spiders dangling in the viscid undergrowth, it hung poised before his fascinated eyes. . . . And that hand was—death. (*VR*, pp. 244–45:262–63)

Just as this hand accompanies Perken's growing visceral awareness of death, so Lenin's hand symbolizes both the dreadful realization that he is powerless to impose his will on others and the physical experience of the separation and strangeness of his physical being as he approaches death.[40]

Garine will finally exit a defeated man—yet overcome not by the enemies of the revolution, nor even by the opposition within the Comintern. Malraux wrote of his protagonist shortly after publication of the novel: "Obviously one must first conquer, but it remains to be seen whether, once victory is obtained, man will not find himself once again face to face with death, and, what is even more serious, perhaps, face to face with the death of those he loves." [41] It is precisely this moment of victory that is unthinkable for Garine; at the termination of life-defining action one is left face to face with his own mortality, so powerfully rendered by the metaphors of sickness and the insect.

"Opposed to society to the extent that it is the *form* of life," [42] the adventurer is thus, by nature, a problematical character. "Engaged in action in order to escape solitude," writes Sartre, "the adventurer finds himself more isolated than ever." [43] Setting out to discover the best possible life, he is forced to redirect his quest toward the best possible death. His life becomes a heroic but inadmissible suicide, for which the most plausible pretext lies in social action. The more he realizes the vanity of action without conviction, the more he begins to live for death:

> The moment of death will be the zenith of his life; he awaits it with ecstasy. . . . In this infinitesimal instant, still living and yet already dead, he will feel himself becoming for others what he was for himself. . . . Living for death and dying to live, convinced of the vanity of action and simultaneously of its necessity, attempting to justify his enterprise in assigning it a goal in which he never believed, searching for a total objectivity of result in order to dilute it in an absolute subjectivity, wishing to build his life as a destiny and yet enjoying only the infinitesimal moments which separate life from death, maintaining incompatible elements in and for himself, the adventurer exists in and for this impossibility.[44]

Concurring with this judgment of Sartre's, Malraux writes succinctly of Garine, "Triumph kills him." [45]

In another discussion of Garine, Malraux concluded:

> The fundamental question for Garine is much less how to participate in revolution than how to escape what he calls the absurd. The whole of *Les Conquérants* is a perpetual quest, and I have moreover insisted on the phrase: to escape the idea of the absurd by seeking refuge in what is human.[46]

But Garine is unable to escape; one does not evade the absurd by flight into or away from the human, but through other means which

Malraux would make the subject of five subsequent novels. Indeed, perhaps the most tragic aspect of the novel is not Garine's solitude but the proximity of the one authentic response to the absurd: "You may live believing in the vanity (*l'absurde*) of all things, but you cannot live in that vanity. . . . You cannot escape it, but neither can you find it if you set out to do so [says Garine]. . . . The only way is to create" (p. 164:230–31). But Garine is unable to dissociate the creative act from what is created, and, plunging once again into despair, cries, "Whether anything can last! Is that the question?" ("La durée—Il s'agit bien de cela") (p. 164:231). *For Garine,* creativity could provide a valid response to the world's absurdity *only if man could defy death long enough to witness the impact of his creation.* Thus this glimpse of what otherwise might constitute authenticity is buried beneath the fact of mortality and the imperative of action.

Finally, Malraux indicates some fundamental confusion about his own creation:

> The level on which Garine interests me . . . is simply the human level. . . . In Garine there remain . . . fundamental feelings which are the test, in my eyes, of the greatness of man, in particular the brotherhood of arms, and virile fraternity. Moreover, Garine represents to a high degree the tragic sense of human solitude which scarely exists for the Orthodox Communist.[47]

Is it not a contradiction to suggest that Garine enjoys "the brotherhood of arms and virile fraternity" while simultaneously suffering from "the tragic sense of human solitude"? It is more valid to recognize Garine as the expression of a basic duality in Malraux's philosophy which would continue to be explored in the subsequent novels. In *La Voie royale,* Malraux would extract his protagonist from the milieu of virile fraternity and revolution against which the hero's individualism (and the entire metaphorical level of *Les Conquérants*) had reacted, and place him deep in the forests of Cambodia to encounter the problems of man outside of society.

THE ROYAL WAY
TO THE SELF

Nothing definite, nothing that allows us to define
ourselves; only a sort of latent power.
—TO, p. 52:91

"Now Claude's obsession mastered him again and he gazed fixedly at the man's shadowed face, straining to get at last some inkling of its expression, against the glow of a ship's lamp behind it (*dans le pénombre*)" (p. 3:11).

The first sentence of *La Voie royale* presents the reader with Claude's difficulty in seeing another man in language which suggests a generalization of the particular problem. The temporal terms "now," "again," and "at last" (*enfin*) imply that this attempt to perceive another is neither sudden nor unfamiliar. The terms "obsession," "fixedly" (*opiniâtrement*), and "straining" convey in turn an intensity of feeling disproportionate to the problem of immediate visual limitation. The evocation of an embattled obsession without prior reference to its object accentuates the importance of that object, "the man (*cet homme*)." This combination of demonstrative (specific) adjective and generic (unspecific) noun deliberately tantalizes the reader, further engaging him in the larger frustration of knowing another person.

It is no artistic accident that, between two men concerned with knowing another, the topic of conversation should be eroticism, which, as Perken explains, is intimately related to knowledge of others—and of oneself:

A man who's still young can make little or nothing of—what's the word for it?—of eroticism. . . . So long as he can't see a woman simply as a vehicle of sex, but takes her sexual function as a mere incidental adjunct of her womanhood, he's all for sentimental love— poor devil! (p. 4:12)

Perken complements his initial distinction between love (which acknowledges the partner as a person) and eroticism [1] (which reduces the partner to a function) with two notions which will become fundamental to his particular eroticism: the "frenzied desire . . . to flay [one's] senses to satiety" (p. 4:12), and imagination: "Memories. . . . They're always taking new shapes. . . . What a queer thing imagination is! Like a foreign body lodged inside us, yet a part of ourselves for all that" (p. 4:12).

The initial movement from the immediate problem of perception to the general problem of cognition both introduces and parallels the transition from the discussion of eroticism as a purely sexual phenomenon to notions of self-testing and self-knowledge. The author makes perfectly clear in the first two pages that La Voie royale must be read on more than the single level of an adventure story. Claude's and Perken's search for lost art treasures may indeed symbolize the "frenzied desire . . . to flay [one's] senses to satiety," and represent the quest for far more than the explicit goal.

Indeed, eroticism as related to self-knowledge, far from a passing concern of the adventurer, permeates the first section of the novel.[2] Interpreting Claude's memories of perversion in a Paris brothel, Perken observes: "The great thing (l'essentiel) is—not to know the woman (la partenaire). She must stand for the opposite sex, no more than that" (p. 7:15). And to Claude's question, "Not to be an individual, you mean, with a life of her own?" Perken replies:

"And that's even truer for the masochists. It's with themselves they're fighting. A man ekes out his imagination as best he can, not as he chooses. . . . In fact there's only one 'sexual perversion,' . . . when a man over-develops his imagination, and nothing in the world, no one, can wholly satisfy him." (pp. 7, 8:15–16)

Though Perken senses the dual function of eroticism (quest for self-knowledge and test of self-limits), he is unable explicitly to relate his erotic obsession to other concerns. In his earlier epistolary-dialogue *La Tentation de l'Occident*, Malraux had attributed Western man's anguish to the realization that God is dead (*TO*, p. 97:166) and the concomitant absurdity of any "attempt to give life a human meaning" (*TO*, p. 34:66). The Westerner's search for "a coherent myth" (*TO*, p. 85:146) and "a plan of the universe [with] an intelligible form" (*TO*, p. 85:146) is doomed for two reasons. Not only is the world *outside* of man incoherent because too "transitory" (*TO*, p. 87:150) but also the world *within* man has been revealed, since Freud, as "a chaotic series of sensations over which I have no command at all, and which are only dependent on my imagination and the responses it calls up" (*TO*, p. 53:93):

> By accepting the notion of the subconscious, and by having become fascinated with it, Europe has deprived herself of her best weapons. The absurd . . . is never completely hidden. . . . If it is possible to judge others on the basis of their actions alone, we can't do the same for ourselves; the real universe . . . is only that place inhabited by other men. Our own is a dream world. (*TO*, p. 49:86)

The Occidental is anguished at both the impossibility of penetrating beyond the "unsophisticated and jumbled procession of the possibilities of act and dream" (*TO*, p. 52:92) and the realization that, within, there is nothing definite (*rien de défini*).[3] This initial failure at self-knowledge through introspection lies at the heart of the erotic quest; not only does the Westerner test his limits and definition in the intensity of the erotic confrontation, he uses eroticism to step outside of himself, to attempt to see himself as others see him:[4]

> The entire erotic game is there: being oneself *as well as the other*, feeling one's own sensations as well as imagining those of the partner. Sadism, masochism, even the feelings aroused by a play, all subject men to this division, final aspect of the ancient forces of fatality. A strange faculty, that of imagining sensations and experiencing them as well; stranger still actually to understand such a game! (*TO*, p. 53:93–94)

To be oneself *and* the other is not so much an attempt to know the other (in fact, Perken explicitly rules out knowledge of the partner) as to replace the introspective, disordered view of oneself by an exterior, more coherent view, or, at least, as Joseph Hoffmann has suggested, to attempt to reconcile these two positions.[5]

The erotic, then, clearly responds to the Occidental's need for self-definition, and, as such, parallels the obsession with the exotic, so fundamental to *La Tentation de l'Occident, Les Conquérants,* and *La Voie royale.* A.D.'s voyage to the Orient, like Ling's to the West and Garine's to Canton, serves as a pretext for self-definition: "How can I find myself, except in an examination of your race?" (*TO,* pp. 39–40:70).

Perken clearly draws the parallel between the erotic and the exotic (as well as between *La Voie royale* and the earlier works) when he argues:

> Try to grasp all that this country really is. Why, I'm only just beginning to understand their erotic rites, the process of assimilation by which a man comes to identify himself, even in his sensation, with the woman he possesses—till he imagines *he is she,* yet without ceasing to be himself! (p. 77:90)

Indeed, for one of the Europeans in *La Voie royale,* the erotic and exotic drives become identical:

> "What brought Grabot to these parts?" Claude asked.
> "Eroticism, principally—though the women here are a damned sight uglier than those in Laos; power means for him, I should say . . . the possibility of abusing it." (p. 125:142)

Perken's heavily weighted initial discussion of eroticism, therefore, seen from the perspective of the earlier works, clearly casts the entire work in the light of the quest for self-definition. The erotic metaphors which permeate *La Voie royale,* moreover, insist on this particular interpretation.

Claude enviously compares Perken's charisma to "a woman's charm" (p. 32:42), identifying the older man with his own idealized self-image. Moments later, reflecting on his discussion with Perken of

eroticism and imagination, Claude senses the relationship between
eros and stretching one's limits, in this case as against death: "The
sense of death's austere dominion, pervaded all his being, persistent as
the throb of blood across his temples, imperious as sexual desire" (p.
44:55).

The link between eros and domination explains many of the metaphors used to describe Perken, who would undoubtedly have sub-
scribed to ideas that appeared in Malraux's later preface to *Lady
Chatterley's Lover:* [6]

> It is a question of . . . . integrating eroticism into one's life without
> losing the force it once owed to sin; to ascribe to it everything that
> was until now ascribed to love: to use it for our self-revelation. . . .
> It is a question of . . . . creating a new myth of sexuality: of making
> a *value* of eroticism.

In this new system of self-revelation,

> . . . woman will become an indispensable instrument of our posses-
> sion of the world. . . . The only way for man to attain a deeper life
> is through eroticism, the only way to escape the human condition of
> the men of his time.[7]

Thus for Perken the erotic reflex becomes automatic and constant.
In the first of several explanations of his motivations for creating a
kingdom of *insoumis* (unpacified tribes), he exclaims: "Yes, that was
what I wanted, just as my father coveted his neighbor's land—or I
want women" (p. 74:87). Moments later, Perken expands the comparison: " 'These women aren't merely bodies; they're . . . instruments. And I want . . .' Claude guessed his unseen gesture, . . . a
hand crushing out life. '. . . as I once wanted to conquer men' " (p.
77;90–91).

When Perken suspects a growing inability to control his kingdom
he again resorts to terms involving women:

> Really what's put me off it, as you say, is . . . my failures with
> women. It's not impotence; don't run away with that idea. Just a
> hint, a menace. Like the first time I noticed Sarah growing old. The

end of something. Above all, I feel my hopes have been drained away. (pp. 75–76:89)

For Perken, the first sign of sexual weakness therefore fatally symbolizes old age and death and begins to undermine his previously unquestioned faith in action.

A corollary of the power-eroticism metaphor arises from the frequent association of intense activity, usually combat, with something like sexual heat. Perken states clearly that sex itself is a form of combat: "Each body that one hasn't yet possessed is—an enemy" (p. 77:90). Hammering away at the Khmer sculptures, Claude feels mounting in him "the sensual thrill (*un plaisir érotique*) which comes of every long-protracted struggle" (p. 110:127).

Like Claude, Perken poignantly relates struggle to sexual drives, especially in the battle against death:

"I've been very near death. And you can't imagine the wild elation of those moments—it's the sudden glimpse of the absurdity of life that brings it—when one meets death face to face, naked"—he made a gesture as of tearing off a woman's garments—"stark naked suddenly. . . ." (p. 145:160–61)

Perken employs a similar image when he decides to confer with the Mois:

But the insistent menace of all those watchful faces made lucid thought impossible. One last, clear vision loomed in his mind: the infinite humiliation of a man caught in the snare of his appointed fate. Grappling with the prescience of his degradation, he felt a rush of sensual rage sweep over him, like an orgasm. (p. 176:192)

Once again sexual fury metaphorically expresses the exultation of the battle against the absurdity of life, the touchstone of man's limits and self-definition.

Malraux relies on the image for a third time in the context of Perken's ultimate battle against death itself: "To his dying freedom he clung with the wild passion of a lover clasping his dying mistress, and in the shadow of its dissolution his will blazed up in a last orgasm of supreme intensity" (p. 181:197).

The relationship between struggle, eroticism, and the absurd so insistently established imagistically illumines a complex but critical area of Malraux's thought. Because "that awareness we have of ourselves is so veiled, so opposed to reason, that any attempt of the mind to understand it only makes it disappear" (*TO*, p. 52:91), Perken seeks self-definition through constraint (his kingdom of *insoumis* defines him objectively as king) and eroticism (the imputation of love feelings to a sexual partner satisfies the self-image of the lover). But both constraint and eroticism constitute fragile and ephemeral means of self-knowledge, since each depends on an involuntary and temporary self-effacement by another: "To compel. . . . To be more than a man in a world of men. To escape man's fate. . . . Not powerful: all-powerful. The visionary disease, of which the will to power is only the intellectual justification, is the will to god-head" (*CH*, p. 228:272).

It will be clear from this examination of the explicit and metaphoric references to eroticism that *La Voie royale* also describes a voyage of self-discovery. Some of the factors which both hinder self-discovery and glorify eroticism (the Orient) are the conformity and constraint imposed by Western social behavior. Claude and Perken attempt to turn away from "human intercourse, from all the absurd or calculated compromises it involves" (p. 21:29), in an attempt to define their own existence, to break out of the strictures "of those who would adjust their lives to a set pattern" (p. 44:54). Acceptance of an arbitrary order inevitably indicates imprisonment in the human condition.[8]

> For the childless, godless modern man such truckling (*soumission*) to the established order impressed him as an abject surrender to the power of death. So he must forge for himself weapons other than the weapons of the herd; and the surest arm for one who feels himself cut off from his kind is courage. (p. 43:54)

The image of the prison is entirely appropriate to a novel of the jungle, whose foliage literally encloses the adventurers within its tortuous trunks and vines.[9] One is not surprised, then, that to Claude, in

anticipation, the jungle appears as impenetrable as the wall of a
prison:

> Now that Claude was almost alone on deck . . . would he once
> again pore over the *Inventory,* and launch his imagination, like a
> man charging headfirst into a brick wall, against those citadels of
> dust . . . that lay within the blue-ringed contours of the Dead Cities,
> and . . . encounter for the hundredth time the obstacles that cut
> across his dream, always at the same point, fatal and ineluctable?
> (pp. 12–13:21)

The philosophical undertone of this image of the wall is soon made
clear. Following a discussion of age, death, and personal liberty, Perken leaves Claude to meditate alone: "Like a cell door the atmosphere of the cabin closed in on Claude once more, and, like a fel-
low-prisoner, Perken's question kept him company. . . . No, there
were not so many avenues to freedom, after all" (p. 43:53–54).
Perken's question concerns the origins of his violent rebellion, origins
which lie, he discovers, in the awareness of death. The vision of a cell
door is provoked when the older man leaves Claude prey to solitary
thoughts about social enslavement and death; thoughts whose very
obsessive insistence constitutes an imprisonment.

Though danger provides the context for the adventurers' pursuit of
an acceptable image of themselves,[10] the irony of man's destiny soon
emerges. In escaping from one prison, society, they only enter another, the forest. Adventure, muses Claude confidently, involves "the
slave's *brief* spell of freedom from his master" ("cette destruction
provisoire des rapports de prisonnier à maître") (p. 45:55; italics
mine). His use of "brief (*provisoire*)" indicates a vague awareness that
adventure, while often an escape from an imprisoning social hier-
archy, does not necessarily release man from the larger prison of the
human condition.

Recurring prison images insist on the forest as man's estate. A solid
wall of foliage confronts Claude and Perken as they approach the
land by boat. Every description of this forest creates the impression of
a walled enclosure:

> The launch cast off and threaded its way (*s'enfonça*) between the
> trees rooted in water. . . . Beyond the leafy *barrier,* through each
> gap, he strained to catch a glimpse of Angkor-Wat . . . but in vain.
> The leaves . . . shrouded the fenlands with a glowing pall. . . .
> Claude could not see more than twenty yards ahead. (pp.
> 57–59:70)

The atmosphere of suffocating enclosure recalls "a blind man chant-
ing the Ramayana" in the center of a circle (*au centre d'un cercle
misérable*) of "beggars and coolie women" (p. 58:70). This vision of
the blind man in a circle not only effectively foreshadows Grabot's
blind journey around his mill wheel but also relates the confinement
of the forest directly to the idea of enslavement:

> What better personification of Cambodia, of this land of decay, could
> he have found than that old singer whose heroic strains had ceased
> to interest any but the beggars and coolie women squatting round
> him? Cambodia, a land possessed, and tamed to humble uses. (p.
> 58:70)

The word "heroic" contributes to the growing premonition that the
hero's adventures will be circumscribed by a circle of enslavement.

No artistic accident provides for Claude and Perken a guide, Xa,
who "has been in jail (*qui sort de prison*)" (p. 65:77), thus complet-
ing the party of prisoners, actual and metaphysical.

As the group penetrates deeper into the suffocating enclosure of the
forest, it becomes increasingly apparent that Claude is cut off not only
from the outside but also from himself: "under its influence, in the
green darkness, he felt himself disintegrating (*la forêt le séparait de
lui-même*)" (p. 84:98). He is also increasingly severed from the universe, or at least "that more *human* universe glimpses of which appeared now and again in a burst of dazzling sunlight" (p. 84:98; italics mine). Even the brief respite provided by these openings fades
away as the jungle continues to close in:

> The track soon disappeared. Pushing their way round a heap of rub-
> ble, they came upon a clump of cane-brake, interlaced like wattles,
> which, rising to a man's height, formed a natural palisade. . . . The

boy shouted . . . his voice rang dead, stifled by the canopy of leaves.
(p. 86:100–1)

To insist upon this already explicit metaphor, Malraux soon complements the comparison when Claude crawls across the insect-ridden
wall, only to find an incompleted monument barren of sculptural dec-
oration: "On their frustrated hope the forest had closed in once more"
(p. 91:106).

Claude is doubly imprisoned by the discovery of the yellow warrior
practicing his savage ritual, "riveted to the sight—by his eyes, by
his hands, by the leaves which seemed to touch him through his
clothing" (p. 93:108). They manage to escape only when they come
"to an opening in the forest (*une nouvelle trouée les* DÉLIVRAIT *de la
forêt*)" (p. 94:109; emphasis added). And when they finally stumble
upon a temple, another "tangled palisade of cane-brake" (pp.
95–96:111) cuts them off from their goal.

Farther along the trail, the branches "form . . . a massive archway,
impervious to the sunlight" above, and the forest reasserts "its prison-
like dominion" (p. 108:124). Later, having freed the coveted stones,
they must again "advance despite the jungle's hostility," for "the forest once again was beginning to assert its domination" (p. 120:136).
The broken light causes Xa to be "striped like a convict by the shadows of the overhanging branches" (p. 117:134), while the adventurers "vanished down a leafy tunnel, like miners entering an adit" with
a "close-woven roof" (p. 121:138).

When Claude and Perken finally come upon important sculptures,
the stones at first defy detachment. Malraux describes one particularly
difficult piece, "Immensely solid, sure of itself, instinct with ponderous
malevolence" (p. 104:120), which Claude metaphorically transforms
into a wall: "So all his obstinacy, his tense determination, the passionate endeavor which had urged him through the jungle had served no
other end than this—to bring him up against this obstacle, an im-
movable stone planted between himself and Siam!" (pp. 104,
105:120).

Moments later he embellishes the image, rendering the stones a prison and casting himself as a prisoner desperate for freedom: "The forest, the temple, the universe were in dissolution. He might have been struggling to bore through a prison wall, and the hammer-thuds have been so many thrusts of a file, rasping persistently against the stone" (p. 107:123). Crazed when his sledgehammer breaks, Claude stands transfixed before the stone: "It held his gaze imprisoned. His hate linked him to it as to an active enemy who barred his way and mounted guard on him" (p. 108:124). Paralyzed by this "active" resistance, Claude again imagines himself a prisoner, forced into the fetal position which Kassner will assume in Le Temps du mépris: [11] "He pictured himself, his arms hugging his chest . . . his body curled up like a sleeping animal; he would lose consciousness utterly" (p. 108:124).

Never arbitrary, images of the prison relate not only to the physical and psychological state but also to the philosophical state of the two men. The power of the forest at times elicits a greatly expanded notion of imprisonment:

> The tall barrier of trees was drenched in shadow and above the great primeval forest brooding round them a host of stars outshone their leaping fire; the slow, tremendous progress of the night overwhelmed Claude with a sense of supreme loneliness, making him feel once more a hunted thing at bay. And in the lambent darkness he discerned an ineluctable indifference, an immanence of death. (p. 141:159)

Here, the word "barrier" relates all the previous forest-prison associations directly to the immensity of the heavens and man's loneliness in the universe, recalling Pascal's celebrated cry of despair:

> Let man then contemplate the whole of nature in her full and lofty majesty, let him turn his gaze away from the lowly objects around him . . . and let him marvel at finding this vast orbit itself to be no more than the tiniest point compared to that described by the stars revolving in the firmament. . . . Let man, returning to himself, consider what he is in comparison with what exists; let him regard himself as lost, and from *this little dungeon,* in which he finds himself lodged, I mean the universe, let him learn to take the earth, its

realms, its cities, its houses and himself at their proper value. What
is a man in the infinite? [12]

This evocation of the larger, metaphysical prison effectively relates
several levels of the protagonists' dilemma, for if the prison reveals
the "immanence of death" for Claude,[13] for Perken the prison signals
man's inability to alter his living destiny:

> "For your sake, Claude, I hope you will die young. I wish it as I've
> wished for few things in my life. You've no idea what it means to be
> imprisoned in one's own life. . . . that feeling of being penned in by
> destiny, by something you can't escape or change, something that
> weighs upon you like a prison regulation; the certainty that you will
> do *this* and nothing else, and when you die you will have been *that*
> man and no other, and what you haven't had already you will never
> have. And all your hopes lie behind you, all those baffled hopes that
> are flesh of your flesh, as no human being, living or to be born can
> ever be."
>
> An odor of corruption wafted from the stagnant marshes hung on
> the air. (pp. 71, 72:84–85)

The forest-prison therefore evokes not only man's "feeble mortal condition, so wretched that nothing can console us when we really think
about it," [14] but also mortality in the sense of irreversible physical decline. Man, in addition to being prisoner of his metaphysical condition and enslaved to his *acts,* is "bound to his body (*enchaîné à sa
chair*)" (p. 208:226), and, as Perken sadly observes, "Death, the real
death, is a man's gradual decline" (p. 42:53).

Malraux underlines Perken's obsession with aging as a universal,
lingering, and malignant sickness (*déchéance*), rendered ineluctable
by time, in a later discussion of "death . . . a standing proof of the
futility (*l'absurdité*) of life" (p. 142:157). Death, Perken explains,
does not consist in the mere fact of suddenly ceasing to exist,

> death is different; it's the exact opposite, in fact. . . . I realized it the
> first time I saw a woman growing old. . . . Then, too, as if that
> warning wasn't enough, there was that time—the first time—
> when I found that I was impotent. . . . I never got that feeling from
> the sight of a dead body. To grow old, that's it—to peter out. Es-

pecially when one's cut off from others. A death-in-life. What weighs
on me is—how shall I put it?—my human lot, my limitations;
that I must grow old, and time, that loathsome thing, spread through
me *like a cancer,* inevitably. Time—there you have it! (p.
142:157–58; italics mine)

Of all the signs of aging in the above passage, only "cancer" is sufficiently concrete and complete to convey the immediacy, the invisible
malignancy and inevitability of the process which obsesses Perken
and inspires his revolt. Sickness, representing an acceleration of the
aging process, thus becomes a particularly pertinent metaphor of this
inescapable erosion of time. A second comparison of time with cancer
emphasizes the relationship with death: Claude could accept a death
resulting from adventure since "at least, he would have had the fight,
if not the victory. But, living, to endure the vanity of life gnawing
him like a cancer; all his life long to feel the sweat of death lie
clammy on his palm . . . unbearable!" (p. 44:55).

Adventure, then, endeavors not only to escape the prison of society
but also to deny the process of age by combating life at every moment.[15] An image of sickness, for example, is used in the specific context of frustrated hope to describe the death of the adventurer Mayrena: Claude ponders "how foiled ambition had gnawed at his heart
like a malignant tumor" (pp. 11–12:20).

References to sickness occur whenever a protagonist encounters a
frustration which throws him back upon himself and on the futility of
discovering a real meaning for life in the face of the march of time.
Such metaphors signal the inevitable conquest of man by time, but
more immediately, they foreshadow Perken's gangrene, itself symbolic.

Claude acknowledges a fixation with the danger and possibility of
death in their adventure: "Claude felt his fixed idea possessing him
again, insistent as a fever in his blood" (p. 26:36). The same metaphor
communicating submission reappears when Claude's hammer breaks,
frustrating the attempt to control the sculptures. He suddenly imagines himself "like a man . . . stricken by malaria" (p. 108:124). Per-

haps the most telling of the comparisons of frustration to disease is Perken's opinion of Mayrena's and Brooke's defeated undertakings as "in a bad way (*malades*)" (p. 76:89).

If deliberate attempts at thwarting the process of time and the absurdity of life can be termed "malades," the routine actions of man in society appear all the more enfeebled. Social man becomes the hyperbole of the infirm, a cadaver: "All the outworn ideas of those who deemed their lives mere stepping-stones towards a nebulous "salvation" were dead ideas—and what had he to do with corpses? Corpse-like, too, the homilies of those who would adjust their lives to a set pattern" (pp. 43–44:54). Since social man, blindly adhering to enforced models, merely submits to the aging process, his whole existence lacks meaning. Entire societies composed of such debilitated and meaningless lives are metaphorically considered contaminated; [16] hence the description of Cambodia as "this land of decay. . . . of all dead lands most dead" (p. 58:70).

Once the equation of sickness to the aging process has been established, the forest (already established by the prison image as a compelling backdrop for the human condition) becomes a constant reminder of sickness and decomposition. Just as the adventurers seeking to escape society found themselves nonetheless imprisoned, so they flee the sickness of society only to encounter in the jungle constant reminders of their mortal infirmity. As Perken concludes his sermon on the inevitable process of natural decay (see above, p. 42), "an odor of corruption (*décomposition*) wafted from the stagnant marshes hung on the air" (p. 72:85). The stench prompts a recollection to the dreadful aging process of Claude's mother: "A picture rose before Claude's eyes: his mother wandering forlornly through his grandfather's old house . . . peering into the little mirror . . . staring aghast at the sagging corners of her lips and her swollen nose, stroking her eyelids with blind, automatic gestures" (p. 72:85).

Other suggestions of decay abound. Claude remains constantly feverish in the oppressive tropical climate: "The heat and the never-ending forest harassed them even more than their anxiety. Like a slow poison, the ceaseless fermentation in which forms grew bloated, lengthened out, decayed, as in a world where mankind has no place, wore down Claude's stamina insidiously" (p. 84:98).

Not only are "leaves rotting" (p. 135:151), but even the termite hills "seemed bred of the corruption of the air" (p. 85:99) and "the village is dilapidated (*pourrie*)" (p. 133:149), graphically illustrating the extent to which everything falls prey to the "foul decomposition (*l'étouffante gangrene*) of the forest" (p. 113:129). Sounds, like every other phenomenon, submit to the "universal disintegration of all things"; the noise of branches striking the carts "seemed muted by the heat (*se decomposait dans la chaleur*)"(p. 95:110). The heat itself assumes the sinister force of the ravenous gangrene: "The growing heat . . . worked like a slow poison, turning their muscles to water, sapping their vitality, while the sweat poured down their faces, mingling with the stone-dust below their glasses in long, viscous streaks like blood-streams trickling from gouged-out eyes" (pp. 106–7:122–23). This passage and the description of Claude's mother refer obliquely to Grabot's blindness, foreshadowing the passage in which he comes to symbolize the entire process of decay and death (see below, p. 49).

Every descriptive detail of the forest contributes to an overpowering image of the metaphysical and corporeal prison to which man must submit. And yet the most compelling image in the novel has yet to be discussed.

When in 1930 Malraux was asked to explain *La Voie royale,* he answered: "I wanted to tell the truth about adventure. First, one truth derives simply from attention to detail. . . . Well, adventure before being a means for a man's exaltation or pleasure, is ants which are crushed under one's palms, insects, reptiles, disgusting dangers at every step one takes in the bush." [17]

The preponderant weight given to insects and reptiles in this vision of adventure is far from arbitrary. *La Voie royale* teems with insects and insect imagery,[18] constantly reinforcing the submission, despair, and terror already evoked metaphorically by the prison and decomposition.

Even before Claude and Perken enter the jungle, they are aware of insects. In the Somali brothels, Perken recalls "the yellow glow of oil-lamps ringed with insects" (p. 5:13). Claude's dreams of Asia include "the marching forth of armies in the scented dusk loud with cicadas, the horses' hooves stirring up dust-clouds dark with slowly veering columns of mosquitoes" (p. 14:22), recalling not only the lines of the damned but the death-dealing army of scorpions in *Royaume farfelu* (p. 150).

Claude's first impression of the jungle is tainted by the menacing presence of insects: "Could a man possibly force his way through that serried undergrowth? Well, if others had contrived to do it, so could he. Against his dubious affirmation the lowering sky and the impenetrable tangle of the leafage, teeming with insect-life, affirmed their silent menace" (p. 46:57).

The relentless mosquitoes compel Xa to warn Claude: "Better keep on the move like I do, Monsieur Vannec, if you don't want to be eaten alive by the damned mosquitoes. It's the worst time of day for them (*L'heure est mauvaise, vous savez*)" (p. 61:73). Although Xa simply refers to the dusk, which always brings the mosquitoes, his ominous "l'heure est mauvaise," underscored by the weighted presence of the insects, contributes to a sense of uneasy foreboding.

The description of the penetration of the forest wall presents a suffocating accumulation of insects and entomological imagery. Palm-covered huts are described as "asquat like monstrous insects on the spongy soil" (p. 83:97). Claude drowses feverishly in a world in which man fades in significance, "And then, everywhere, the insects" (p. 84:98). Animal forms concede to the dominion of the insects:

The other animals came from . . . that more human universe glimpses of which appeared now and again in a burst of dazzling sunlight. . . . But the insects lived by and on the forest—from the globular black creatures which the draught-oxen squashed under their hooves, and the ants zig-zagging up the porous tree-trunks, to the spiders hooked by grasshopper-like claws to the centers of their huge webs, four yards across, whose silken filigree caught up the light that lingered near the soil. (p. 84:98–99)

So pervasive are the insects that one form can effectively be compared only to another, hence the spider's "grasshopper-like claws." [19]

The insects continue to assimilate all other forms to their own:

Amid the welter of the leafage heaving with scaly insects only the spiders kept steadfast vigil, yet some vague resemblance linked them, too, with the other insects—the flies and cockroaches, the curious little creatures with heads protruding from their shells crawling upon the moss—, with the foul virulence of bacterial life seen on a microscopic slide. (p. 85:99)

The malaise experienced in the presence of this virulence of microscopic life recalls Pascal's vision of the two infinities, the immensity of the universe and "all the conceivable immensity of nature enclosed in this miniature atom." [20]

Three pages of description of this "world where mankind has no place" (p. 84:98), terminating with a further reference to "high gray anthills . . . like mountain peaks on some dead satellite" (p. 85:99), culminate in Claude's awestruck cry, "Here what act of man had any meaning, what human will but spent its staying power?"(p. 85:99). Pascal, on considering the "universe" of the infinitesimally small, had exclaimed, "For, after all, what is man in nature?" [21] The two confrontations with an aspect of nature that abandons man to the meaninglessness of his own acts convince both Pascal and Malraux of the absurdity of human endeavor without God.

Malraux associates insects with death even more explicitly when Claude muses that "gangrene is as prevalent (*aussi maîtresse*) as vermin (*l'insecte*) in the jungle" (p. 87:102). Since gangrene signifies an omnipresent threat of death, the comparison clearly extends a comparable power to insects. Thus, in addition to foreshadowing Perken's final illness, this image extends the insects' power to include metaphysical anguish.

Indeed, at one point, insects constitute a barrier between Claude and the sculptures. Crawling along a narrow wall, "Before him he saw the overhanging branch of a tree, silhouetted across the gap; over the green bridge a troop of ants was passing, their bellies showing

clearly against the light, their legs invisible" (p. 88:103). Claude
must pass under this bridge of living enemies to reach the end of the
wall, where, however, it is immediately noted, other red ants may be
lying in wait: "pretty foul it'll be if there are red ants about" (p.
88:103). The primordial fear totally independent of Claude's will is
underscored again moments later when "something sticky was smeared
upon his hand, a mush of brittle molluscs and tiny eggs squashed to a
pulp" (p. 89:103), so that "his nerves were conscious only of the mass
of squashed insects, responded only to the nausea of their contact" (p.
89:103). His unreasoned fear is further supported when Malraux once
more explicitly associates insects and death: " [Claude] glanced down
for a second at the stones below; teeming with insects; on those
stones he might easily crush out his life" (pp. 89–90:104). The insects have so shaken Claude that his voice and nerves respond irra-
tionally.

After the successful disengagement of the Khmer stones (a passage
which is permeated by the foreboding presence of "dull-hued ants"
and swarms of "gray wood lice" [pp. 101, 103–4, 110:117–20]),
Malraux surrounds the adventurers, at every point at which they encounter serious difficulty or danger, with "mosquitoes think as motes in
sunlight" (p. 120:137), "a hum of insects" (p. 122:143), "the hume of
myriads of insects" (p. 137:152).

Two further analogies link insects even more explicitly to the destiny of the two men. When Claude proposes to push on without a
guide Perken rejoins: "If you're quite determined to end up as a little
heap of garbage alive with maggots, your idea strikes me as sound
enough" (p. 120:137). And, in a quieter, more philosophical moment,
the older man reflects: "D'you see all those damn-fool insects making
for our lamp, obeying the call of the light (*soumis à la lumière*)? The
termites, too, obey the law of the anthill (*soumis à leur termitère*). I
. . . I *will not obey* (*Je ne veux pas être soumis*)" (p. 142:158).[22]
Perken's language leaves no doubt as to the power of the insect image
and its associations with submission to death.

The degree of terror inspired by the insect image cannot be attrib-

uted merely to its reinforcement of the prison and sickness themes. In
La Tentation de l'Occident, Malraux had suggested the dreadful fascination derived from contemplation of other forms of existence without links to our own:

> The idol of the many arms, the dance of death, these are not at all *al-
> legories* of the perpetual flux of the universe. They are beings,
> impregnated with an inhuman life *which has made those arms nec-
> essary.* They should be contemplated as giant crustaceans brought up
> from the depths of the sea are contemplated. Both are disconcerting
> to us, show us suddenly how much simplicity there is in us, inspire
> in us the idea of an existence without ties to our own. (*TO,* p.
> 86:147–48)

The fascination of this otherness clearly works on Claude in the
forest where "he felt himself disintegrating (*le séparait de lui-même*)
like the world around him. . . . everywhere, the insects. . ." (p.
84:98). That Claude should be *separated from himself* by the contemplation of this otherness suggests a sudden conscious split of his own
subconscious as distinct from his conscious mental activity. That this
awareness is linked to the double-consciousness elicited by the erotic
act becomes evident when the attraction of the insect is likened to a
kind of repressed sexuality: [23]

> Here everything frayed out, grew soft and flabby, tended to assimilate
> itself with its surroundings, which, loathsome yet fascinating as a cre-
> tin's eyes, worked on the nerves with the same *obscene power of at-
> traction* as the spiders hanging there between the branches, from
> which at first it had cost him such an effort to avert his gaze. (pp.
> 85–86:99–100)

This powerful and irrational attraction-revulsion is again forcefully
demonstrated when Claude and Perken suddenly catch sight of "a yellow warrior . . . stark naked, and in a state of erection" (p. 93:108).
The fright is compared to one of Claude's obsessive childhood traumas involving beings fraught, as we have seen, with significance:
"Claude . . . felt himself riveted to the sight . . . by that feeling of

panic which always used to come over him, as a child, whenever he saw a live crab or lobster, or a snake" (pp. 93–94:108–9).

The reference not only recalls the passage in *La Tentation de l'Occident* just cited but relates the insect and erotic motifs even more closely. The Westerners travel beyond Pascalian (metaphysical) despair and the discovery of the body's inescapable submission to aging and decomposition, to the realm of the subconscious—that unreasoned fear and chaos within man which for Malraux reveals the absurd.[24] If the journey is one of self-discovery through the erotic and exotic, as the parallel with *La Tentation de l'Occident* and the structure of the metaphoric language suggest, one can reasonably expect at the heart of this forest of darkness a symbolic vision of the essential in Western man.

When the adventurers, at the end of this voyage of self-discovery, encounter the Mois (the intriguing coincidence between the name of the tribe and the French first-person pronoun is worth noting) they enter a prison of the savages' encirclement within the prison of the jungle. Descriptions of the village abound with allusions to the prison; the adventurers are illuminated by "a . . . shaft of sunlight (*une barre de soleil*)" (p. 155:171); the interior of the mill becomes an "airless darkness of a prison cell," where one bar of light penetrates "like a ray falling from the loophole of a dungeon" (p. 159:175). Finally, within this obscure prison of the subconcious, the adventurers come upon that symbolic expression of the Westerner toward which their entire search had been directed. Grabot, the prototypical erotomaniac, now blind, a slave, revolving mechanically around the millstone of his prison,[25] defines Western man as more a grave (Grabot) than a living being: he is, explicitly, "the reminder of his own human lot (*cette preuve de sa condition d'homme*)" (p. 170:186). He becomes a Sisyphean image of the absurdity of life.

Not merely captive and blind, Grabot is also described in terms of decomposition (pp. 159, 163, 169, 176:175, 179, 185, 192). For Claude, gradually acknowledging an existence however "corpse-like"

(p. 163:179), Grabot is "a mighty wreck (*une puissante ruine*)" who, like the temples of Asia, "has fallen on evil days (*pourrissaient sous l'Asie*)" (p. 169:185). The spirit of adventure, "that last infirmity of courage (*cette lèpre du courage*) which had brought Grabot low (*qui avait* DÉCOMPOSÉ *Grabot*)" (p. 175:192; emphasis added), was unable to circumvent the aging process.

Instead of rejecting this "proof of the human condition," Claude and Perken ally themselves with Grabot, accepting him as person and symbol. The three barricade themselves in one of the native huts and there await the attack of the Mois. This scene of armed conflict between the social and metaphysical image of man and the savages from the deepest recesses of the jungle reunites all of the novel's major images of despair (insects, prison, sickness, and eros), and also serves as a microstructure of the entire work.

Even when freed of his millstone, the blindman continues to circle interminably in the surrounded hut, following submissively the symbolic model imposed by society and assuming a double significance, that of social man, and of aging-dying process: "Grabot was twice a corpse (*un double cadavre*)" (p. 179:195).

Surrounded by an ever increasing number of Mois, Claude senses that he is "as much a prisoner now in his private universe of forms as Grabot in the darkness of his eyeless head" (p. 166:182). The implicit comparison of the prisons of Claude's and Garbot's interior chaos with the prison imposed by the savages constitutes yet another sign that the Mois may symbolize the consciousness of self, "a chaotic series of sensations over which I have no command at all" (*TO*, p. 53:93).

Until the Mois could be appeased or repressed, "there was no escaping from the forest's dark dominion" (p. 175:192). Claude senses the interplay between the social, psychological, and metaphysical imprisonment of the three men:

> The passing minutes seemed immured within the ring-fence of those bestial faces, in which eternity was incarnate—an obdurate barrier that *nothing happening in the outside world* could cross, *nothing*

could permeate. It seemed to Claude as if to live, and to watch the progress of the prisoned hours . . . could only mean ever to grow more cruelly aware that they were hemmed in by a barrier of living beings aligned before another barrier, the towering stock-ade; each hour was bringing them a clearer and still clearer re-alization that their detention was but the prelude to slavery. (pp. 170–71:187; italics mine)

The threatening Mois recapitulate the forms of the menacing for-est. Claude formulates all fears in terms of the obsessive insect:

Once again, as if nothing could subdue the onset of the forest and its forms of life, Claude felt himself transported into an insect-world. From the scattered huts which, only a moment before, were silent and seemingly unoccupied, now, through invisible exits, a swarm of Mois was emerging; with nimble, wasp-like movements they streamed along the path, brandishing their mantis-like weapons. Now and again the spears and cross-bows stood out against the sky clean-cut as waving antennae. (pp. 163–64:179)

The Mois thus metamorphose into insects whose every movement is described in terms of flowing or swarming. They advance "like ants" (p. 171:187), their ranks "buzzing like a wasps' nest" (p. 172:188), and display "curved bows projecting like a row of wooden beaks (*mandibules*)" (p. 173:189–90).

The threat of death provokes an urge for a brutal retaliation which verges upon sadism. Once again, metaphor weaves together insects, death, and erotic sadism: "No, there was nothing they could do— except kill as many Mois as possible. He remembered the way the leeches squirmed and shriveled up when he burnt them alive on the end of a match" (p. 174:190).

Malraux here presents a situation of ultimates: death is imminent —the Mois will attack at nightfall—and the triply-charged meta-phoric system of imprisonment with a blind, circling erotomaniacal "cadaver" suggests not only the social constraints from which Claude and Perken had originally emancipated both themselves and meta-physical despair, but also the confrontation with the double destiny of sickness unto death as symbolized by Grabot as a degraded external image, and the disorder within man as symbolized by the Mois as the savage insectlike subconscious.

Confronted with this microstructure of their entire adventure, Perken recapitulates the reactions and the basic metaphor which had brought all three Westerners into this new prison: he gambles on action.

Perken had originally hoped that the return to the Cambodian forest would conquer the vanity of his existence, "make a sport of it" (p. 45:55). He uses the image of the wager most explicitly in a series of clairvoyant pronouncements on the nature of his involvement in Cambodia. His leadership of a group of Cambodian tribes (*insoumis*) barring the advance of Western hegemony had constituted not so much a political move as a bid for immortality in "the great game I'm playing against death." With enough men and military force, argues Perken, "I could set on foot the great adventure (*le jeu pourrait être joué*) . . . to survive for many men, and perhaps for a long time; to leave my mark upon the map of Asia" (p. 74:87).

References to gambling in the face of despair recall Pascal's wager: "il faut parier," as well as the use of the same image in his discussion of the need for *divertissement* to suggest the necessity of passion (even if artificially inspired) in man's activities.[26]

Perken also emphasizes the necessity for high stakes: "Men of my sort should always have the forces of a State to play with" (p. 219:237). Instinctively, however, Perken knows that his own life against death constitutes the real stakes, and that he who gambles risks losing, especially when playing against Death. "To live defying death," muses Perken in a discussion of suicide. "It seems to me sometimes that I am staking myself, all that I am, on a single moment —my last" (p. 144:160). And, emphasizing the degree to which this wager represents an affirmation of life and not simply a desperate act, he adds: "When I think about my death it's with a view to living —not to dying" [27] (p. 145:161). Nor should one forget the degree to which Perken's fellow prisoners are gamblers; for not only have they too taken the risk of adventure, but both insist on the necessity of gambling in the face of death and the absurdity of life. Grabot had said: "I'm playing a poker game all by myself—see?—that the other fellows won't cut into; the mere idea of breaking their precious necks sets 'em jittering" [28] (p. 126:143–44). Claude realizes that "he was risking much, but whether he won through or lost, he could but gain in hardihood by the venture (*en un tel jeu*), and sate his thirst for courage, his deep awareness of the world's futility and human wretchedness" [29] (pp. 210–11:229).

Considered in the light of this image pattern, Perken's decision to leave the hut and advance toward the Mois clearly represents a leap to action: a wager that, in the face of death (whether actual or psychological), only action is capable of defying "destiny." Indeed, as he approaches the line of Mois, Perken experiences "wild elation at the thought that he was risking (*jouer*) more than death" (p. 177:193), that on his action rode the entire meaning of his existence.

This microstructure of imprisonment followed by a leap to action reproduces the larger structure of the novel: just as Perken's desire to leave a scar on the map will be thwarted by his own mortality, here he liberates Claude and Grabot, only to incur his own death. The entire passage is proleptic of Perken's death. Amid a variety of other elements metaphorically charged with despair, he wounds himself on a poisoned stake—allowing the "maîtresse de la forêt," gangrene, slowly to destroy him. The natives confronting Perken display certain insectlike characteristics, as, for example, the chief's "embryonic thoughts which in the dark recesses of its skull were squirming into life, like flies' eggs hatching in a dead man's brain" (p. 185:201–2), and the conference of the Mois which becomes "a drone of voices . . . like a buzzing swarm of insects circling over squatting mummies" (p. 192:209). The last image in the series, perhaps the most prophetic in terms of Perken's eventual death, compares the blood trickling from the skull Perken has shot to an insect:

"The moving blood, spreading in crooked tentacles, looked like some living creature, a large red insect gripping the bluish bone in token of possession" (p. 195:212).

This blood, signaling temporary victory over the immediate threat by duping the Mois into crediting Perken with magic powers, nevertheless casts his victory into the shadows of ambiguity.[30] The blood, after all, is Perken's own flowing from a fatal wound which will eventually undermine his ability to prolong the natural process of life over death. The image of the "gros insecte" (exactly the term used to designate the character Death in *Lunes en papier*) [31] here insists on the omnipresent possessiveness of death and reveals his victory as ephemeral if not illusory. Bargaining for his life, Perken realizes that "his fate, his future, were staked on that lump of squalid flesh" [32] (p. 184:201), and although "cette masse vivante" apparently refers to the tribal chief, the double meaning is clear: Perken's destiny ultimately resides not in heroic action but in his own mortal flesh.

Given the importance of eroticism in Perken's evaluation of and hold on life, his demand for a prostitute on learning of his fatal wound becomes easily comprehensible. The jeopardization of action creates the need not only to reaffirm his manhood through constraint but also to project his biased view of his situation onto another and then to accept that view as objective. But "being oneself as well as the other, feeling one's own sensations as well as imagining those of the partner" can only result in loneliness and failure.[33] Although Perken "possessed [her body] as he might have struck it" (p. 213:231), "Never, never would he apprehend, never share, this woman's sensations; never could the frenzy which thrilled her body be for him anything but a proof of the unbridgeable gulf between them. Without love there can be no possession" (p. 214:232).

Following this discovery of the inauthenticity of eroticism as a defense, Perken forces himself for a third time toward the leap to action despite its previous pessimistic overtones. Although dying, he insists on returning to the forest to organize his *insoumis* to resist the mechanized invasion of the Westerner, the railroad whose absolutely regular tracks replace the royal way. Obsessed with leaving a scar on the map, he doggedly hopes to escape the imprisonment of his decaying flesh by leaving behind something enduring of himself.

The final pages of the novel unite all previous image patterns into a multifaceted image of the defeat of Perken's hopes. Constrained by society, Perken had sought escape in adventure only to discover that his original prison had simply been exchanged for others, the ultimate one being an incarceration within a dying body. In seeking to deny this incarceration through a sort of terrestrial immortality, Perken discovers that he is "at once bound to his body and detached from it, like the criminals of old time who were condemned to death by drowning, tied to a corpse" (p. 208:226). Hoping to escape this corporeal prison by simply willing to ignore the disease, Perken is caught by "a look from Claude [which] brought him back to his body, to himself" (p. 208:226).

As they proceed toward Perken's *insoumis,* the two men notice "pillars of smoke . . . clean-cut as tree-trunks" (p. 219:234), "rising shafts of smoke each like another bolt shot home to bar their progress" (p. 240:258). That this new incarceration is to be understood as physical (separating Perken from his *insoumis*) as well as metaphysical (locking Perken off from all hope of leaving his mark) becomes abundantly clear in one apocalyptic passage:

> Ever more numerous, towering high against the molten glare of noon, pillars of smoke ribbed the skyline with a gigantic palisade (*grille*); and in his mind the heat, the lurching cart, his fever, the baying of the dogs, the twinges of his wound, the sleepers falling like so many clods of earth upon his body—all seemed mingling indistinguishably with the barrier (*grille*) of smoke, the empire of the forest and of death, in an inferno (*emprisonnement surhumain*) of abandoned hopes. (pp. 243–44:261–62)

Death and the forest, together with the railroad representing the mechanized constraint of the West which they had originally fled, culminate in the immense and final prison. Even the sounds of the forest, filling in the spaces between the bars, intensify the claustro-

phobia: "dogs were howling . . . and their clamor echoed through
the forest to the horizon's edge, filling the interspaces of the smoke
with sound" (p. 244:262). Perken remains to the end "a prisoner still,
penned in the world of men as in a dungeon, a mad world (*cette absurdité*) of smoke-wraiths and lurking perils like dim creatures of the
under-earth" (p. 244:262).

The entire prison-image pattern, as circular and as absurd as Grabot's endless journey around the millstone, contributes to a final
tragic despair which is reinforced by the parallel culmination of the
images of sickness and decay.

All the various sickness images converge in Perken's final struggle
against the gangrene. The original wound had almost immediately assumed metaphysical importance through personification: "It seemed
to Perken that he was being wrenched away from his body, that irresponsible body of his, intent on leading him to death" (p. 207:225).
But, refusing to surrender to death, he deludes himself that the fatal
wound is simply one more adversary, which he is confident of con-
quering: "For all his burning impatience Perken felt no distress. Once
more he had an overt enemy to face, were that enemy none other
than his flesh and blood" (p. 207:225). The outcome of this struggle
against his own blood cannot remain in doubt given the alliance of
pain and death against Perken's will: "Pain and death . . . work in
concert; one is the never failing herald of the other" (p. 208:227).
They leave Perken a mere piece of flotsam stranded on the beach of
his dying flesh: "The wave of agony ebbed, and with it passed the
mental effort he had made against it" (p. 208:227).

Perken is made poignantly aware of the disjuncture of his will and
dying body when he attempts to move his own foot, "but its dark
mass seemed independent of him—it was as if he suffered in another's flesh—and he made no effort to move it away" (p.
223:240–41).

Although Perken continues to resist any acceptance of his condition ("Perken felt furiously alive, up in arms against this affirmation
of his failure [*sa déchéance*]" [p. 224:242]), he gradually realizes

that the will does not outlive the body ("Man's will had come into its own, taken command again . . . in the service of death" [p. 224:242]). He thereby admits the powerlessness and absurdity of his position. Perken's life has discribed one long decline.[34] A final dreadful image summarizes the futility of his battle and his horror of the fatally diseased flesh: "All he had achieved lay dead before his eyes —like his own corpse" (p. 224:242). Thus, "his bitterest foe—the knowledge of his downfall (*la déchéance*)" (p. 238:256) forces Perken to acknowledge that death vitiates all the courage and energy of life: "Fever was decomposing all his ideas like carrion rotting underground" (p. 241:259).

The dying man's final awareness of the inanity of existence ironically renders him *less* absurd since he harbors no more illusions about the possibilities of life. Reflecting this realization, Perken muses as he lies dying, "to be a living man was even more absurd than dying" (p. 243:261).

Insects irrevocably link the dying man's fate to the idea of submission: Perken's death is attended by an almost unbearable "plague of monstrous insects" (p. 234:252). Prostrate before the approach of the army about to destroy his kingdom of dissidents, Perken watches as the mosquitoes appear to weave his shroud:

> Close to his ears humming mosquitoes wove their tracery of subtle sounds, spreading a tingling mesh of tiny stabs upon the deep-set throbbing of the wound. . . . A soft pattering caught his ear and, looking round, he saw his fingers, frenzied by the insect-bites, drumming feverishly on the woodwork of the cart; till now he had not known that they were moving. (p.241:259)

Feeling his control over his body diminishing, this expiring being suddenly perceives his hands as part of the dreadful otherness: [35]

> He had seen his hand thus several times before—as something apart, something quite independent of him. . . . That hand of his, that white thing yonder, with its fingers higher than the heavy palm, its nails clawing the threads of the trouser-seam, somehow recalled the spiders hooked to their webs in the warm leafage. (p. 244:263)

This comparison of hand and spider immediately recalls Garine's vision of Lenin (see above, p. 27) and all the concomitant futility of *Les Conquérants*. The insect, hyperbole of otherness, and the death which it symbolizes fall upon Perken almost simultaneously: "A mosquito settled on an eyelid; he could not move" [36] (p. 246:264).

A last insect metaphor establishes an irrefutable equation between death, the insect, and the futility of existence: "Men walked the earth, men who believed in their passions, their sorrows, their own existence—insects under the leaves, a teeming multitude beneath the far-flung canopy of death" (p. 246:265).

The uniting of various imagistic patterns throughout *La Voie royale,* especially in scenes of particular tension, testifies to Malraux's novelistic maturity in this second major work of fiction. The work does more, however, than masterfully weave a coherent fabric of metaphor; the author had discovered a tension between abstract concepts and metaphoric language, a tension which would remain characteristic of his work through *Les Noyers de l'Altenburg.* Each of Malraux's novels poses abstract (metaphysical, psychological, or political) problems. The author's ability not only to illustrate the problems posed but actually to bring them to some resolution through tensive and symbolic language is a major novelistic achievement. Thus, in *La Voie royale,* although Perken suggests certain problems common to all Westerners (the erotic conflict, enslavement to a meaningless social order, and futile rage directed against the aging process), his arguments are left unresolved in explicit terms; they are dealt with only in the symbolic and Pascalian universe of the Cambodian forest during this dark voyage of self-discovery. The conclusions are far from optimistic. The novel testifies to the failure of Western man to find a meaning or permanence purely through adventurous action or escape. "Seeking oneself and fleeing oneself are equally senseless activities" (*TO,* p. 59:111). It was this failure of action in isolation which would bring the novelist back into the domain of society to test the value of his beliefs in the context of a Marxist revolution.

THE IMPRISONING OBSESSION
OF THE HUMAN CONDITION

It is no longer a question of painting a world, as they said of Balzac, but of expressing through images the development of a personal problem.—"L'Attitude de l'artiste," Commune, November 1934

The thrust of Tchen's dagger, which impales Tan-yen-ta on his bed in the opening scene of *La Condition humaine*, provides a sharp contrast to the first scenes of Malraux's two previous novels. The substitution for the telegraphed reports which had opened *Les Conquérants* of a scene of compelling and violent action suggests a parallel movement from Garine's philosophical distance from Communism to a new context of fervent and unquestioned dedication to a Marxist revolution.

And yet, the murder accomplished, Tchen immediately realizes that "to assassinate is not only to kill" (p. 4:12), and that, far from entering the world of the engaged militant ("Tchen had not even given it a thought" [p. 8:17]), he feels only separation from "the world of men" (p. 3:11). His isolation "in this night in which time no longer existed" intensifies as he becomes aware that "beneath his sacrifice to the Revolution lay a world of depths" (p. 4:12) which cut him off from "the world of the living" (p. 6:10), from "the life of men who do not kill . . . millions of lives [which] all now rejected his" (p. 7:10). Forever branded by this "world of murder," Tchen cannot cast off his sense of isolation even when reunited with his comrades.

Every attempt to explain this new sense of separation has resort to the same metaphor. Tchen returns to Kyo and Katow: "Little by little it seemed as if he were discovering them—like his sister the first time he had come back from a brothel" (p. 12:22). Confused by this preliminary association, Tchen seeks the advice of Gisors, who asks, "The first woman you ever slept with was a prostitute of course? . . . What did you feel afterwards?" Tchen replies only, "Pride . . . at not being a woman" (pp. 57–58:72–73). Since the Western-educated Tchen feels his own sensations and imagines those of his partner (cf. *TO,* p. 53:93), his scorn for the other would result from the projection of his own feelings of self-alienation derived from his earlier auto-eroticism: "From half-confidences, it seemed that the acquaintance of prostitutes and students had made him overcome the only sin that had always been stronger than Tchen's will-power, masturbation; and with it, a constantly recurring feeling of anxiety and degradation" (p. 63:78). For Tchen as for Perken, the erotic act is evidently a moment of self-definition through constraint. Whereas Perken's early sexual experiences had defined his control over the world, Tchen's experiences lead only to projection of his own self-degradation and ultimately to anguish.

Tchen's sense of isolation is finally elucidated by a further recourse to erotic imagery. He says to Gisors: "You were right to speak of women. Perhaps one thoroughly despises the man one kills. But less than the others . . . than the ones who don't kill. The weaklings (*puceaux*)" (p. 58:73). For Tchen both killing and the sexual act, involving the sadistic degradation of another being, leave the aggressor feeling not merely disdain for the submissiveness of the victim but even greater contempt for the virgins who have never dared to commit themselves.

More than simply a key to Tchen's social attitudes, as Lucien Goldmann has claimed,[1] the erotic attitude provides a sure indication of Tchen's attitudes about himself, his sense of isolation, and ultimately the anguish which destroys him.

Already in the assassination scene (which itself, in light of the language of eroticism, approaches a sexual act) [2] Tchen's solitude takes on Pascalian overtones: [3] "In his anguish the night seemed to whirl like an enormous smoke-cloud shot with sparks; slowly it settled into immobility. . . . Between the tattered clouds, the stars resumed their endless course" (p. 7:16). Confronted by this immensity, Tchen comes face to face with his problematical status. In the absence of any authentic value—God, Christ, or commitment to other men [4]—he chooses death. Still another erotic metaphor serves to elucidate Tchen's suicidal decision to flee his anguish: "I know what one does with women when they want to continue to possess you: one lives with them. What about death?" Gisors retorts: "Then, you must think it through and carry it to the extreme. And if you want to live with it . . ." which Tchen interrupts with "I shall soon be killed" (pp. 58–59:73–74).

Tchen's suicidal passion for terrorism is finally related to the problem of alienation in the description of the proposed assassination, which clearly reflects Tchen's awareness of its erotic nature: "In the business of murder the difficult thing isn't to kill—the thing is not to go to pieces: to be stronger than . . . what happens inside one at that moment" (p. 146:178). Clearly one must not look inward, for "one can always find terror in himself. One only needs to look deep enough: fortunately one can act" (p. 148:180). This rejection of introspection in favor of action immediately precedes the equation with sexual expression of Tchen's projected assassination of Chiang Kai-shek. Must he be the executioner? "No . . . and yet I wouldn't want to leave it to another. . . . Because I don't like the women I love to be kissed (baisées) by others" (p. 149:181). Together these passages elucidate Tchen's "downward ecstasy" toward his own death (p. 147:179). His discovery both that action is merely an avoidance of the inner self and that murder, like the sexual act, only projects an inner degradation onto the world leaves Tchen no respite from himself. The subsequent scorn of others *and* of self leads to an increasingly tragic sense of isolation, an anguish whose final solution becomes self-annihilation. Thus, for Tchen, "seeking oneself and fleeing

oneself are equally senseless activities" (*TO*, p. 59:102), for each mer-
cilessly forces him to acknowledge his problematical isolation.

The effectiveness of erotic attitudes and metaphors [5] as a key to individual authenticity is well demonstrated by Malraux's treatment of
Ferral's affair with Valérie. Their relationship remains devoid of love
since "the difficulties which beset [Ferral's] present life drove him
into (*l'enfermaient dans*) eroticism, not into love" (p. 114:139). This
suggestion that eroticism derives from weakness rather than power (as
suggested by his insistence on constraint) in turn explains Ferral's
sense of isolation (whence the verb *enfermer*). The affair takes on dis-
tinctly existential overtones with Ferral's observation, "No one can be
adequately explained by his life" (p. 114:139), despite his avowed
search for such an explanation: "in this game he was involving what
was most essential to him in life" (p. 114:139).

Ferral's obsession with eroticism clearly derives from his need for
self-definition: "He went to women to be judged, he who counte-
nanced no judgment" (pp. 229–30:274). Seeking judgment yet simultaneously refusing to be judged by others, it is small wonder that
he contends, "To give herself, for a woman, to possess, for a man, are
the only two means that human beings have of understanding anything whatsoever" (p. 117:143), and, as a corollary, "man can and
must deny woman" (p. 227:271).

Ferral's entire philosophy of social relations directly parallels his
definition of intelligence: "the possession of the means of coercing
things or men" (p. 225:268). He therefore depersonalizes Valérie into
a "living adversary." To Valérie, a woman is first of all a human
being. "To her, perhaps; not to him. A woman, a human being! She
is . . . an enemy" (p. 230:274). In his effort to strip his sexual partner of any personality, Ferral reduces women first to "shadows" (p.
213:255) and finally to nonexistence (p. 230:274).

To verify this domination of his partner, Ferral needs the evidence
of Valérie's complete submission, at the level of "what was deepest,
most secret in her" (p. 118:144). However, his attempt at penetrating
to her most private core by "destroying a mask" results only in the

creation of a second mask of sensuality, underneath which lies resentment.

Ultimately Ferral is thrown back on the prototypical mode of eroticism, projection: [6] "He imagined himself as her, inhabiting her body, feeling in her place that enjoyment *which he could experience only as a humiliation* . . . she was nothing but the other pole of his own pleasure" (p. 119:145; italics mine). The ambiguity of Ferral's humiliation (either his interpretation of Valérie's submission or, more likely, a recognition of his failure to dominate her completely) and the identification of Valérie as a projection of his own desire indicate a growing awareness of the impossibility of dominating anything more substantial than a creation of his own imagination. Ultimately, "Ferral never went to bed with anyone but himself" (p. 231:275–76), introversion which recalls Tchen's isolation.

Valérie easily demonstrates the bankruptcy of a philosophy dependent entirely upon domination for purposes of self-realization. In publicly refusing Ferral, "She had struck him at his most sensitive point . . . she denied him" (p. 214:257). Since he had engaged what was "most essential to him in life—his pride" (p. 114:139), Valérie's actions effectively deny his definition of self, so carefully constructed in the erotic encounter. It takes only one unconquerable being to undermine the conqueror's control over the world. For the explicit explanation of this failure, Ferral, like Tchen before him, turns to Gisors, who teaches him:

> It is very rare for a man to be able to endure . . . his condition, his fate as a man. . . . There is always a need for intoxication: this country has opium, Islam has hashish, the West has women. . . . Perhaps love is above all the means which the Occidental uses to free himself from man's fate. (p. 227:270–71)

At the suggestion that eroticism replaces authentic acts through its comfortable system of self-judgment by the denial of others and the projection of one's own feelings, Ferral claims: "A man is the sum of his actions, of that he has *done,* of what he can do. Nothing else" (p. 228:271).

This claim, however, not only directly contradicts his previous assertion that "no one can be adequately explained by his life" (p. 114:139), it avoids the whole problem of judgment. In fact, Ferral is convinced that he alone may judge his acts and that the only valid form of action is domination. Gisors corrects him:

> Man has no urge to govern: he has an urge to compel, as you said. To be more than a man, in a world of men. To escape man's fate, I was saying. Not powerful: all-powerful. The visionary disease, of which the will to power is only the intellectual justification, is the will to god-head; every man dreams of being god. (p. 228:272)

Ferral's game of domination is doomed when Valérie refuses to submit, and exposed when Gisors demonstrates that only God can always dominate; every conqueror must eventually fail. In the company of a courtesan, Ferral realizes that eroticism is "the humiliation of oneself or of the other person, *perhaps of both*" (p. 231:275), and that

> he had lived, fought, created; beneath all those appearances, deep down, he found this to be the only reality, the joy of abandoning himself, of leaving upon the shore, like the body of a drowned companion, that creature, himself, whose life it was necessary each day to invent anew . . . his will to power never achieved its object, lived only by renewing it. . . . He needed the eyes of others to see himself, the senses of another to feel himself. (pp. 230–31:276)

His efforts at domination are, as Gisors has demonstrated, merely games invented to provide him with an identity but at which, like Garine and Perken before him, he is destined to fail.

Just as Tchen and Ferral couch their fundamental aggressiveness in sexual metaphors, so Clappique uses erotic imagery to describe the fragmentation of his inner self. His sexual relations, like his other human contacts, are grounded in a refusal of reality. After a disastrous evening at the gambling table, attempting to "flee himself by any means," he takes up with a prostitute, realizing that "I am like a woman who doesn't know what a new lover is going to get out of her" (p. 248:296). He reiterates Tchen's parallel between erotic activities and the escape from self by relating his inner inconsistencies to the variety of sexual responses from a single woman.

Clappique's most significant sexual encounter, deleted from the final work but published separately as "A l'hôtel des sensations interdites," [7] describes his attempt to seduce an alluring but anonymous nude. Begun in darkness, the affair ends in panic. He rushes out, imagining others in the room with him—a concrete expression of his inner dispersion and reduplication. Of Clappique it might almost be said, "He never went to bed with anyone but his various selves." [8]

Thus far, the theme and imagery of eroticism have consistently demonstrated the problematic aspects of each character. One would therefore expect that if, as Lucien Goldmann claimed,[9] Kyo *as militant* fulfills Malraux's requirements for a nonproblematical character, one in possession of authentic values, he will be subject to neither the interior anguish nor the erotic obsessions of the others.

Refusing to capitulate to society's absurdity, the militant views collective action as a means of radically improving the human condition. His positive goals provide a guarantee against eventual disillusionment at the moment of defeat or victory, for their scope precludes the possibility of attainment within any single lifetime. The ideal militant immerses his sense of self in both a historical process and a collectivity. He voluntarily submits to a higher authority, which, by demanding his total commitment, absolves him of a degree of responsibility.[10]

One would then expect that the militant's human relationships would reflect his positive and untroubled stance, and that his love relationships in particular would be free of the need for erotic manipulations. A more careful examination of the Kyo-May relationship, however, reveals a number of problems which seriously undermine the concept of Kyo's fundamental authenticity. His father, Gisors, observes before the insurrection begins:

> Kyo had chosen action, in a grave and premeditated way, as others choose a military career, or the sea. . . . The heroic sense had given

him a kind of discipline, not a kind of justification of life. He was
not restless. His life had a meaning, and he knew what it was: to
give to each of these men whom famine, at this very moment, was
killing off like a slow plague, the sense of his own dignity. (pp.
63–64:79–80)

Gisors's testimony apparently constructs the perfect Marxist militant,
but this assessment of his son includes the reflection: "Individual
problems existed for Kyo *only in his private life*" (p. 64:80; italics
mine). Indeed, Kyo's first reactions to May's infidelity are sadistic,
jealous, and ultimately erotic:

> The revelation of what he wanted finally flashed upon him; to lie
> with her, to find refuge in her body against this frenzy in which he
> was losing her entirely; *they did not have to know each other* when
> they were using all their strength to hold each other in a tight em-
> brace. (p. 50:64; italics mine)

Kyo's denial of the need to know May brings to mind Perken's insistence that "the essential thing is not to know the partner" (*VR*, p.
7:15), as well as Ferral's inability to accept Valérie as anything more
than the opposite pole of his desire. Like Ferral, whose eroticism ultimately leads to a crisis of identity, Kyo then wonders:

> "But I, to myself . . . what am I? A kind of absolute, the affirmation
> of an idiot: an intensity greater than that of all the rest. To others, I
> am what I have done." To May alone, he was not what he had done;
> to him alone, she was something altogether different from her biog-
> raphy. (p. 53:67)

What is this thing altogether different from biography? "The madman, *the incomparable monster, dear above all things, that every
being is to himself and that he cherishes in his heart*" (p. 53:67; italics mine). Malraux had earlier identified this "incomparable monster"
as the subconscious, and concluded that any attempt exhaustively to
define oneself would result in the Absurd:

> Our consciousness of what is distinctive about our lives is not com-
> municated to us by facts. It resides in the deepest part of us; when

one of us thinks "I," it is not acts which he conjures up. . . . It is an image in which our special deformation of the world is given free rein. . . . To attempt to define the ego amounts to forcing it to disperse in various probabilities. . . . Doctrines which are attached to personality decorate our deepest self with a clever mythology, especially noteworthy for the quality of its constantly changing lies. To push this search for oneself to the limit, *while accepting one's own world,* is to verge on the absurd.[11]

Far from the paradigm of the unproblematic, Kyo encounters a fundamental crisis of identity triggered by the discovery of his erotic tendencies and intensified by his obsession with the unfamiliar sound of his recorded voice. From Gisors, Kyo learns that whereas one listens to others with one's ears, one hears oneself with the throat.[12] This discovery that one applies different criteria to the examination of self than to the scrutiny of others closely parallels the erotic game and indeed constitutes a displacement of the anguish of the search for self-definition in eroticism:

His torment returned, and he remembered the records: "We hear the voices of others with our ears, our own voices with our throats." Yes. One hears his own life, too, with his throat, and those of others? . . . "But I, to myself, to my throat, what am I?" (pp. 52–53:67)

Unlike Ferral, Kyo does not rely completely on eroticism to *replace* awareness of his primitive inner life [13] with projections of his partner's admiration. Like Ferral, however, he refuses real judgment from others: "My kind are those who love me *and do not look at me"* (p. 53:67; italics mine). Kyo thus discovers simultaneously a relationship with May based on blindness rather than understanding and a paradoxical need and refusal to define himself which conspire to isolate him in an irresolvable anguish.[14]

Katow is the sole combatant who appears to escape the existential problems posed by the erotic obsession.[15] Katow's freedom from this obsession and his thorough commitment to the revolution would appear to cast him as the sole nonproblematical character in the novel.

I have insisted on the erotic theme in *La Condition humaine* beyond its purely metaphoric development because it most clearly establishes a key to individual attitudes toward one's self and the world. In the case of every erotic obsessive the failure of the sexual experience forces a return to the world of action to reassert a waning ability to control, possess, or define. Malraux frequently resorts to the image of gambling at these moments of crisis to suggest the desperation of such action.

Ferral, the most erotically obsessed and thoroughly defeated character, proves the true heir of the gamblers Perken and Garine in his frequent resort to gambling imagery when he attempts to escape from his failure with Valérie through successful participation in the world of men. During their first encounter, Ferral reflects, "He was not unaware that *in this game* he was involving what was most essential to him in life—his pride" (p. 114:139; italics mine), while Valérie asserts even more explicitly, "It's a game" (p. 117:143). Ferral mentally defines their relationship even more candidly: "His pride called for a hostile pride, as a passionate player calls for another player to oppose him" (p. 213:255).

Politically, Ferral gambles on the card most likely to favor his personal advancement, considering his activities in the Far East only a temporary diversion: "He was playing a waiting game here" (p. 83:104). Projecting a triumphal return to Paris, "he did not intend to play the same game again; he was going to change the rules" (p. 83:105). "It was his dream to return to France . . . to get back into the political *game* and, having cautiously reached the cabinet, to pit (*jouer*) the combined forces of the cabinet and a bought public opinion against the Parliament" (pp. 84–85:106; italics mine).

Economically threatened by the Communists' intended nationalization of foreign investments, Ferral decides to buy Chiang's favor, acknowledging that "today he was among those through whom the fate of Shanghai was being decided (*se jouait*). All the economic forces, almost all the consulates were playing the same game as he" (p. 112:137–38). Gambling images permeate Ferral's every consideration of the political situation in Shanghai (cf. pp. 211–12:254).

Ferral's vocabulary reduces the negotiations at the Paris meeting of the consortium, following the repression of the Shanghai revolt, to a poker game whose chips represent industries and corporations. Fantasizing that he "holds the Havas Agency among his cards," Ferral muses with satisfaction that "the State can no more play seriously against the banks than the banks against the State" (pp. 325–26:389). Though Ferral's efforts will be rejected by the Paris group, he recalls with satisfaction an adversary's earlier characterization of him: "Ferral always wants a bank to be a gambling house" (p. 328:392).

The similarities between Ferral's and Perken's insistence on the theme of gambling (including the imperative of high stakes) throw a Pascalian light upon the Shanghai adventure and on Ferral's attempts to relieve his despair through constant *divertissement*. As Malraux's first two novels demonstrated, such a maneuver ultimately leads to disillusionment and defeat.

Certain flaws in Kyo's militancy revealed in the discussion of eroticism leave him vulnerable to fundamental doubts. His impasse in the quest for self-knowledge, coupled with the abandonment of his Shanghai organization by the Comintern, produces "the anguish of being nothing more than a man . . . who suffers and who knows he is to die" (p. 144:177). A moment later Kyo quotes his father: "the essence of man is anguish, the consciousness of his own fatality" (p. 148:180). It is at this point that Kyo takes up the image of gambling to express his despair: "Kyo had once and for all accepted the fact that his life was menaced (*il* JOUAIT *sa propre vie*)" (p. 147:179; emphasis added). The phrase recalls Perken's "It seems to me sometimes that I am staking myself, all that I am, on a single moment—my last" (*VR*, p. 144:160); like Perken, Kyo will repeat the metaphor when confronted with the certainty of death.[16]

Gisors, introduced as an embodiment of the antithesis of action, is nonetheless forced to gamble. Addicted to opium, which he equates with eroticism as an escape from the human condition (p. 227:271), Gisors, like the erotic obsessive, finds ultimate escape impossible.

Opium cannot eradicate the painful awareness of his son's impending arrest. Like Ferral and Tchen, Gisors must become involved. Having sent Clappique to intercede in a hopeless cause, he realizes that "Clappique was neither an interpreter nor a messenger—he was a card. The card had been played—he had lost. He would have to find another" (p. 269:320).

Ironically it is Clappique who crystallizes the gambling image, although he gambles hoping to *avoid* action. His evening in the casino provides not only a concretion of the image pattern but also the key to the entire pattern.[17] Clappique quickly realizes that financial need as a pretext for gambling is absurd; the real reason involves the need for risk.

> To win, no longer in order to take flight, but to remain, to risk more, so that the stake of his conquered liberty would render the gesture even more absurd! . . . he was discovering the very meaning of gambling, the frenzy of losing. "It's r-remarkable," he thought, "how people can say that the player's sensation is caused by his hope of winning! It's as if they said that men fight duels to become fencing champions." (pp. 241, 243:288, 291).

Clappique's basic conclusions may be applied to all of the gamblers in the novel. At one point he pauses long enough to consider passers-by beneath the casino window as "weak, stupid lives . . . shadows: voices in the night," and decides that "those who did not gamble were not men" (p. 240:287–88). This imperative to gamble when juxtaposed with Clappique's other major discovery that "gambling is a suicide without death" (p. 242:290) clearly demonstrates the impasse of action in Malraux's world.

Seen retrospectively, each decision to gamble follows closely upon the discovery of an impossible conflict: in the cases of Tchen, Ferral, Clappique, and Gisors a failure to control reality through erotic constraint or opium and finally failure to find positive self-definition. For Kyo the conflict arises between the desire for, and the refusal of, self-knowledge. Like Garine, Grabot, and Perken before them, each stakes his life on the proposition that action will provide a definition of self where other means have failed. In the light of Garine's and Perken's disillusionment, however, and with Gisors's definition of action as "the illusion of being able to do exactly as they please . . . [an] elaborate self-deception" (pp. 228–29:272–73), Malraux clearly indicates that the decision to gamble one's life can only represent suicide on the installment plan.

The alternative to suicidal gambling in *La Condition humaine* is hardly more attractive. The refusal to act, or the impossibility of action, is communicated on the personal level by the Belgian Hemmelrich, and on the symbolic level by the helpless agony of Hemmelrich's child. Afflicted with incurable mastoiditis, the child is "hardly more than a baby. . . . All he knew of life so far was suffering" (p. 175:214). Sustained by Hemmelrich's submissive poverty, the disease invites interpretation as a symbol of the ills of poverty-ridden China, contaminated by Western colonialism.

On a more limited and personal level, the sick child represents for Hemmelrich the impossibility of action. Restrained from revolutionary participation by responsibilities to his family, he wastes his life in helpless frustration and anger. This loss of liberty creates an impression of mortal illness: Hemmelrich "looked like a boxer gone to seed (*boxeur crevé*)" (p. 11:20). Only Katow understands Hemmelrich's agony: [18] "He knew from experience that the worst suffering is in the solitude which accompanies it. . . . he suffered above all from himself" (p. 208:250).

When, near the end of the insurrection, the Belgian finds his shop bombed, he discovers that "he was especially afraid of having to stand by and watch a slow death, powerless, only able to suffer, as usual" (pp. 252–53:302). His suffering is equated to that of his wife and child and, like Garine's and Perken's sickness, menaces him with a gradual decline which he feels powerless to combat. The elimination of his child's incurable disease ironically signals an end to the sickness of submission which had so long incapacitated Hemmelrich. His immediate reactions to the loss of his family are given in terms of healing: "He knew he was suffering, but a halo of indifference surrounded his grief, the indifference which follows upon an illness or a blow in the head . . . now he was no longer impotent. Now, *he too could kill*" (pp. 253–54:302–3).

Appropriately, imagery recalling Perken's fatal wounds also translates moments in which Ferral's consuming need for the power to constrain and dominate others is compromised or defeated. The Shanghai revolution threatens the entire life of the consortium, Ferral's only source of political power and, ultimately, of pride. As the insurrectionists pound on his automobile windows, Ferral feels physically attacked: "Just as he would have meditated upon the meaning of his life had he been wounded, so now that his enterprises were menaced he was meditating upon them" (p. 83:104). This reference to existential anguish in the presence of physical disability creates still another link between Ferral and Perken.

Sickness images no less effectively portray Clappique's compulsive mythomaniacal behavior as a debilitating submission to an inner dispersion. Into the frivolity of his various impersonations Clappique injects a note of tragicomic irony to describe his own behavior: "You see my face? That's what twenty years of hereditary whimsicality lead to. It resembles syphilis" (p. 25:36). The comparison, suggesting more than the cancer of aging experienced by Perken and Garine, conveys the decomposition of Clappique's free will through the escapism of his lies.[19] Yet because he is "one of those rare beings who had no [reality]" (p. 262:313), "Clappique's affliction was independent of him, like that of a child; he was not responsible for it; it could destroy him, it could not modify him" (pp. 262–63:313). This reference to the suffering of a child clearly alludes to Hemmelrich, whose invalid son constitutes a barrier to authenticity. Clappique's distance from his own suffering, his inability to discern true feelings and/or values from mythical ones, constitute a similar obstacle to authentic action.

From *La Voie royale* we recall that Perken's first sense of his own mortality arose from the realization of the aging of his wife. Echoes of

Sarah's dilemma reverberate throughout the Kyo-May misunderstanding. Kyo's love for May is "the only thing in him that was as strong as death" (p. 54:68); the erosion of their love would therefore constitute an acceptance of death which would in turn rob his revolutionary action of meaning. With his first doubt of her love, images of sickness threaten him with spiritual extinction. Lying with May at his side, Kyo sees himself "like a sick man being nursed by her" (p. 46:60). In terms which again recall Sarah's effect on Perken,[20] Kyo considers that

> nothing, however, prevailed against the discoloration of that face buried in the depth of their common life as in mist, as in the earth. He remembered a friend who had had to watch the disintegration of the mind of the woman he loved, paralyzed for months; it seemed to him that he was watching May die thus, watching the form of his happiness absurdly disappear like a cloud absorbed by the gray sky. As though she had died twice—from the effect of time, and from what she was telling him. (p. 46:60)

Another comparison renders the Kyo-Perken parallel even more explicit: "He was suddenly separated from her . . . by a feeling that had no name, as destructive as time or death" (p. 49:64). Moments later "he was before her as before a death-bed; and as towards a death-bed, instinct threw him towards her: to touch, to feel, to hold back those who are leaving you, to cling to them" (p. 50:64). The more the notion of time ("a cancer" [VR, p. 142:158]) is associated with May's imagined death the more Kyo resembles Perken and the more problematic his status.

Finally the image of "their love, so often hurt, uniting them like a sick child" (p. 46:60), reiterated in the phrase "With her alone I have this love in common, injured or not, as others have children who are ill and in danger of dying" (p. 53:68), establishes an implicit comparison with Hemmelrich. Although, in each case, the general sense of the image denotes unity, the negative connotations of the sick child (especially in the context of the Kyo-Perken parallel) overshadow any positive value of such words as "uniting," "love," and "in common." Kyo's "sick child," like Hemmelrich's, confines him to problematical preoccupation with aging and death.

Through the metaphor of eroticism which leads to the confrontation between the image of the wager (action as suicide) and that of sickness (refusal of action as a passive form of suicide), Malraux once again encounters an insurmountable obstacle in his development of a personal problem through imagery. Two other major patterns of imagery in the novel contribute their pessimistic weight to the impasse.

Insect imagery, as in *Les Conquérants* and *La Voie royale*, forcefully communicates the obsessive presence of death in the opening scene of the work, as Tchen undertakes his first political assassination. In the darkness of the hotel room, Tchen first examines Tan-yen-ta's fragile netting which his knife will render ineffectual against both insects and death. Fascinated by the resiliency of flesh, Tchen compulsively drives the knife into his own arm. As the sleeping man suddenly shifts, Tchen shudders: "an insect was running over his skin! —blood trickling down his arm" (pp. 4–5:13). From the first scene, death, blood, and the insect are suggestively associated to produce a sensation of both fascination and horror.[21]

The concurrence of the arrival of death and the presence of an insect continues throughout the novel. Finding himself in the first minutes of the insurrection alone in a street filled only seconds previously with the bustle of midday marketing, Ferral is immediately aware of "the silence . . . [which]seemed to forbode the end of the world. . . . A silence full of lives at once remote and very near, like that of a forest saturated with insects" (p. 86:108). This evocation of *La Voie royale* poignantly isolates the Westerner in a hostile and potentially fatal environment.

A more explicit development of the insect metaphor occurs as the members of the Comintern assemble at Party headquarters in a last futile attempt to resist the Kuomintang. Hemmelrich, now liberated by the death of both wife and child, enters amid the furious activity of the doomed men: "Like a nest of insects, the vast hall was alive with an activity whose meaning was obscured but whose movement was clear" (p. 255:305).

After Chiang's forces have destroyed the Party headquarters, Hemmelrich's attempt to escape is momentarily thwarted by an enemy soldier suddenly looming over tangled barbed wire, a symbol of his destiny:

> He was watching that mass passing from one wire to another. . . . Like an enormous insect, it hung to a wire, fell back, attached itself again. . . . It seemed to Hemmelrich that the monstrous insect might remain there forever, enormous and knotted, suspended against the gray light. (p. 274:326)

The suspicion of imminent death provoked by this sinister metamorphosis is soon generalized into all the forces of destiny:

> The monster—man, bear and spider combined—continued to disentangle itself from the wires. . . . Hemmelrich felt himself at the bottom of a hole, fascinated less by the creature that was moving so slowly, approaching like death itself, than by everything that followed it, everything that was once more going to crush him, like a coffin-lid screwed down over a living person; it was everything that had choked his everyday life, which was now returning to crush him with one blow. (pp. 274–75:326–27)

The spider here not only heralds death, it recalls all that had robbed Hemmelrich of liberty and rendered him a living corpse.

The insect also expresses submission to other forms of destiny. After his disastrous evening at the Casino, Clappique falls prey to an anguished presentiment of death. Unable to banish this disquiet in an erotic encounter, he is metaphorically transfigured into the symbol of his morbid obsession: "Slumped on the bench, legs crossed and arms held tightly to his sides like a delicate insect" (p. 246:295), Clappique submits completely to "his lie . . . the fictive world he was creating."

Whereas Clappique demonstrates a morally weak capitulation to his mythomania, Tchen exemplifies the opposite extreme, submission to an *idée fixe*. His life revolves exclusively around the idea of death and the conviction that he alone has the right to eliminate Chiang. To Kyo such a narrow and obsessive aim constitutes a restriction of one's freedom of action, a form of enslavement equal to physical incarceration. As Kyo leaves Tchen on the docks at Han Keou, he considers his friend's decision, despite Party opposition, to kill Chiang: "He knew some terrorists. They asked no questions. They composed a group: murderous insects, they lived by their bond of union in a tragic narrow group (*un étroit guêpier*)" (p. 149:181; emphasis added). In an image reminiscent of both Perken and Garine, Kyo sees his friend, and gradually himself as well, as each subservient to his personal destiny:

> Each of Tchen's gestures brought him nearer again to murder, and things themselves seemed to be pulled along by his destiny. Moths (*éphémères*) fluttered about the little lamp. "Perhaps Tchen is a moth (*un éphémère*) who secretes his own light—in which he will destroy himself. . . . Perhaps man himself . . ." Is it only the fatality of others that one sees, never one's own? Was it not like a moth (*éphémère*) that he himself now wanted to leave for Shanghai as soon as possible to maintain the sections at any price? (pp. 155–56:189)

This comparison insists on the submission incurred by any overly rigid or dogmatic stance, through the explicit vocabulary "pulled along by his destiny," "destroy himself," and "at any price"; through the generalizing fragment "Perhaps man himself"; and through its deliberate recollection of Perken's description of the insects drawn to the camp light, "in complete submission to that light." [22] Kyo himself hesitates between two alternative forms of submission: an obedience to the Party which amounts to suicide, or a total commitment to his own rigid determination to maintain the fighting capacity of his cadres. Unable to formulate a rational response to the dilemma, Kyo seeks an answer in the surrounding night:

> Along the banks, near the street-lamps crackling with insects, coolies lay sleeping in postures of people afflicted with the plague. . . . He felt, as he had a while ago with Tchen, that on this very night, in all

China, and throughout the West, including half of Europe, men were hesitating as he was, torn by the same torment between their discipline and the massacre of their own kind. (p. 156:189)

The overwhelming negative weight of the insect's fatal light tropism, associated with the plague-ridden coolies, overshadows Kyo's choice between discipline and massacre and reveals the irresolvable nature of his dilemma.

Kyo reinvokes the insect as a powerful metaphor of physical submission during his imprisonment among a group of caged, dehumanized beings. To express the terror and fascination felt before the submission of these "worms," Malraux resorts to the most fundamental of his insect images, that which derives directly from childhood traumata, for the third time in his writings: [23] "Those obscure beings who stirred behind the bars, disturbing like the colossal insect and crustaceans in his childhood dreams, were no more human" (p. 281:337).

What disturbs Kyo is not so much the affront to dignity in these cages as his own morbid fascination:

> Kyo was . . . looking, hardly able to see anything. . . . "Compassion or cruelty?" he wondered, terrified. What is base, and also what is susceptible to fascination in every man was being appealed to with the most savage vehemence, and Kyo was struggling with his whole mind against human ignominy—he remembered the effort it had always required of him to get away from tortured bodies seen by chance: he had literally had to tear himself away. . . . It was the same paralyzing horror, quite different from fear, an all-powerful horror even before the mind had appraised it, and all the more upsetting as Kyo was excruciatingly aware of his own helplessness. (p. 282:338)

The metaphor of the insect couples the theme of submission with that of an incontrollable subconscious in an indictment of Kyo's authenticity. As with the recording of his voice, Kyo falls prey to interior forces which erode his militancy.

The association of the insect with the imprisoned men is doubly effective since, as has been seen, insect and prison present parallel images of man's submission, whether to external destiny or to involuntary acceptance of inner chaos.

Images of the prison which illumine the physical, psychological, and metaphysical restrictions within the human condition continue to develop from *La Voie royale*. Malraux describes Tchen, Ferral, and Clappique, whose actions are frequently dictated by an overpowering obsession, in terms of captivity. After Tchen's disquisition on the necessity of terrorism, Gisors reflects: "He had thrown himself into the world of murder, from which he would never emerge: with his passion, he was entering upon the life of a terrorist as into a prison" (p. 60:75–76). His subsequent recollection that "in order to live . . . [Tchen] needed first of all to escape from his Christianity" (p. 63:78) emphasizes the insistent presence of the prison in the younger man's life.

In each case Gisors relates the psychological confines of Tchen's obsessions to the other prison to which those obsessions inexorably lead. When Tchen pushes his obsession to the limit by throwing himself, bomb in hand, under Chiang's car, he encounters that larger imprisonment to which Gisors alluded. Regaining consciousness, he discovers only his indifference to Chiang's fate and the loss of all meaning in a larger circle of destiny: "Everything was turning, slowly and inevitably, along a great circle—and yet nothing existed but pain" (p. 235:279). In a book so explicitly grounded on Pascal's image of the human condition (see below, p. 80), this reference to a great circle of inevitability must allude to Pascal's despair at the disproportion between man and "the vast orbit described by the stars revolving in the firmament." [24] Tchen's last seconds of consciousness are filled with the sense of his own nothingness in "this little dungeon . . . the universe." [25] His imprisonment is complete.

Whereas Tchen's obsession is terrorism and Ferral's is domination,[26] Clappique's obsession takes the form of evasion through mythomania, flight from the responsibilities of a fixed identity by imagination and artful impersonation.[27] He also avoids involvement by passionately immersing himself in roulette. At first conscious of the passing time, he becomes captivated by the tiny ball spinning as inexorably as Grabot moving around his mill. He throws down his last chips as if hypnotized and actually chained to the ball: "He tossed it with his right hand; he no longer moved the left one, as if the motionlessness of the ball were somehow holding it tied" (p. 238:286). As if fate has destined him to remain at the wheel, he refuses escape from the table: [28] "To win, no longer in order to take flight, but to remain, to risk more, so that the stake of his conquered liberty would render the gesture even more absurd!" (p. 241:288). Clappique's passion for gambling ironically involves more than one imprisonment: [29]

> Now he was playing his last cent, his life and that of another, especially that of another. He knew he was sacrificing Kyo; it was Kyo who was chained to that ball, to that table, and it was he, Clappique, who was that ball, which was master of everyone and of himself. (p. 242:290)

Once outside, Clappique (like Tchen before him) discovers a surrounding immensity in terms which again evoke Pascal's little dungeon of the universe:

> . . . the serenity of the night seemed to have put to flight . . . all the anxieties, all the griefs of men. . . . The moon had just emerged from a tattered bank of clouds and was slowly drifting into an immense, dark and transparent hole like a lake with its depths full of stars. Its light, growing more intense, gave to all those sealed houses, to the complete desertion of the city, an extra-terrestrial life as if the moon's atmosphere had come and settled in the great sudden silence together with its light. . . . Death, even his own death, was not very real in this atmosphere, so inhuman that he felt himself an intruder. . . . the moon reached the opposite bank, and all fell back into darkness . . . the anxious night in which the street-lights, just now blurred by mist, formed large tremulous circles on the sidewalks. (pp. 243–44:291–92)

In this night whose immense panorama of stars mirrors the tremulous circles of streetlights, Clappique's life and death lose all proportion.

The prison of his personal destiny symbolized by the roulette wheel is engulfed by the larger prison of the universe. The entire scene, uniting the prison image with the theme of gambling, forcefully reiterates the impossibility of escape from the human condition.

A last futile flight from reality leads Clappique to disguise himself as a sailor and to stow away on a steamer bound for Europe, which represents not liberty but an ironic return to the original social enslavement from which he, like Garine, had sought escape: [30] "Europe, he thought; the feast is over. Now Europe. It seemed to be coming towards him with the bell that was approaching, no longer as one of liberation, but as of a prison" (p. 295:352).

Even Kyo encounters a sense of imprisonment before his actual incarceration by the Kuomintang. After the disastrous interview with Vologin in Hankow, Kyo and Tchen suddenly face the certainty of death if they return to Shanghai, and with "the anguish of being nothing more than a man . . . who suffers and knows he has to die." This awful realization unites Kyo and Tchen in "a prisoner's friendship" (p. 145:177).

Although Tchen, Ferral, and Clappique are never physically restrained, each is doomed by his particular egoism—terrorism, eroticism, or mythomania—to an even greater sense of separation than the militant Katow, who can find dignity and fraternity even within prison walls.

The scene in which Kyo and Katow are forced to watch their comrades led off to a fiery death in the furnaces of a locomotive whose whistle signals each succeeding execution is central to an understanding of the novel. In addition to including the death of the two protagonists, the scene constitutes a powerful fictional transcription of Pascal's image of the human condition, to which the title of the novel alludes:

> Imagine a number of men in chains, all under sentence of death, some of whom are each day butchered in the sight of the others; those remaining see their own condition in that of their fellows, and looking at each other with grief and despair await their turn. This is an image of the human condition.[31]

Less pessimistic than Pascal's image, the scene derives its impact from a basic ambiguity. That so bleak a novel, with its many references to night and fog, should culminate in the darkness of a crowded prison indicates a fundamental pessimism. The idea that "each of these men had wildly seized as it stalked past him the only greatness that could be his" (p. 300:358) does little to dispel that pessimism, for the phrase "as it stalked past (*au passage*)" suggests the impermanence of their efforts; and "the only greatness that could be his" leaves the impression of a makeshift last resource.

Nor does Kyo's death alter the negative mood of the scene. Although he attempts to infuse his suicide with a positive value ("It is easy to die when one does not die alone" [p. 304:362]), and though the words "love," "fraternal love," and "fraternity" accompany the event (pp. 302–3:361–62), an equally powerful negative vocabulary describes the prison milieu: "prison, place where time ceases," "separated from everybody (*séparé des vivants*)," "pain . . . absurdity . . . humiliation," "the Revolution . . . was receiving its death stroke" (p. 303:361). Confronted by this prison darkness, Kyo takes his life, simply because "it is fine to die by one's own hand, a death that resembles one's life. And to die is passivity, but to kill oneself is action" (p. 302:360); thereby falling back on the tried and untrue philosophy of Garine, Perken, Grabot, and Tchen. The ambiguity continues in Kyo's final attempt to justify death:

> He had fought (*il aurait combattu*) for what in his time was charged with the deepest meaning and the greatest hope; he was dying among those with whom he would have wanted to live; he was dying, like each of these men, because he had given a meaning to his life. What would have been the value of a life for which he would not have been willing to die? (p. 304:362)

As Roger Stéphane has pointed out,[32] the conditional mode casts some doubt on the absolute validity of Kyo's choices. The notion that death must retroactively validate life creates an irresolvable and paradoxical tension between authenticity and annihilation.

Only Katow seems to escape this impasse through the selflessness of the true militant. At first "thrown back into a solitude which was all the stronger and more painful as he was surrounded by his own people" (p. 305:363), he proves that the anguish of death can be overcome by self-sacrifice for the immediate benefit of others. In offering his cyanide to two comrades he demonstrates that "a man could be stronger than his solitude and even, perhaps, than that atrocious whistle" (p. 306:365), that is, death itself.

In *Antimémoires* Malraux suggested the relationship of the heroic acceptance of torture and the vindication of the human condition:

> The man who kills himself . . . "becomes free." But the man who accepts the risk of torture—even if *only* for his own arbitrary conception of himself and, more deeply, for a cause which is not the defense of his own kin but the human condition—does not commit himself alone . . . but the human condition, like Prometheus. (p. 321:473)

Before the double impasse of the sickness of inaction and the suicide of action, only Katow emerges as the Promethean hero in defense of the human condition. Ironically—or necessarily?—Katow is the least developed of Malraux's protagonists to the date of writing *La Condition humaine.* His apparent authenticity is subject to neither the pressures nor the intensive scrutiny leveled upon the other characters.

The basic tension of this re-creation of Pascal's vision of the human condition, between the fully developed problematical stance of Kyo as intellectual and the victory of the barely sketched Katow as militant, reemerges in the final scene of the novel.

May returns to Gisors to convince him to reenter the struggle, for she still believes that through action men

> may work and know why. . . . The humiliation of the slave, the work of the modern worker suddenly becomes a *value,* when the oppressed ceases to attempt to escape this humiliation, and seeks his salvation in it, when the worker ceases to attempt to escape this work, and seeks in it his reason for being. (p. 330:394)

But May's contention that "the value of men lay only in what they had transformed" (p. 331:395) too quickly recalls Perken's desire to leave a scar on the map to qualify as a thoroughly unproblematical Marxist vision of man. In addition, May's renewed conviction, undermined by the novel as a whole and by the tensive language in particular, is opposed by Gisors's well-founded pessimism:

> One can fool life for a long time, but in the end it always makes us what we were intended to be. . . . Men should be able to learn that there is no reality . . . all is vain. . . . It takes fifty years to make a man, fifty years of sacrifice, of will, of . . . of so many things! And when this man is complete, when there is nothing left in him of childhood, nor of adolescence, when he is really a man—he is good for nothing but to die. (pp. 333, 334, 337–38:399, 400, 403)

Out of this renewed tension between the militant's faith in action and existential pessimism emerges a new belief in music [33] and in the possibility of a "serene accord" with the world:

> For the first time the idea that the time which was bringing him closer to death was flowing through him did not isolate him from the world, but joined him to it in a secret accord. . . . Every man is a madman . . . but what is a human destiny if not a life of effort to unite this madman and the universe. (p. 335:400)

The novel thus closes on a double ambiguity. Although both militancy and this new serenity are opposed to the predominant anguish of the isolated prisoner, neither is ever sufficiently developed to permit a definitive solution to the tension. Malraux's subsequent novels are therefore dedicated to a resolution of the apparent impasse of *La Condition humaine*. In *Le Temps du mépris* and *L'Espoir*, Malraux was to reexamine in greater detail Katow's militant answer to man's anguish, while in *Les Noyers de l'Altenburg* he would pursue Gisors's thirst for a serene harmony with the world.

LE TEMPS DU MÉPRIS
RECAPTURED

*The greatest mystery is not that we have been flung at
random between the profusion of the earth and the galaxy
of the stars, but that in this prison we can fashion
images of ourselves sufficiently powerful to deny our
nothingness.—NA, p. 74:99*

Every major character in Malraux's fiction up to Kassner in
Le Temps du mépris illustrates his thesis that the modern
novel represents "the development of a personal problem
through images." [1] Each novel elicits its successor, for each protagonist encounters a final philosophical dilemma to which he is incapable
of providing an answer. All Malraux's heroes prior to *Le Temps du
mépris* clearly represent what Georg Lukács and Lucien Goldmann
termed the problematical character.[2]

Kassner, however, has been interpreted as Malraux's paradigm of
the true revolutionary, whose absolute faith in the *fraternité virile* of
the Comintern enables him to undertake any sacrifice. No matter how
shattering the physical discomfort and isolation, his faith in the massive solidarity of the Party remains unshaken. His integration into the
greater fraternity of the Party and his devotion to its cause appear to
provide neither the occasion nor the excuse for the agonizing ontological and existential doubts of his predecessors. Goldmann thus considered Kassner Malraux's unique nonproblematical character, within
the context of a community which is itself nonproblematical.[3] Even

death, which had stymied the earlier characters, would appear, there-fore, to present no intolerable enigma for Kassner, who sees his own life as an integral part of an independent collectivity which will con-tinue to function without him.[4]

This interpretation, then, considers Kassner's problems to be practi-cal rather than philosophical, more concerned with the prison's limi-tations on his political activity than with the imperative to justify his existence, with what Comte Rabaud, in *Les Noyers de l'Altenburg,* calls the "eternal . . . in man . . . his divine quality . . . his ability to call the world in question." [5]

With this view of the novel, questions raised by the earlier novels would appear to be circumvented. The only solution apparently pro-posed to man's confrontation with death and the absurdity of life would involve a total loss of self within the ideology of a larger group, a solution, it must be borne in mind, which the author himself never embraced. Even more disconcerting than the nature of the par-ticular doctrine is the presence of *one* overriding ideology which, as Irving Howe has observed, "reflects a hardening of commitment, the freezing of opinion into system." [6]

This interpretation, however, is undermined by one overpowering consideration: one entire stratum of the work, the level of metaphori-cal language, belies the protagonist's nonproblematical status just as significantly as this level established the problematicity of Malraux's earlier works. The most compelling indictment of the nonproblemat-ical interpretation is to be seen in Malraux's decision to situate nearly two-thirds of the novel in prison, rather than in scenes either actively depicting the corruption of society or extolling the achieve-ments and fraternity of the Party. This in itself would not necessarily require a critical about-face had the prison not proved such a preg-nant metaphor in Malraux's earlier works. Although Kassner never explicitly questions the human condition, although his values and beliefs preclude the anguish of a Garine, the central situation of the novel once again revolves around the quintessential Pascalian image. Kassner's prison inevitably evokes incidents and metaphors of imprisonment from *Les Conquérants, La Voie Royale,* and *La Condition humaine,* in the last of which the scene of the execution of Kyo and Katow so obviously derives from Pascal's image of the human condition as prison.[7]

Three key passages in rapid succession elaborate on this Pascalian theme. As Kassner falls prey to a flood of associative thoughts threatening to dissolve his will and carry him over the frontiers of sanity, Malraux compares the loss of reason to the prescribed movement of the heavens: "His youth, his suffering, his very will, all was vanishing, revolving in the motionless cadence of a constellation" (p. 45:54). This preliminary identification of the enslavement of the mind to overpowering forces with the unvarying rhythm of the constellations is soon developed. Moments after Kassner's first panic, Malraux amplifies the comparison with two additional metaphysical themes: man's own insignificance in the universe, and an overwhelming sense of *destin:*

> Beyond time, there was a world . . . in which all that had made up his life glided with the invincible movement of a cosmos in eternity. . . . he now felt his lean body mingling, little by little, with the boundless fatality of the stars, his whole being held spellbound by the army of the night careening towards eternity through the silence. (pp. 46–47:56)

Kassner's prison is invested with a double significance; the passage first recalls Pascal's "this little dungeon . . . I mean the universe." [8] When Kassner compares his life (destiny) to the boundless fatality of the stars, he moves from a sense of his own meaninglessness to one of enslavement and finally to a kind of universal determinism. These two aspects of the prison image, together with the fact of physical imprisonment, are united in the novel's most powerful image:

> The fervor of life and death just now united in the musical harmony was swallowed up in the world's limitless servitude: the stars would always follow the same course in that sky spangled with fatality, and those captive planets would forever turn in their captive immensity, like the prisoners in this court, like himself in his cell. (p. 50:59–60)

Here the centrifugal expansion of Kassner's awareness outward toward the constellations is reversed in a dramatic series of references to enslavement telescoping centripetally, starting from a universal vision, moving to the specific group of stars, converging on the tiny group of prisoners, focusing finally on the smallest element, assaulting Kassner with Pascal's realization that he is "no more than the tiniest point compared to that described by the stars revolving in the firmament." [9] The centripetal movement strongly insists upon Kassner as a more metaphorical and metaphysical than merely physical prisoner. By so obviously re-creating Pascal's image of the human condition, Malraux suggests that even the militant Kassner, faced with the possibility of a solitary death, is recast into the problematical world of his predecessors Garine, Perken, and Kyo. In thus resurrecting the existential questions so crucial in his first three novels, Malraux intimates that the answers of the militant may finally prove inadequate in certain critical contexts. An analysis of other image patterns in Le Temps du mépris will clarify this observation. When Kyo is imprisoned in La Condition humaine, he experiences a gradual, then accelerated metaphorical regression from man, to beast bound for slaughter, to tortoise, and finally to worm.[10] The overwhelming impact of these seriated metaphors communicates the loss of dignity incurred through imprisonment. Robbed of liberty and constantly forced to submit to physical brutality, the prisoner is stripped of his fundamental virility and humanity.[11] In 1935 Malraux declared, "It is not at all certain that confidence raises man up from the dust, but it is sure that scorn will trample man in the dust for ever," [12] a statement which casts doubt upon the novelist's belief in the unproblematical nature of the Party and its militant adherents.

As a result, it is much more logical to view Kassner, as Malraux viewed Ernst Thälmann (undoubtedly the model on which Kassner is based) as one of "those few intellectuals who mean to recover for the abused word *dignity* its most profound meaning." [13] The novel's imagery repeatedly insists that the most heinous aspect of the prison consists not in its interference with political activity (which is put aside for two-thirds of the work) but rather in its encroachment on human dignity. Throughout the novel, each prison reference carries the metaphorical weight of such an impairment of dignity, implemented, as in so many other passages of Malraux's previous fiction and especially *La Voie royale,* by the insect.[14]

Kassner quickly descends metaphorically to the level of the insect when the prison is described as "a seething nest (*une fourmillière*) of tiny sounds" (p. 29:37). The prisoner reacts not so much to the entry of guards themselves as to their shadows "like enormous spiders" (p. 33:42) cast by a small lantern onto the low ceiling. The implication is clear: if the prisoners themselves are reduced to "tireless centipedes" by the "life-like quality of a creature's shell" of this "black termite's nest" (pp. 35, 92:45, 103), the guards who enforce this dehumanization become degraded into mere abstractions, shadows once removed of one of the lowest forms of life.

Throughout the novel, then, the insect metaphor becomes an objective correlative of the defeat of dignity. When Kassner, fearing that his tumultuous and uncontrollable thoughts verge on insanity, decides to take his life,

> He began to pace the floor. . . . The hour that was approaching would be the same as this; the thousand smothered sounds that teem like lice beneath the silence of the prison would repeat to infinity the pattern of their crushed life; and suffering, like dust, would cover the immutable domain of nothingness. (pp. 74–75:85)

The element of submission, compellingly communicated by the insect metaphor, is deliberately reinforced by the existentially affective phrase "the immutable domain of nothingness," which insists once again upon the prison as human condition.

Aside from symbolizing the humiliation so destructive to the militant, the insect also communicates the frustration of the prisoner's attempt to impose a vital order on his thought. For the militant, the insect would signify only the inhumanity of other men, an exterior infliction of suffering. Yet for Kassner the insect embodies the demon within, the subconscious which threatens to cast him irretrievably into mental chaos. The insect, a particularly appropriate image of such self-alienation, has always carried in Malraux's work a connotation of the unknowable and incomprehensible *other,* the content of hallucinations and childhood traumas.[15]

The demon of self-alienation—one for which even the militant can provide no answer—emerges with the ebbing of Kassner's former strength: "His strength, grown parasitic, was gnawing him relentlessly" (p. 36:46).

Of the factors which constantly threaten Kassner's sanity, one of the most obsessive is time, without a clear sense of which order is impossible. Kassner, threatened less by political realities than by the subtle invasion of both past and future into his sense of the present, slides into a perpetual sense of "forever" which destroys perspective and coherent thinking. Time metamorphoses into a dreadful black spider driving Kassner to the level of the subhuman:

> Only a sly submissive kind of sub-human creature grown utterly indifferent to time could adapt itself to the stone. Time, that black spider, swung back and forth in the cells of all the prisoners as horrible and fascinating for them as it was for their comrades who were sentenced to die. (p. 51:61)

If sleep represents momentary escape, insomnia promises certain insanity: "He knew the world of insomnia, and had been haunted by sensations of distress inexhaustibly reiterated, with an insect's precision" (p. 80:88).

At moments when Kassner is in greatest danger of losing his lucidity, *le destin* is presented through the metaphor of the insect. Such an image hovers hauntingly over his difficulty in concentrating on the coded tapping from a neighboring cell: "He could not drive from his mind the image of a hand vainly trying to catch a fly on the wing" (p. 55:65).

Recovering sufficient control to apply his mind to deciphering the code, Kassner encounters the frustration of succeeding in retaining the order of the numbers only to face their incomprehensibility, of coming close enough to hope but not close enough to succeed. This renewed frustration illuminates the growing dichotomy between the former assurance of the unproblematical militant and the submissive weakness of the problematical prisoner. Faced with this impasse Kassner undergoes a Kafkaesque metamorphosis: "He felt like an insect squeezed in its hollow stone, avariciously contracting its legs over its accumulated wealth—just as his fingers against his chest at this moment were contracted over those numbers, which were tokens of friendship" (pp. 83–84:93). Tantalizingly close to meaning and yet resisting interpretation, the numbers themselves behave like spiders: "Hanging by some imperceptible and precarious thread in back of his eyes, they nevertheless flooded the darkness, flowed over him as though he should have to hold on to them to save himself, and his hands were repeatedly missing them" (p. 84:93).

Hours later, with the code still undeciphered, the problematical Kassner is "eaten away by the ant-like numbers" (p. 87:96). Only when he overcomes his mental chaos long enough to unravel the cryptic message does he regain his lost will, finding dignity in a sense of fraternity which momentarily overrides the sense of submission. But the victory proves illusory; with the removal of the comrade in the neighboring cell, Kassner is immediately replunged into his solitary battle against insanity. The lesson is clear: fraternity is a valid defense against the power of the existential milieu only as long as the militant is in direct contact with another. The entire decoding exercise constitutes merely a form of Pascalian "diversion," [16] nothing more than a delay in Kassner's ultimate confrontation with himself. Alone, Kassner will be forced to search *within himself* for answers at variance with the notions of solidarity which had sustained him in the political world.

It should be evident from the discussion of this persistent metaphor that the practical problems of the militant as militant have been eclipsed by more difficult problems specific to the prisoner. Protected by the Marxist values of his Party from existential anguish and reflection, Kassner the militant never considers his mortality a threat to the meaning of his life. Death, for the militant, is problematic only in so far as it obstructs his further contributions to the revolution.

As we have just seen, however, Kassner, in the metaphorically charged prison, confronts not simply death but rather the necessity of maintaining his sanity in the face of death, the problem of "diversion." Kassner realizes, once his neighbor disappears, the awful proportions of the problem that "man . . . does not know how to stay quietly in his room." [17]

It is here that we witness the emergence of Malraux's new hero, the artist. The adventurer and militant proving unable to resolve the problem of man face to face with this solitary destiny, it is left to the potential artist in man to reach within himself to find a solution to the crisis.

The appearance of the artist figure is revealed through the series of metaphors whose vehicle is water. Malraux underlines the presence of water the moment Kassner enters his cell: "the wall exuded (*suait*) human destinies" (p. 29:38), as though it had dissolved many before Kassner who were now being slowly exuded through the wall's subterranean pores. Kassner himself soon feels the effect of this dissolution: "While he remained motionless his limbs and his flesh seemed to dissolve in the darkness" (p. 47:56–57). All sounds are perceived as "something confused and distant, like sounds under water" (p. 91:102). These metaphors create the impression of suspension in a pool, and, though the sexual interpretation is not developed, the implications of a return to the womb are enormous for Kassner the militant; such a powerless and dependent state again suggests the denial of manhood and virility imposed by the prison. To a militant, containment and constraint amount to death and confront him with a problematical situation in which his militancy is no longer relevant.

Representing the stream of consciousness, the image is even more prevalent and refers consistently to the emerging artist. Close upon Kassner's first suspicion of his own insanity, music, although initially presented as a salvation, inspires a series of increasingly chaotic apocalyptic visions:

> Uneasy waves, torpid like his wounds, began to stir in the depth of his consciousness, and little by little the solemnity of the deep began

to settle over them . . . the chant fell and suddenly rose again . . .
lifting him like a ship to the very crest of suffering. (pp.
43–44:52–53)

The torrent of images oriented toward a Rimbaldien apocalypse flows
into a vision of "life and death merged in the immobility of the starry
sky" (p. 46:55) before being "submerged beneath a flooding death
chant" (p. 45:54). This cosmic vision of destiny subsides before a
calmer indifferent oblivion: "All memory was dissolving in an endless
rain which fell over things as though it were sweeping them into the
remotest reaches of the past" (p. 46:55).

This vision of destiny as an eternally dissolving rain gradually cascades into an ocean of aimless images threatening to drown the life of
the mind: "his life . . . wholly submerged in solemnity as his body
was now enveloped by the darkness, as these shreds of memories were
flooded by these sacred harmonies" (p. 46:55). Kassner, totally sub-
sumed by the flow of his mind, is abandoned by the music which had
originally carried him away, "all this music born of his mind which
now gradually was withdrawing, ebbing away with the very sound of
human happiness, leaving him stranded on the shore (*comme un pois-
son mort*)" (pp. 50–51:60–61).

Recapitulating Kassner's experience, the author resorts to more
water imagery to suggest the involuntary dissolution of the will:

> Ikons, stoles, chasubles, dalmatics and crosses . . . finally dissolved
> into nothingness. This struggle against stupor and the slow hours
> went on relentlessly, at a tempo which was gradually decreasing, and
> Kassner would live through it here to infinity, with those orthodox
> ornaments in the depth of his obsession as if in the hold of a sunken
> galley, to a slower and slower rhythm, more and more drawn out,
> like circles in the water, until all was nullified in the silence of com-
> plete mindlessness. (p. 52:62)

Kassner, though momentarily shaken from his stupor by insistent
tapping from the neighboring cell, is soon plunged anew into "a jum-
ble of images," every one of which ends in dissolution. Although Kassner's sense of hearing registers the tapping on the wall, his mind in-

corporates these sounds into the memories of the revolution, each of
which in turn becomes a literal correlative of the dissolving fluidity of
Kassner's stream of consciousness. Thus, the "Trans-Siberian grounded
like an ocean liner in the forest" (p. 56:67): "the convent . . .
[which] drifts with the dreary clouds like a phantom ship, far from
its dead crew" (p. 68:78); "the muffled pounding, its hurried beat
gradually slowing down to the rhythm of a steamboat engine"
(p. 70:79–80); "the long wave-like gallop of creatures . . . carried
away by their own momentum like sails before the wind" (pp.
70–71:80); "this convulsed fleet whose motion rose and fell; both
fleet and sea filled the street from end to end" (p. 71:81); and "the
earth that was as living as the rivers and the sea" (p. 72:82). Although initiated by several similies whose tenor recapitulates the
sound of tapping ("steamboat engine," "muffled pounding," "gallop"),
this series of comparisons is gradually emancipated from any nonfluid
association, suggesting that Kassner's mind has been set adrift and is
now cut off from outside stimuli, subject only to its own flow.

Once the destructiveness of the uncontrollable stream of consciousness has been so closely identified with the image of water, anguish itself is transposed into water imagery: "it was the tide of anguish rising at each peal of the bells in his temples" (p. 68:77).

Time, Kassner's most dangerous and elusive enemy in the prison, is
both compressed and expanded into an amorphous sense of perpetuity.
When this timelessness is sporadically interrupted by specific sounds,
the floodgates of the present seem to open; with the sudden steps of a
guard "time was rushing like a boiling torrent towards Kassner, was
tearing out the tiniest fibres of his nerves" (p. 88:98). Finally, all the
various elements eroding his mental stability culminate in vast and
sweeping "waves of madness" (p. 81:90).

Water images, the most extensive and complicated pattern in the
novel, thus point up Kassner's temporary inability to control the
direction of his thoughts. He discovers the imperative of channeling
the tides of his subconscious in order to resist the invidious temptation to surrender to the comfortable prison of insanity, submitting to

the "world's limitless servitude" under "that sky spangled with fatality" (p. 50:59–60). Just as Montaigne had reined in the "runaway
horse" of his mental chaos by composing the *Essais*,[18] so Kassner decides to compose a speech, not for the purpose of communication,
since it cannot be heard, but rather to channel and manipulate his
thoughts into a coherent structure:

> Deprived (*vidé*) of brotherhood as he had been of dreams and
> hope, Kassner waited in the silence which hung over the desires of
> hundreds of men in that black termite's nest. . . .
> "Comrades in the darkness around me. . . ."
> For as many hours, as many days as were needed, he would pre-
> pare what could be told to the darkness. . . . (pp. 92–93:103).

The only means of salvation lies in creativity. Kassner discovers what
Walter would express ten years later in *Les Noyers de l'Altenburg*:

> In the prison which Pascal describes, men manage to drag out of
> themselves an answer which . . . cloaks those who are worthy of it
> with immortality. . . . The greatest mystery is not that we have been
> flung at random between the profusion of the earth and the galaxy of
> the stars, but that in this prison we can fashion images of ourselves
> sufficiently powerful to deny our nothingness.[19]

It is the artist who redeems the militant when the latter, like Perken,
Garine, and Kyo before him, is thrown face to face with death and
destiny. Kassner's composition of his speech constitutes what Berger
will call "a rectification, a humanisation of the world." [20]

With freedom, Kassner's world is radically transformed. As darkness yields to light and mental chaos is replaced by resolute assurance,
the artist once again accedes to the militant. This transformation en-
tails a reversal of the previous symbolic patterns. As mental turmoil
subsides, its metaphorical expression as a rushing stream of consciousness is superseded by the image of water as purification. As the door
opens, "the full light of the corridor . . . streamed over his whole
body, washed away the darkness which glued his eyelids" (p.
103:112). He proceeds from cell to guardroom "through great yellow
waves of light" (p. 104:113), where "a ray of sunlight full of motes

glittered like a canal in the wind" (p. 105:114). Once outside, Kassner is ritualistically purified of the darkness of the prison: he finds himself "in the clear air washed by great blue streams" [21] (p. 106:115).

The last insect image in the novel parallels the more optimistic outlook of these later water images. Waiting for his eyes to reaccustom themselves to light, Kassner realizes that "his mind remained attached to the cell by a thousand delicate spider-webs" (p. 113:123). The metaphor is brilliant; imprinted on Kassner's memory are the brutal affronts to the dignity and mental stability of the prisoner. Yet, with his freedom, these memories begin to fade before the new duties; they have become mere spider-webs, the fragile reminder of a once all-consuming danger.

The artist-militant duality in the character reflects Malraux's interests and activities at the time he was writing the novel. While politically maneuvering to free Thälmann and Dimitrov,[22] Malraux simultaneously and passionately pursued his notion of the artist as final defender of culture in the West. His speeches of the period extol the heroism of the artist daring to defy the hypocrisy and corruption of Western society.[23] He proclaimed, for example, that

> the important thing is to possess *the world of solitude,* to transform what had been suffered into conquest for the artist. . . . Art lives in as much as it permits men to escape from their human condition, not by evasion but by possession. All art is a means of possession of destiny. . . . Like imprisoned or free men, imprisoned or free civilizations reorder the past which they have undergone. (Italics mine) [24]

In his world of solitude, the prison, Kassner transforms submission into conquest not by a futile attempt to escape destiny but rather by confronting and possessing it. In Malraux's eyes, the possession of destiny through art comes to assume an equal importance with revolution: "From day to day and thought to thought, men re-create the world in the image of their greatest destiny. Revolution gives them only the possibility of their dignity; it is for the individual to make of this possibility a possession.[25]

Through his discovery of the creative act as a response to ontological despair, Kassner emerges as a correlative of the novelist himself, and indeed of all creative artists. Camus was to write of Proust's *Le Temps retrouvé:*

> He has demonstrated that the art of the novel can reconstruct creation itself, in the form that it is imposed on us and in the form in which we reject it. . . . . But still more profoundly, it is allied to the beauty of the world or of its inhabitants against the powers of death and oblivion. It is in this way that his rebellion is creative.[26]

The passage would apply equally well to the novel under consideration. Kassner's metaphysical revolt, no longer simply political reaction, leads inevitably to the proposal of the creative act as a positive assertion of man's control over his world.

Despite a discovery as fundamental as that of art, Malraux was as yet unwilling to abandon his philosophy of action and virile fraternity. The last third of the novel contains a structurally identical retranscription of the prison experience. Aloft in a tiny plane piloted by a co-militant, Kassner is resubjected to a confrontation with "destiny." Again a flood of water imagery suggests a menacing tide of destiny which threatens to sweep Kassner away to death in the tiny enclosed cell of the cockpit. The sky, a "mist-covered sea" (p. 125:134), contains "tidal waves" (p. 129:139) which threaten to "submerge" (pp. 122, 125:130, 136) the plane, become "battle ship" (p. 122:130) or "sperm-whale" (p. 129:139). In this tiny prison, Kassner again executes the circles of destiny, as "in the center of the cyclone the plane was spinning on its own axis" (p. 128:137), and it is natural for Kassner to discover other links with his recent imprisonment: "The inscriptions in the cells, the screams, the knocks on the wall, the craving for revenge were with them in the fuselage against the hurricane" (p. 126:136). Once again, Kassner is confronted with a Pascalian sense of his own finitude:

> Only the memory of the prison darkness enabled Kassner to realize the surrounding immensity. . . . The silent throngs of his comrades

who had filled the darkness of the prison seemed to people this region of fog, the immense gray universe. . . . In the midst of the fog, which was now constant, time was disappearing in the strange sleep-like struggle. . . . Before the immense black cloud . . . Kassner became once more acutely conscious of his infinite smallness. (pp. 122, 123, 124:132, 133)

And again the lesson is double: Kassner discovers anew the fraternity of combat ("It occurred to Kassner that only the proximity of death entitles one to get sufficiently close to a man to know that child-like look which he had just seen, and that this man too was about to die for him" [p. 130:139]): but he also senses a much deeper lesson, the "simple consciousness" (p. 134:144) necessary to perceive life and capture it in art. Having reaffirmed his sense of militant fraternity and artistic consciousness, Kassner is at last ready for his discovery of the earth,[27] of its "rhythm of life and death" (p. 133:144), and for his return to his people and reunion with Anna.

It should be evident that the two natures of the protagonist of *Le Temps du mépris,* the revolutionary and the artist, are necessary and complementary. Unable to survive within the solitary confines of the prison, the militant calls from within himself the artist. Yet once having come to grips through art with the existential problems raised by the prison, the militant and the revolution regain the foreground. It is no artistic accident that Kassner is ultimately freed through the self-less fraternal act of a co-worker.

This artist-militant dichotomy is clearly visible in the distribution of the tensive language, the bulk of which occurs in the prison scenes and throws into relief the previously unrecognized problematical artist. But neither artist nor militant is ultimately rejected. When the artist has dealt with the anguish of a solitary destiny, the militant must again take up the arms of the political arena. Man must come to grips with his existential situation before he can fearlessly enter the world of action. Though the novel ends with the reunification of the militant with Anna, and the realization that he must renew his political activity, it is the artist, more representative of Malraux as novelist, who was forced to question the world's meaning, and to transform his destiny into consciousness. It is the artist in Kassner who can claim, "I have refused the beast in me and have become a man without the help of the gods." [28]

Le Temps du mépris, therefore, stands as an eloquent fictional transcription of Malraux's words to the International Congress for the Defense of Culture in 1935:

> Every work of art is created to satisfy a need, but only a need passionate enough to give birth to it. . . . Each of us must re-create in his own domain and through his own quest the heritage of the phantoms which surround us . . . and to create out of the hopes and wills . . . a human consciousness with the age-old suffering of men.[29]

Kassner the prisoner becomes, however briefly, this artist. Led to a confrontation with destiny by the militant, this Promethean figure,[30] capable of denying the nothingness of the universe through creativity, has exemplified Malraux's most eloquent statement of man's objective. "The entire destiny of what men call culture can be summed up in one idea: to transform destiny into *conscience* (conscience *and* consciousness)." [31] This phrase from 1935 would become the slogan of the protagonists of *L'Espoir* and *Les Noyers de l'Altenburg,* just as the duality of art and action inherent in Kassner would become the basis of Malraux's subsequent thought.

THE TENSION OF HOPE
IN *L'ESPOIR*

*He realized with a rush of agony how similar are all
the tragedies of man's estate, each circling his sad
small orbit of despair like a madman turning in his cell.*
—E, p. 338:348

Malraux's dedication of *L'Espoir* to "mes camarades de la
bataille de Teruel" carries two important implications about
the work: an intensification of the author's personal involvement in the events described unequaled in any of his previous work,
and his sudden confrontation with the masses. Such expansion in the
degree and breadth of involvement in turn implies a shift in narrative
structure. For the first time Malraux constructs numerous and extended scenes of full-scale battles involving a collective hero, and creating a dichotomy between rapid dramatic action and the moments of
concentrated pure reflection that follow.

These changes in structure necessarily affect Malraux's established
arrangements of imagery. Whereas in previous works the image patterns are oriented around particular characters and their problems,
imagery in *L'Espoir* operates more broadly, generated by situations of
collective or historical movement rather than by an individual protagonist.

At first glance, therefore, this novel appears to present a problematic stage in the "development of a personal problem through im-

ages." It will be necessary briefly to examine several other structures in the work to gauge the significance of the imagery.

The dichotomy between scenes of action and those of reflection is no structural accident: the title of one section of the novel, "Être et faire (Action and Reaction)," crystallizes its predominant moral issue. Garcia elucidates the problem for Hernandez:

> The communists, you see, *want to get things done.* Whereas you and the anarchists, for different reasons, want to *be* something. That's the tragedy of a revolution like this one. Our respective ideals are so different; pacifism and the need to fight in self-defense; organization and Christian sentiment; efficiency and justice—nothing but contradictions. We've got to straighten them out, transform our Apocalyptic vision into an army—or be exterminated. That's all. (pp. 181–82:191) [1]

Yet Hernandez cannot understand why men should undertake a struggle unworthy of them: "What's the point of the revolution if it isn't to make men better?" (p. 180:190).

On the explicit level, therefore, the basic structure of *L'Espoir* is dialectical; each character is defined and developed according to his response to the dilemma "being *vs.* doing." Puig, the heroic anarchist, exemplifies the "être" option; for him, "every political crisis resolved itself into a test of character and courage" (p. 23:31). Puig soon dies heroically and uselessly, representing in a tragic way the Anarchists' belief in the Apocalypse, the "illusion lyrique" that revolution can be sustained by enthusiasm alone. At the opposite end of the spectrum, the Communists Vargas, Manuel, and Heinrich recognize that "this war's going to be a war of mechanized equipment. . . . The people is magnificent, absolutely magnificent—but helpless. . . . We haven't any organization" (pp. 98, 99:105, 106, 107).

Between these antithetical viewpoints stand the artist and the intellectual. Magnin, Garcia, Scali, and Alvear all come to realize that

> the great intellectual is a man of subtleties, of fine shades, of evaluations; he is interested in absolute truth and in the complexity of things. He is . . . "antimanichean," by definition, by nature. But all

forms of action are manichean. . . . Every true revolutionary is a born manichean. The same is true of politics, all politics. . . . There are just wars . . . but there's no such thing as a just army. . . . One can have a policy that's just, but there's no such thing as a just party (pp. 335, 339:345, 349).

Because action is imperative, however, an antimanichean stance becomes impossible.

The same dialectical structure governs the level of action: whereas the first section, "L'Illusion lyrique (Careless Rapture)," portrays heroic gestures, Part Two (The Manzanares) describes the dehumanizing burden of organization and discipline. No pragmatic solution emerges from the confrontation of these equally impossible stances, however, because of the simultaneous necessities of the moral victory of humanism and the military victory over Fascism.

To the extent that this conflict remains purely ideological it defies explicit resolution. Irving Howe has noted:

The novel tries to confront experience in its immediacy and closeness, while ideology is by its nature general and inclusive. Yet it is precisely from this conflict that the political novel gains its interest and takes on the aura of high drama . . . forcing upon the novelist *a concentration of those resources that are needed to overcome it. . . .* To the degree that he is really a novelist, a man seized by the passion to represent and to give order to experience, he must drive the politics of or behind his novel into a complex relation with the kinds of experience that resist reduction to formula.[2]

The only means capable of resolving the "Être-faire" conflicts in *L'Espoir* are found precisely at the level of imagery. It is the imagery which enlarges the scope of the moral issue beyond the Spanish war, and intimately links it to Malraux's earlier confrontation with man's fate.

In their first serious discussion of motives, Ramos and Manuel are engulfed by "the tide of darkness flooding the . . . great plain of Madrid" (p. 73:81). In the midst of this immensity, Ramos confesses that, like Perken before him, his involvement springs from the fear of growing old (p. 74:82), an admission of his problematic status in keeping with their surroundings. Later, Manuel is again awed by the immensity of his surroundings, this time as he watches his men "floundering deeper and deeper in the deepening mud":

> Long lines of ancient furrows streamed down to a deep valley that climbed again toward a draggled horizon, grey in the wan morning light that looked like nightfall. That skyline seemed to end the world, but behind it lay the vast Segovia plain, like sea beyond a cliff-wall, stretching out to infinity. (pp. 302–3:312)

Contemplation of such vastness confronts man with his insignificance within the cosmos. In *La Tentation de l'Occident,* the contemplation of such disproportion consistently inspired the same reaction in Western man: "The work of our mind is to experience lucidly our fragmentary nature and to draw from that feeling a sense of the universe." [3] This appreciation of man's fragmentary nature issuing from a contemplation of the universe constitutes still another paraphrase of Pascal's "What is man in the infinite?" [4] Malraux phrases the question: "What human gesture would not have seemed trivial and inadequate?" (p. 187:196).[5]

Spain defines a setting whose immensity threatens to engulf the combatants,[6] a vastness most compellingly experienced by the aviators. Just as Kassner translated the panorama of the sky into images of water,[7] so the Pelicans consider their world above the clouds as an ocean in which they are lost. Magnin, for example, "had grown used now to the primordial peace (*paix de commencement du monde*) of that high world, so aloof from man's restless strivings" (pp. 393–94:401), and the simple peasant accompanying him further generalizes the scope of the war in noting the "vast peaceful spread of sky between the sun and the sea of clouds" (p. 393:401). Each further reference to the clouds in this scene alludes to water, "the impassivity (*l'indifférente*) of the sea of clouds" (p. 394:401), or "dark rectangular patches like night-blue lakes" (p. 394:402). When the plane bursts through the clouds, the rooftops of Teruel appear as various creatures of the deep:

Roofs appeared through it, now on one edge of the stain and now on
the other, like goldfish motionless against a moving background. . . .
And immediately, yellow and tawny red in the leaden light, a cluster
of roofs like the scales of some huge fish filled the hole in the clouds.
(p. 394:402)

During the bombing of the Italian motorized column, tensive language reduces the tiny beings seen from above to watery or submar-
ine forms, minimizing their importance and humanity. When the first
truck is hit, for example, the column disperses into "a torret flowing
around a rock" (p. 87:95). From Sembrano's viewpoint, the over-
turned trucks resemble "dead fish rising to the surface of a dynamited
pool" (p. 88:96).

Bombs released over the main square of an occupied town "sped on
with the free movement of torpedos (torpilles)" (p. 89:97); in French,
torpilles denotes both military projectiles and a species of fish. This
image recurs in a later aerial attack; Leclerc observes bombs dropping
from the bomb bays "shining like fish in the moonlight" (pp.
185–86:195). Approaching enemy Junkers appear to the Republican planes above as "submarines" (p. 90:98), and a Junker hit by Republican fire goes "floundering (nageotant) down across the fields" (p.
90:98). After Sembrano's plane is downed, his wounded crew experiences a fellowship of "naufragés [shipwrecked men]" (p. 379:386).

Both armies flow forward and back with the rhythmic regularity of
tides, in which individual wills and actions are irrevocably dissolved.
In Barcelona, the first line of Fascists rushing the Republican gun
"streamed back . . . like jetsam flung by a wave along the foreshore"
(p. 17:25).[8] Here Malraux revitalizes the cliché which links military
attack and wave by extending the metaphor to include elements rejected by the sea. Each new attack on the hotel leaves "its driftsam of
the dead" (p. 23:31).

The inexhaustible flow of men into vain battle continues as Gonza-
lez is "borne forward on the same tide of hard, fraternal exaltation"
(p. 201:210–11). In the battle of Madrid, a heavy rain again contributes to the sensation of general dissolution:

Across the paroxysms of the riven earth roaring up to the streaming
clouds, vomiting across the downpour great cascades of clods and
stones and blood, Manuel could see a wave of enemy troops advancing, with fixed bayonets. They had no sheen, for the rain melted to
liquid slime all that was hurtling up into it from the sodden plain.
. . . in the dim chaos of the deluge . . . the enemy . . . were surging back, as though repulsed not by the old milicianos, but by the
never-ending rain (*la pluie éternel*), which was . . . sweeping
away towards their unseen trenches the attacking waves, in a seething spate of dissolution, across the welter of a cloud-burst shud-
dering with explosions countless as the rain-drops. (p. 309:319)

The passage is remarkable not only for the density of the metaphoric
language but also for its spatial and temporal permutations. The cross-
hatching of vertical elements (blood rising to meet rain) and hori-
zontal (troops surging back and forth) locks the men in a figurative
web rendered timeless by the allusion to the flood and by the adjective "never-ending." The armies seem ultimately to dissolve altogether as the rain sweeps away waves of enemy soldiers and explosions themselves become raindrops.[9]

The civilian population is caught up by this apocalyptic surge in
massive floods of flight. Patrolling Madrid during the bombing, Garcia is suddenly swept up in "the unseen river bearing the crowd on its
futile way" (p. 263:272).[10] A larger and even more futile exodus precedes the Fascist advance on Teruel. Attignies appeals for aid to this
"surging mass (*la coulée*) of fugitives . . . punctuated by the pulsing
of the sea" (p. 372:380), and suddenly feels as though "the whole
world . . . was moving (*coulait*) in the same direction" (p. 373:381).
This "stream of humanity" (p. 374:382) plunges helplessly into a dark
tunnel where "the rumbling of carts through the rock was like an underground river" (p. 374:382). Attignies's claustrophobia in this tunnel produces a series of watery images strikingly similar to those used
to describe Kassner's fears in the womblike obscurity of his cell:

Attignies felt half-stifled in the tunnel. . . . Perhaps he had died on
the way . . . perhaps the cart and donkey were phantasms of an un-
expectedly gentle dissolution? A moment ago he had been in the

water; now he was drifting into a close and airless world in the bowels of the earth. More cogent than the consciousness of life in living
men, that sense of death beginning in the blood-drenched plane was
with him now in the airless, soundless tunnel; all that his life had
meant was dissolving like an idle dream into a vast, desolating tor-
por; the points of lights became so many deep-sea fishes in the hot,
darkness, and the political commissar was wafted, motionless and im-
ponderable, far beyond the confines of death, across a mighty river of
sleep. (pp. 374–75:382–83)

This universal dissolution culminates in a complex tripartite operation: the physical transition from the water and blood of the submerged plane to the dark womblike tunnel; a mental disintegration
from lucidity and determination to the overwhelming tide of fatigue;
and, finally, the loss of individuality and self in the "flood of fugitives
(*la coulée de peuple en fuite*)" (p. 375:383), which "surged (*bouillon-
nait*) around the first village, leaving innumerable evidences of its
passage around the first houses, as an ebb-tide reveals a beach littered
with pebbles and debris" (p. 375:383).

The image of water, appearing regularly in moments of battle, destruction, flight, injury, and death,[11] consistently emphasizes the
meaninglessness of individual life, and elevates the perspective of the
war to a brutal study of man's struggle against a larger destiny. This
enlargement of perspective makes clear that *L'Espoir* does not abandon the examination of the variety of basic attitudes toward existence
which characterized the four previous novels. The war, in fact, provides a hyperbolic expression of the human condition which spotlights
the alternatives most vividly.

Water is not the only element in the work which communicates
this disproportion of man in the larger struggle against destiny. Although man is dwarfed by all the machines of war,[12] the most overwhelming element he must face is fire.

The death-dealing incendiary bombs in Madrid ironically assume
an independent, almost personified, vitality. Ramos gradually realizes
that only fire lives in this city: "sleek scarlet flames were scurrying
like a hungry beast of prey . . . [with] irrepressible vitality" (p.

294:304). Powerless in the face of this fiery exultation, the entire city is consumed: "Though the bombers had flown back . . . under the roofs innumerable fires were surreptitiously alive (*le feu continuait sa vie propre*), creeping from floor to floor" (p. 294:304). The fire continues its metamorphoses: Ramos watches in despair "flurries of bright sparks that raced along the streets like mad patrols" (p. 296:306), "a horde of little restless wisps of fire, battening on the houses like a plague of insects" (p. 294:304). For Mercery, attempting to extinguish the fire in the Hotel Savoy, the blaze becomes, simply, the enemy: "Never, at the front, had he faced the enemy as he had been doing here during the last twenty hours. . . . He stood . . . watching each nest of flames as if it were an enemy advance-guard he were fighting" (p. 340:350). The awesome potency of the flames, however, forces him to reevaluate the adversary:

> It was an enemy with more life in it than any man, more life than anything else in the world. Combating this enemy of a myriad writhing tentacles, like a fantastic octopus, Mercery felt himself terribly inert, as though made of lead. But, for all its tentacles, he would best the monster (p. 342:352).

Having overcome one fire, Mercery turns to contemplate "the distant fires, flapping, like bull-fighters, their scarlet capes across the darkness" (p. 342:352). At the height of its destruction, the conflagration attains apocalyptic dimensions; Lopez senses this new dimension when an entire building is "inhabited by the elemental fire (*le Feu*)" (p. 320:329). Slade, observing a city in which "nothing seemed alive except the dancing flames" (p. 329:340), is also stunned by this "elemental chaos":

> A huge burst of flames shot through a roof . . . the flames slithered along the house-front downwards to the street. . . . As the fire approached the buildings which were already gutted, it lit them up from behind. They showed as gaunt, phantasmagoric skeletons, against the flames that prowled behind the ruins like beasts of prey loath to leave their kill. The ghastly twilight seemed ushering in another Age of Fire. (p. 330:340) [13]

Like the images of water, this return to the primordial Age of Fire underscores the metaphorical generalization of war as the quintessential representation of man's estate, a Pascalian vision of his disproportion in the world.

Several others of Malraux's most prevalent metaphoric themes further expand this indictment of the inhumanity of the human condition. Although Manuel realizes that war consists of riddling "enemy flesh with shreds of iron" (p. 78:86), Malraux had learned from Goya that "the way to express the unusual, the frightening, that is the inhuman, was not to attempt the careful representation of a spectacle, real or imaginary, but to use a treatment capable of representing it without yielding to its component parts." [14] Thus he turns to the image of the insect once again to infuse the horrors of war with the awful dilemma of man's submission: to transpose the inhumanity of the war beyond the physical to the metaphysical, beyond the individual to the universal.

With the first shots in Barcelona, the insect, harbinger of both death and submission, hovers over battle, particularly in the guise of bullets, which "zipped past like a swarm of dragon-flies" (p. 15:23). Repeatedly, "bullets were capering like crickets (*sautaient comme des insectes*)" (p. 20:28); "the air was alive with bullets zzz-ing like angry wasps" (p. 56:64); or, again, "bullets sped past them with a wasp-like drone" (p. 110:118). The shell punctures in Sembrano's blood-spattered bomber create another, even more sinister effect: "The bullets wove a pattern of red streaks like a spider's web around their plane" (p. 370:379).

Larger effects of war are compared to an invasion of insects which recalls the scorpions of *Royaume farfelu*. Surrounded by death and agony during the bombing of Madrid, Ramos helplessly watches "a horde of little restless wisps of fire battening on the houses like a plague of insects" (p. 294:304). As he searches for the wounded, Ramos's own flashlight becomes "an insect's feeler" (p. 297:307) each time he encounters helpless suffering.

Even more horrible than equating insects to instruments of war,

the entymological metamorphoses of the soldiers themselves frequently suggest the hopelessness of their situation. As if to support
Ximenes's dictum that "it's far more important to get definite results
than to set an example" (p. 145:154), the most striking example of
heroism in the novel terminates in futility rendered bitterly acute by
one compelling image. In Barcelona the Anarchists are surprised by
the furious honking of two Cadillacs, careening "like cars in gangster
films" toward the Fascist gun emplacements:

> The front car . . . scattered the soldiers on either side, and raced be-
> tween the two eighteen-pounders, crashing against the wall just be-
> side the mountain gun, which presumably had been its objective.
> Black, blood-spattered wreckage; a squashed fly on a wall. The gun-
> ners went on firing . . . (p. 21:29).

The reference to gangster films which opens this suicidal incident implies a vainglorious futility which is confirmed by the final image of
the crushed fly.

Even as the *milicianos* organize and fewer self-inflicted martyrdoms
occur, the insect imagery insists on submission to a random destiny:
the universal vulnerability in war.

In a haunting example of the cinematic close-up technique that
Malraux had endorsed elsewhere,[15] the author endows the creeping
line of tanks with the terrible aspect of an advancing insect colony:

> Gonzalez dropped back on the ground. "His" tank must be some four
> hundred yards away, but the tall grass level with his eyes concealed
> it. . . . Already, he noticed, some ants and a tiny spider were crawl-
> ing on [the grass]. On the ground, in their grassy forest, other crea-
> tures were going their small, warless ways. Then, just behind a pair
> of ants, loomed up the lurching, roaring bulk of a swiftly moving
> tank. (p. 201:211)

The frantic rush of men into battle may evoke the frenetic, apparently futile activities of the insect, but when Manuel sees men of his
division deserting the enemy lines, the insect image assumes the double significance of submission to destiny and the ignominy of treason:

"Behind the small dark specks running with their arms above their heads, like insects waving their antennae, the ground sloped . . . all the way down to Madrid" (p. 305:315).

The enemy barricaded in the besieged university hospital in Madrid appears to the *milicianos* as a doomed insect colony. Watching the artillery pound the hospital, Maringaud notes that "a close-up view of the windows gave it the look of an abandoned beehive" (p. 354:363). Yet the hive is not empty, for as the bombardment continues, Maringaud catches sight of the Fascists evacuating: "from the smashed beehive a swarm of insects was pouring out" (p. 355:364).

Although war consistently dehumanizes the soldier, particular moments of degradation and defeat are often spotlighted by the metaphor of the insect:

> The soldiers began to retire, crawling back, pressed to the ground, as if they had all been hit in the stomach. Squirming like a wounded cockchafer, a man was dragging a comrade behind him, moving back slowly, with a look of terror on his face, but refusing to abandon his friend. (p. 305:315)

Manuel's men, insufficiently armed and nervously awaiting the Moors' advance, are "embedded like insects [in] the low walls" (p. 419:426). Insect imagery once again insists on the dehumanizing conditions of battle: "The Dimitrov battalion . . . slept huddled together like flies . . . against the cold" (p. 418:425).

Above all this carnage fly the planes. From their aerial perspective, Magnin and the Pelicans naturally compare the furious futility of the tiny men below to the swarming of insects. The first Republican aerial victory occasions an extended comparison between the Fascist disorder below and the disruption of an insect colony. As the planes first spot the motorized column, the long winding vehicular formation suggests the slow undulations of a worm; though bombs sever this body, its movement is uninterrupted: "Like the head of a cut worm crawling off by itself, about a third of the column, its vanguard, pressed steadily on" (p. 87:94). The final scattering of the individual trucks transforms the column into smaller bugs: "Seen from the plane, the lorries seemed stuck to the road like flies on a strip of flypaper. . . . Scali saw them in imagination buzzing up into the air" (p. 87:95). The troops scattering for cover beget an even more powerful metaphor: "Darras had a glimpse of a welter of lorries sprawling bottom upmost under the thinning smoke clouds. . . . Darras saw only, flying for their lives, little specks of khaki dotted with the white turbans, like panicked ants carrying away their eggs" (p. 88:95–96). The striking identification of white turbans with ant eggs becomes an objective correlative for the Moors, continually reinforcing the absurdity and inhumanity of these struggles.

Though Magnin and Scali constantly view the men beneath them as "ant-like forms with round white hats" (p. 124:134), or frightened Fascists as "tiny specks on the crestline of the rock, clinging to it like flowers (*comme des mouches*)" (p. 203:213), the reverse perspective is also brought into play.

The plane accompanying Le Jaures is compared to a tiny fly; the huge searchlights of Baleares crossing wildly before it reduce the encounter to ridiculous proportions: "like using thin wands to catch a fly" (p. 234:244). When Scali's craft crashes into a snow-covered mountain, recalling the fate of the Cadillac in one of the first battles of the war, the plane and crew are pathetically reduced to "a drunk wasp dashing itself to pieces (*assomée*) against a wall" (p. 401:409).

In addition to their function in battle scenes, insect metaphors underline the dehumanizing submission which, as Kyo so quickly discovered, the prison imposes. Although Moreno, Hernandez, and other true Republicans can maintain their courage in prison, the little postman and other pseudo-revolutionaries compromise for survival:

> The authentic revolutionaries kept their mouths shut—because they were revolutionaries; the others, men who fancied they were revolutionaries because those about them were, and had discovered, faced with death, that all they really clung to was life—life on any terms—kept silent too. Silence is the prisoner's safeguard; thus insects try to be indistinguishable from the leaves on which they live. (p. 212:221)

The insect reappears as Garcia recalls a conversation with Caballero about the latter's imprisoned and condemned son:

> They had sat at the table facing each other. . . . Through a window open on the autumn sun a grasshopper had blundered in and fallen upside down on the table between them. Half-stunned, the insect tried to keep from moving, but its brittle legs were quivering and, as Garcia watched it, both men had kept silent. (p. 270:279)

The stricken grasshopper foreshadows the boy who, like Hernandez and his fellow fifty, will "sauter en arrière [leap backwards]" into a muddy ditch and quiver until dead.

Thus, despite the determination of the fighting men, the insect image repeatedly contradicts any assumption of courage or hope. Despite occasional Republican success the presence of the insect reminds the reader not only of the shadow of death that darkens this war but also of an even more pervasive pessimism concerning man's fight against the overpowering forces of his destiny.

At the end of the novel, Manuel pauses to listen to an old man's story of "le Cid Campéador." Concluding this narrative of Spain's vanished grandeur, the old peasant muses, "Yes, all this business here, and all those cardinals, even the Grecos, and the tourists, and the whole caboodle, when one's had twenty-five years of them—and this war too, after six months of it . . ." As if to dismiss the story, the grandeur, the hope, and the war, the man "waved his hand towards the south-west . . . like a man brushing away a swarm of flies (p. 430:437). This single eloquent gesture, culminating such a strong and extended pattern of images in one stroke, recapitulates the dehumanization of war.

War, the construct of a series of elemental forces united in opposition to human dignity, joins Malraux's other major symbol of man's fate, the prison. Although not as predominant as in the earlier novels, prison images and experiences nevertheless function significantly in the over-all structure of the novel. War has been seen to serve in *L'Espoir* as a hyperbolic metaphor of the human condition: submission, death, and a sense of disproportion have weighed upon all of

Malraux's characters. Prison situations, metaphors, and allusions operate in precisely the same fashion. Le Negus, for example, sees the oppressed proletariat as perpetually imprisoned by their early humiliation:

> When a man comes out of prison, nine times out of ten his gaze
> doesn't . . . doesn't *settle;* see what I mean? He's lost the way of
> looking at people like a man. In the proletariat, too, there's lots of
> folk can't look at people steadily. . . . They're free today. They've
> never been that before. I'm not thinking of political freedom, but an
> other kind. . . . What we are out for is to live the way men ought to
> live, right now and here; or else to damn-well die. If we fail, there's
> an end of it. (pp. 170–71:180–81)

The most eloquent prisoners, Moreno and Hernandez, have also
known "those horrors that the universal anguish of mankind instantly
recognizes: humiliation . . . prison." [16] For Hernandez, however,
prison signifies much more than subjection—it becomes the locus
of his confrontation with his mortality: "Prison life was another matter. . . . Boredom set him thinking, and a condemned man's thoughts
all turn to death" (p. 213:222–23). He discovers from his prison
contemplations that "the principal thing about death is that it makes
all that has preceded it irremediable, eternally beyond redress" (p.
214:224). The simple realization of the inevitability of death and the
universality of inhumanity and suffering echoes Pascal's question,
"What is the meaning of life *since* man is mortal?" [17]

Moreno's experience in prison contributes a further philosophical
implication for the human condition. Men pass their time flipping
coins to "determine" whether they will die.[18] In 1950 Malraux wrote,
"The state of mankind (*la condition humaine*) is also a prison, and
the people in it that [Goya] loathes first are the traffickers in
hope." [19] The need of these "traffickers in hope" to gamble on an inevitable outcome, the need of hope where no hope is possible, infuriates Moreno (though he himself later abjectly joins in the game) because it represents a refusal to deal responsibly with the one reality
which the prison forces on man, the inevitability of death.

Moreno's and Hernandez's experiences represent the core of the prison symbolism in *L'Espoir,* but they are generalized to apply to other groups of characters by a series of individual images. When Hernandez leaves his cell for interrogation, he notices that "the prisoners walked round and round the yard, hag-ridden each with his own destiny (*son destin empoisonné*)" (p. 212:222). The circular movement of prisoners and the word *destin* recall both the "captive planets" turning in "their captive immensity" of *Le Temps du mépris* (p. 50:59–60) and Garcia's grim reflections while Madrid burns: "Garcia was thinking of Hernandez. And, as he watched the flames rising above Madrid, he realized with a rush of agony how similar are all the tragedies of man's estate, each circling his sad small orbit of despair like a madman turning in his cell" (p. 338:348). That same tiny infernal circle has been traced by Grabot, Kassner, and Hernandez in their respective cells, the circle of universal determinism and the ineluctable mortality of the human condition.

Small wonder, then, that the Pelicans wait for an overdue plane "like prisoners at exercise" (p. 129:139), for each will soon return to the cell-like cockpit of a plane whose obsolescence condemns him to eventual death at the hands of the enemy.

House escapes from just such a feeling of inevitable death when he learns from Magnin that his wounds will not leave him permanently crippled. Magnin senses "a resistless tide of joy surging up from the bed, the joy of a prisoner set free, mysterious in its immobility" (p. 94:102). The prison allusion here recalls the close relation between sickness and incarceration as forms of submission.

Images of sickness, though not so frequent as in previous works, nevertheless effectively second the prison motif by forcefully communicating the metaphysical anguish produced by the war.

In their first engagement in the Sierra, Manuel and Barca suddenly find their brigade pinned down behind a truck by an enemy machine gun. One thought preoccupies them all: "Nothing would have suited them better than an attack from the fascists; a straight fight rather than this sick suspense—like the ordeal of a doctor's waiting-room (*cette attente de malades*)" (p. 53:61). They experience for the first time one of war's fundamental verities which Malraux develops later in the work through Moreno, just released from prison:

> After the first ten days you're an automaton, a sleep-walker. You see too many men die, there's too much of the machine in what's against you: tanks, artillery, planes. Fate takes charge, and you're only sure of one thing—that you haven't a dog's chance. You're like a man who's drunk a poison that kills after a certain number of hours. . . . Your life is over. (p. 316:325–26)

The comparison of the effect of a slow poison with the situation of the soldier, like the prison image, implies a constriction of normal activity and a total concentration on the nature of existence and the inevitability of death.[20] Once again, the war is revealed as a telescoped hyperbole of life; it is made clear that man must decide basic questions of life, ideals, and action in the context of an awareness of mortality. In this light, images of sickness extend the decidedly existential themes of *La Voie royale* and *Les Conquérants*. Those in *L'Espoir* who are condemned to death or a life of inaction appear sick in the eyes of their fellows.

When Shreiner is refused permission to fly for lack of the necessary reflexes, the other pilots move aside "like men shrinking from the sight of a child's agony" (p. 63:71). Shreiner's failing is tantamount to condemnation to the inactive useless life of the infirm.

Manuel is also condemned to an even more agonizing moral drama, the loss of humanity necessitated by command. Manuel wrestles with the dilemma which compels him to condemn other men, taking the problem to his mentor, Ximenes, "as a sick man seeks the company of a fellow invalid to discuss death" (p. 348:358). The comparison indicates that Manuel's feeling of his own humanity is just as surely condemned by his role of leader as Perken's is by his gangrene. As Garcia points out, however, wishing for impossibilities constitutes another form of sickness: "Thinking about what ought to be instead of what can actually be done is a mental poison. For which, as Goya said, there is no antidote" (p. 183:192).

All of the images discussed thus far help to enlarge the major concerns of *L'Espoir* from simple questions of military or political practicality to a fundamental examination of the human condition. We can better understand, then, when Garcia says of the "being-doing" dilemma, "The question is far from being a trivial one . . . it raises the whole problem of civilization" (p. 336:347). Imagery not only raises the day-to-day problems of war to a metaphysical level but also proposes a solution to the dilemma of being *vs.* doing which remains unresolved in explicit debate.

Images of theater, the most extensive in the novel,[21] denounce ephemeral heroism undertaken merely for the sake of example, the desire for being unaccompanied by definite results.

Ximenes might have included in his sermon denouncing heroics Malraux's epigrammatic statement that "a man's most effective weapon lies in reducing the curious side of his character (*sa part de comédie*) to a minimum" (*NA*, p. 38:49–50),[22] so closely is fruitless heroism identified with a masquerade.[23] Theater imagery ridicules the Cadillacs' foolhardy attempt to overpower an entire Fascist artillery: "with a syncopated stridence of horns and klaxons two Cadillacs tore up the road . . . wildly zigzagging like cars in gangster films" (p. 21:29).[24]

Such senseless bravado plagues the Republican army throughout the war; the disciplined Communist leaders expend as much energy on curbing the Anarchists' enthusiasm as on combating the enemy itself. As long as the militia prefers *being* to doing, it cannot be organized into a truly effective fighting unit. Trapped behind the truck in the Sierra, Manuel desperately watches his men courageously hurl themselves at the Fascist crossfire. The young girl suddenly appearing to exhort the men to even greater bravery underscores the uselessness of the sacrifice. It is no coincidence, then, that her voice takes on a "theatrical intonation" (p. 53:61). As Garcia laments, men can still play at being soldiers in a desperate situation (p. 432:439). Throughout the work, hints of play-acting manifest themselves in such phrases as "the anarchist reappeared, like an actor entering abruptly from the wings" (p. 378:386). A wounded bombardier wears an "air of high romantic dignity (*un masque romantique*)" (p. 411:418). Even the sober Scali reminds one of "an American film comedian. . . . the disproportionate shortness of his legs . . . gave him a 'Charlie-Chaplin' walk" (p. 118:127). Dressed for flight, Scali resembles "an American comedian taking part in a film about aviation" (p. 243:253). Other theatrical transformations include Alba's, Leclerc's, and Nadal's "comedy" (pp. 144, 246, 249:153, 256, 259) and Siry's "gestures of a comedian" (p. 283:253).

Magnin and Manuel both mistrust men whose lack of seriousness renders them undisciplined and unfit for battle. To Magnin such types are "extras from a film studio" (p. 236:246); Manuel realizes that a Republican army composed of such heroes alone would be only a "comic-opera army" (p. 74:82).[25]

Indeed, Madrid, Toledo, and the Alcazar appear as settings of fantastic theatrical productions.[26] After the first Republican victory, "Bathed in the bright glare of its streetlamps, gay with the motley of the Revolution, Madrid looked like an enormous film studio" (p. 36:44), in which "men with rifles under their arms were drifting in bringing the latest news, like the film actors who drop into a studio bar, in costume, between two takes" (p. 32:40). Searchlights douse a square in Toledo with "the fierce light of a film studio," and the narrow streets with "a vivid, theatrical effulgence" (p. 161:170).

Each time the weight shifts toward the mere fact of being, images of theatricality reappear. Discussing Hernandez's generosity toward Moscardo, which Garcia had considered play-acting ("every revolution is inclined to melodrama, at its early stages" [p. 176:185]), Mercery dramatically exclaims: "Whatever happens, Hernandez, you've given a fine, a noble example. In the name of the League of Peace and Justice to which I have the honour to belong, I take off my . . . my *képi* to you" (p. 174:183). Garcia, present at this theatrical homage to courage, becomes confused: "Since the day of the flame-thrower attack when they first had met, Garcia had been puzzled by Mercery's personality. Must idealism, he wondered, always involve play-acting?"

(p. 174:183). It is no coincidence, then, that Mercery exemplifies the extreme of vainglorious heroism when he audaciously directs his fire hose against an oncoming Fascist fighter plane and is shot from his ladder into the flames of Madrid.

Observing Hernandez's active involvement in the military affairs of Madrid, the disillusioned Moreno asks, "From the point of view of the revolution . . . what's your real opinion of all this play-acting?" (p. 192:202). Though Hernandez, clinging to an idealistic vision of dignity, at first responds, "It's more than play-acting" (p. 192:202), he later admits to having been caught up in "the comedy of honor" (p. 218:228). The whole war appears to the condemned man as an immense and tragic farce: "And, at this hour in half the land of Spain, young men were playing their grim part in the same tragic comedy . . . falling sheer or leaping back into a pit. . . . It struck Hernandez that he had never seen men turn back-somersaults before except at circuses" (p. 219:229).

The element of theatricality is eloquently summarized by Garcia's theory of the motives behind combat: [27] "Pugnacity forms part of the play-acting which almost every man indulges in, and it leads men into war just as almost every sort of play-acting leads us right into life" (p. 432:439). This extremely significant observation generalizes the image of the mask from heroes to all soldiers, and from war to all of life. Once again the images broaden the scope of the novel with war as a hyperbole of the inauthenticity men continually substitute for efficacy.

On the other hand, the pitfalls of action, of the all-consuming drive for efficacy of the Communist ideology, are amply illustrated by Manuel in one particularly symbolic episode. Following his condemnation of two volunteers accused of desertion, Manuel confesses to Ximenes, "Every step I've taken towards greater efficiency, towards becoming a better officer, has estranged me more and more from my fellow-men. Every day I'm getting a little less human" (pp. 347–48:358). He recounts the condemned man's desperate accusation that he had no voice for their concern (p. 333:343), but he fails to admit to Ximenes that "as it so happened he had, at that moment, lost his voice" (p. 348:357–58). The importance of the loss-of-voice image derives in large part from Manuel's instinctive repression of his mutism. Malraux was to write in *Les Voix du silence:*

> We know that a man's consciousness of himself functions through channels other than those of his awareness of the outside world; every man's self is a tissue of fantastic dreams (*monstre de rêves*). I have written elsewhere of the man who fails to recognize his own voice on the gramophone, because he is hearing it for the first time through his ears and not through his throat; and because our throat alone transmits to us our inner voice, I called this book *La Condition humaine.* (*VS*, p. 630:628)

Although Manuel can voice his fears for his humanity, his loss of voice or loss of contact with his inner being paradoxically communicates his predicament even more forcefully.

Traditional imagistic and symbolic patterns have led to a dialectical impasse in which compromise seems impossible.[28] And yet, through the introduction of a new symbolic element, Malraux adumbrates a solution for the agonizing personal problem he had been developing since *Royaume farfelu.*

As Magnin hurries up the mountain toward his wounded comrades, the path suddenly changes direction:

> The point where it changed direction was an apple tree, outlined against the sky, in the centre of a minute field, recalling a Japanese landscape. Its apples had not been picked. Strewn on the ground, they formed a dense ring round it, which merged gradually into grass again. This apple tree was the only living thing among the rocks, living with the mute ageless indifference of endlessly reincarnated plant-life. (p. 406:414)

No further observations are made about the tree as Magnin passes. But during the descent from the mountain, surely the most fraternal and certainly the most vivid scene in the novel, the author again singles out this lonely tree for even more telling attention.

The light was failing. Like an equestrian statue, Magnin was sitting askew on his saddleless mule, gazing at the little apple-tree sur-rounded by its dead fruit. . . . In the silence suddenly grown murmur-ous with the sound of rippling water, the ring of decaying fruit seemed to typify the passage from life to death that not only was the doom of men but was an immutable law of the universe. . . . With-out his quite knowing why, the deep gorges into which they now were plunging, as if into the bowels of the earth, seemed imbued with the same agelessness as the trees (*s'accordait a l'éternité des arbres* . . . *l'éternité des pommes épaisses sur la terre*). (p. 414:421–22)

This single tree, directly recalling Kassner's vision of "tall straight apple trees in the center of their rings of dead apples" as he rediscov-ers the earth in *Le Temps du mépris,* and prefiguring Berger's sudden encounter with the walnut trees in *Les Noyers de l'Altenburg* (see below, p. 143), signals a pivotal turning point for both Magnin and Malraux. Magnin's encounter with the eternal rhythm of life and death mirrors Malraux's discovery of *L'Espoir* (both as novel, i.e., creative process, and as a possible solution to man's anguish). Like the opposition of dying fruit and renascent seed, the dialectical structure of the novel confronts "l'illusion lyrique" with "l'exercise de l'apocalypse" to produce "l'Espoir." In a sense this structure recapitu-lates all stages of Malraux's development to date. The lyrical illusion represents the tragedy of man's deceptive sense of triumph over his destiny; the exercise of the apocalypse suggests the possibility of the transcendence of this tragic situation by means of collective organized action which almost necessarily results in the loss of soul.[29] Hope arises not so much from a reconciliation of these two conflicting tenden-cies as from an acceptance of the necessity of their opposition.[30] It is for the artist, fictional and actual, to transform the experience of this dialectic into consciousness and conscience.

The novelist accomplishes this transformation by constantly juxta-posing philosophical dialectic with a more emotional and intuitive at-titude which occasionally supports, but more often contradicts, the ra-

tional conclusions. However perceptive and accurate, reason
frequently appears tragically inadequate in the face of the people's anguish; however "necessary," Communist insistence on organization
often appears mere petulance when confronted with the indigenous
and determined fraternity of the people. Hope lies in the unresolved
tension between the distance of dialectic and the immediacy of crisis,
between the necessity of being and that of doing.[31] Thus the hope
that one could not find in the political realities of Spain in 1936 is
transmuted into images of optimism and life.

For Manuel, of all Malraux's characters most hopelessly immersed
in the "sad small orbit of man's despair (*le petit cercle infernal des
drames des hommes*)" (p. 338:348), the discovery of hope occurs simultaneously with that of "the infinite possibilities of their destiny"
(p. 438:445), of life itself and of the rhythm of the beating of his
heart and the tramping of prisoners' feet.

The solution lies neither with the anarchist-adventurer nor with
the militant, but rather with the intellectual and the artist. "Converting as wide a range of experience as possible into conscious thought"
(p. 338:348) becomes the password not only for Garcia but for the
author himself, for from the anguish of war and impossible dialectic
the author created a novel and a possibility of optimism more fundamental than any historical event could be.

THE DISCOVERY OF TRANSCENDENCE
IN *LES NOYERS DE L'ALTENBURG*

*To reflect upon life—life in relation to death—is
perhaps no more than to intensify one's questioning. . . .
And it is possible that, in the realm of human destiny,
the depth of man's questioning is more important than his
answers.—A, pp. 1, 6:10, 17*

"I cannot make out the shape of the cathedral," reflects Berger in the opening sentence of *Les Noyers de l'Altenburg* (p. 11:13). Chartres, once an expression of transcendental aspiration, has been transformed into a prison, symbolizing metaphysical darkness. Enlarging the scale of this prison, Malruax quickly generalizes place into concept through tensive language. Chartres becomes "this *world* from which all news has vanished" (p. 12:14–15; italics mine); the reaction to a report of "a million and a half prisoners" expands the prison to immense proportions: "Laughter all around: why not ten million?" (p. 13:16). As with Grabot, Kassner, and Hernandez, the circle motif amplifies Berger's prison to cosmic proportions.[1] Berger sees "vast circles of faces leaden from hunger and sleeplessness (*plombés de faim et de nuit*)" (p. 15:19), in which the association of circle and night evokes Kassner's dire equation of prisoners and fixed constellations.

Malraux once again situates his protagonist in the quintessential Pascalian symbol of the human condition, into which the cathedral injects a poignant irony. Every detail resonates with the absurdity of social concerns. Deprived of civil rights and food, the men nevertheless establish property and build cooking fires. In this pervasive anguish, the men recapitulate Garine's and Perken's views of society: [2] "restlessly stamping and shuffling round like any other animal starving in a cage . . . two million French prisoners are waiting for the effect of their destiny to wear off" [3] (pp. 17, 22:21, 27).

Other images of despair reiterate the potential absurdity of this microcosm. In *La Voie royale* a mosquito alights on the dying Perken's eye to affirm the victory of death and the absurd. Here flies establish their dominion over the weakest of the prisoners: "By my side an Algerian rifleman blankly watches the flies that come to settle on his face. . . . Behind my head voices growing fainter and fainter talk of treachery" (pp. 11–12:14). The insect, therefore, is early associated with imprisonment, sickness, a gradual weakening, and, finally, man's ignoble betrayal of his fellow men.[4] Moments later, an insect-crustacean image reduces the whole to less than the sum of its parts,[5] vividly contrasting with the pairs of German and Russian soldiers in a later scene (see below, pp. 151–52): "Another tank-corps casualty and I move up, leaning on each other like a pair of entangled crabs" (p. 13:16). The crabs not only reaffirm the element of submission but reinforce the malaise of the original crustacean trauma,[6] the alienation of man from himself.

Self-alienation is immediately related, as it is in *La condition humaine,* to the impossibility of knowing others. The two wounded men traverse the immense nave of the cathedral prison only to discover that the promise of communication with their families is impossible.

Nor is the letter episode univalent; the hope for communication between the world of the prison and what is beyond, like the subsequent illusory hope for armistice (p. 19:23) or for any form of freedom, merely frustrates "those who traffic in hope." [7] When the chance to communicate with the outside world is announced, "delirious once more . . . leaving trails of blood (*filets de sang*) behind them, the wounded surge (*déferlent*) towards two voices" (p. 14:17).

The author immediately reemphasizes the image of water through a juxtaposition with infirmity: "The hoard of casualties slithers (*glisse*) towards us, surges (*roule*) round this highest of high places on earth" (p. 14:17). These waves of prisoners bring to mind the futility of the soldiers' efforts in *L'Espoir* and lay bare the illusoriness of metaphysical hope. "God is dead," Malraux had proclaimed in *D'une jeunesse européenne;* [8] he here reiterates the impossibility of Christian transcendence.

Two other highly charged themes complete this devastating picture. Immediately before noting the flies on the sick Algerian's face, the narrator laments the extent of his own wounds: "My legs, which have become a yielding, paralyzed sheath from the wound in my hip, melt away (*se dissolvent*)" (p. 11:14). Any kind of infirmity in Malraux's work has consistently communicated submission to destiny. Indeed, every prisoner seems paralyzed; within the cathedral, men's faces take on "the pathetic gaze of paralytics" (p. 13:16). Sickness and exhaustion, "that delirious weakness (*cette maladie d'halucinés*) which kept us marching on with gaping fish-faces" (p. 13:16), in the context of a reference to crustaceans, twice establish a formula of overwhelming despair. The failure of transcendence, together with the alienation from self and the world and with physical deterioration, threatens to dissolve human will in an ocean of collective despair.

Against this somber view of man's estate stands one positive act and the one positive image engendered by it. Berger sees men who refuse to renounce composing letters which they have learned will never be delivered. This determination despite the absense of hope offers Berger the hint of a response to the images of despair which surround him:

> There are now three of them writing on their knees. . . . Is it the same animal endurance that keeps the others writing today? Pencils, paper, purple tongues are in evidence in every cabin . . . and even outside, where a few isolated figures are pinning the paper to their knees with their left hand so that the wind may not blow it away with the torn-up letters. . . . How many days have I watched them

like this in the barrack-room, filling page after page? (pp. 20–21:26–27)

Berger witnesses the simple but fundamental discovery of these uneducated prisoners: "In this place, writing is the only way to keep alive" (p. 24:30). This recapitulation of Kassner's postulation of art as an anti-destiny, not, as might be expected, among intellectuals, but from men who "have been living from day to day for thousands and thousands of years" (p. 23:28), confronts Berger with Man himself.[9] The prisoners' intuitive response to their destiny illuminates man's eternal ability not merely to endure but to surpass his destiny:

> Peeping out from underneath that age-old familiarity with misfortune is man's equally age-old ingenuity, his secret faith in endurance, however cluttered with disasters, the same faith perhaps as the caveman used to have in the face of famine. . . . In this den of ours, drowsy in the noonday sun of eternity, the whispering voice of prehistoric man. (p. 21:26)

This first suggestion of the fundamental in man elicits a metaphorical transformation of this prison experience into primeval terms. An extended series of metaphors throughout the last several pages of the episode transposes these simple unheroic men into Eternal and Universal Man through a geographical, almost universal expansion in both space and time.

Observing the frenetic letter writing, Berger envisions a primeval African man: "Now these huts, these fires, these wandering Senegalese . . . begin to assume some eternal quality in the noonday sun and the wind" (p. 20:24–25). Each of the succeeding metaphors evokes the golden age of a past civilization: the primitive enclosures suggest a "Roman-camp stockade" and a "Babylonian hovel" while men are "crouched like Peruvian mummies" (p. 20:25), stretching the scope of the vision from prehistory to the present, from Asia Minor to South America. While one prisoner takes on the appearance of "a pioneer" (p. 21:25), others present "Gothic faces" (p. 21:25) and inaugurate a progression backwards through history to a consideration of the eternity of man's past which overshadows imprisonment:

What now emerges from the wild crowd that can no longer shave is *not the penal settlement,* but the Middle Ages. That applies even to those from the Mediterranean whose faces I expected to be those of Greek fishermen, Roman builders; perhaps because the Middle Ages undertook to represent men, and we are not in the sort of place that yields gods. But the Middle Ages are only a mask concealing their past, a past so long that it prompts dreams of eternity. (p. 23:28; italics mine)

The appreciation of man's permanence begets a rediscovery of anthropocentricity. Berger acknowledges that in a world without God, man must become the measure of all things.

A second suggestion of the permanence of man evokes not only his endurance in time but also the limitless depths of emotion and resourcefulness: "Their joy, all blows and outbursts, has not changed since Brueghel, since the fairy-tales . . . [and] issues from depths more fathomless, more intriguing than all the knowledge we have of the human race, as intriguing as its endurance!" (p. 23:28). Lost amid the thousands of prisoners ignorant of their fate yet possessed of the courage and resiliency to carry on, Berger discovers humanity's dark primitive stock. Berger exclaims: "Every morning I watch thousands of shadows in the restless light of dawn and I think: 'It's mankind' . . . [with his] age-old ingenuity, his secret faith in endurance" (p. 22, 21:27, 26). Whereas "shadows" and "restless" first convey the anguish of dehumanization by the dark prison of destiny, the subsequent "light of dawn" and "It's mankind" point up once again Berger's dawning awareness of fundamental man. Malraux unites the personae of author and narrator with the question, " 'As a writer, by what have I been obsessed for the last ten years, if not by mankind?' Here I am face to face with our basic essence (*la matière originelle*)" (p. 23–24:29). The permanence of this obsession [10] can be explained by the narrow single-mindedness of Malraux's attempt to discover the essence of man by studying only individuals: Perken, Garine, Kyo, Kassner, Manuel. The cure for this obsession lay in both the discovery of man's "matière originelle" and the subsequent realization that "it is not by any amount of scratching at the individual that one finally comes down to mankind" (p. 24:29).

This brief introductory episode thus presents a well-balanced dialectic between basic images of man's fate as they had evolved over the previous five novels and, more significantly, a suggestion of the possibility of Art as an anti-destiny, and a new vision of fundamental man.

Malraux's writing previous to *Les Noyers de l'Altenburg* had forced upon him two fundamental and pessimistic insights; first, "all action was soiled by its very nature," and second, "as for the absolute, triumph is ridiculous, but so is the triumpher." [11] Repeated experiments in his life and fiction had proved to Malraux that action could not accomplish man's peace with the world and with himself. He was still faced with the twofold problem of alienation: [12]

> We know that we did not choose to be born, that we would not choose to die. That we did not choose our parents. That we can do nothing about the passage of time. That between each one of us and universal life there is a sort of . . . gulf. When I say that every man is deeply conscious of the existence of fate, I mean that he is conscious—and almost always tragically so, at certain moments, at least—of the world's independence of him. (p. 96:127)

If any solution to this alienation were possible, it obviously lay elsewhere, not necessarily in a total rejection of action, but conceivably in the subordination of action to an operative philosophy which could somehow close this crevice between man and the world.

Almost unconsciously, Malraux's protagonists had progressively been evolving toward such a philosophy. Despite a sense of total alienation and a growing awareness of mortality, Gisors had glimpsed the possibility of a serene harmony between man and the world. Deep in his cell, Kassner had discovered the only means of defeating humiliation and insanity, the composition of a glorification of the virile fraternity of his fallen and future comrades. In the midst of a hopeless and dehumanizing war, Magnin had been drawn toward the most compelling image of the indomitable life-cycle,[13] and Garcia had learned that man's highest achievement consisted in transforming experience into consciousness. It remained for Berger to develop in more explicit terms this germinating idea of artistic creation as an active response to destiny.

Vincent Berger (the narrator of the middle sections of the work) and his son (the narrator of the Chartres and tank corps episodes) are unique among Malraux's characters in their penchant for observation rather than participation. An original tendency toward activism in Malraux's protagonists is succeeded by a need for synthesis. Having accumulated the necessary "expérience aussi large que possible," they dedicate themselves to transforming that experience into art. The contemplation of man and the reaffirmation of his "new vision of man" [14] constitute the quest of the artist-protagonist, who is situated somewhat closer to author than fictional character, between literary creation and reflective conceptualization.

Malraux's last novel, then, systematically searches for the essential in man in the face of a series of situations and philosophies which seek to deny and destroy him. The structure of the novel consists of a series of juxtapositions of fundamentally pessimistic experiences, involving three generations of the Berger family, countered by optimistic visions of the creative and enduring qualities of man.

This series is architecturally arranged with the Altenburg episode in the center followed by Vincent's exhilarating rediscovery of life before the walnut trees (see below, p. 145). The Altenburg episode is central not only physically but also in that the colloquy poses in cold rational terms the fundamental questions, "What is man?" and "How can he resolve the problems of his existence?" On either side of this central structure stand two series of confrontations between man and the problem of destiny. The first series is composed of four episodes. The first of these, as we have seen, describes the prison in Chartres in which the attempt to humble man into abject submission is countered both by Berger *fils*'s sweeping vision of history and by the discovery of the creative act. The father's anguished encounter with Ottomanism (which Lucien Goldmann sees as a metaphor for Malraux's own experience with Communism),[15] the second episode, is countered by the "retour sur terre" of an evening in Marseilles, a sudden reassuring vision of a greater community of mankind "on earth, towards the end of the second millennium of the Christian era" (p. 60:79). The third incident, Dietrich's suicide, is followed by the symbolic darkness of an endless tunnel in which, however, Nietzsche creates his "chant sublime" (p. 72:96).

Following the central colloquy, two other confrontations between man and attempts to refute him occur. The alarming inhumanity of Professor Hoffmann, inventor of the nerve gas, is overshadowed by the irrepressible humanity of the men in the trenches. The lethal gas cannot overcome the fundamental humanity of the soldiers, who return to German lines carrying a Russian enemy on their shoulders, each pair "greater than the sum of its two parts." [16] The final episode, again narrated by the son, confronts "waiting for a shell to fall in a tank trap [which] seems a piercing denial that life has any meaning" with "the depth of peasant life, which was attuned to death as day is to night." Here Berger regains "the discovery of a simple sacred secret . . . life . . . as powerful as the darkness and as powerful as death" (pp. 224, 223:292, 290–91).[17]

THE OTTOMAN ADVENTURE

Lucien Goldmann has exposed Berger's brief alliance with Ottomanism as an allegory of Malraux's involvement with official Communism and national ideology.[18] Berger's lectures on Nietzsche had convinced him to abandon abstract philosophical speculation in favor of action. Vincent explains his gravitation toward Ottomanism in much the same way that Perken and Garine justify their involvement in Asia:

> The origin of this enthusiasm was . . . mixed up with the need to get away from Europe, the lure of history, the fanatical desire to leave some scar on the face of the earth, the attraction of a scheme to which he had contributed not a few of the finer points, the comrade-

ship of war, friendship. "Activity which is fostered by dreams instead of being blighted by them is hard to find." (pp. 49–50:64)

Just as the Chartres camp presents a general review of Malraux's images of destiny, this episode recapitulates the problematic attempts of the adventurers and militants of Malraux's five previous novels to provide an answer to that destiny. In his turn, Vincent quickly discovers that his first political idealism must fall before the cold, calculated politics of efficacy and that Enver Pasha's political program consists only of a thinly disguised rationalization for his drive for personal power. Thus, rather than realizing his aspirations for meaningful action, Vincent discovers that a "false idiotic Central Asia . . . rejected its own destiny" (p. 57:74).

This episode, an allegorical résumé of the experiences of his previous protagonists, denies Malraux's original philosophy of collective political action as an anti-destiny.[19] This rejection is effected on three different levels: the literal level of Vincent's own experience within a collective ideology, the transposition of this experience into an allegorical expression of the experiences of other protagonists, and finally on the level of imagery.

The most remarkable stylistic feature of the episode is its imagistic sterility, a quality which at once communicates the sterility of the entire experience. Compared with the metaphoric density of the previous works, the tone and style of this passage suggest a formalistic history text; for seventeen of the twenty pages (pp. 36–53:47–69), the only semblances of tensive language are two historical comparisons.[20] When Malraux does turn to imagery, traditional themes of despair convey the absurdity and barrenness of the venture.

As a young man, Vincent had insisted on the necessity of seriousness: "Bear in mind that a man's most effective weapon lies in reducing the curious side of his character to a minimum (*c'est d'avoir réduit au minimum sa part de comédie*)" (p. 38:49–50). Vincent had originally dedicated himself to Enver's Ottomanism at least in part because of the lack of serious responsibility demonstrated else-

where. When Abdul Hamid and Mohammed V desert Vincent without acknowledging his services, Vincent is "angry but not surprised
—the game had been played according to the rules" (p. 44:57).
Without a specific ideology, the mercurial shifts of power, revolutions,
and counterrevolutions in the Middle East appear to Vincent's eyes
just one more ritual played according to established, albeit unwritten,
rules. Vincent's final disillusionment with Enver's integrity takes the
form of another image of game-playing: "Enver was a gambler; my
father was depriving him of his trump card, and the General held it
against him not so much because he believed that my father was mistaken but because he was afraid he was not mistaken at all" (p.
56:73–74).

The process of Vincent's disillusionment accompanies the first rela-
tively dense cluster of symbols in the entire episode, all of which reinforce the dominant barrenness of the Mideast experience:

> He met with the same meticulously ambiguous speeches, the same
> uneasiness, *the same nothingness.* And . . . coming back from the
> sands of the South where, in the thorn bushes, *crickets larger than
> crayfish* raise the antennae on their knight's helms at the sound of a
> caravan passing, he reached some *bone-coloured* town. Under the
> gateway made of clay and bristling with beams, horsemen in rags sat
> dreaming, . . . at the foot of buildings veiled like women, horses'
> skulls and scaly fish-bones glittered in the dust of the windowless
> streets. Out of doors . . . the walls, the sky, and God. "After three
> years . . . you forget *the desert is empty.*" (p. 53:69–70; italics
> mine)

Just as Ottomanism allegorically mirrors previous militant involvement, this passage structurally corresponds to the Cambodian jungles
in which Perken meets his destiny. Like the forest, the desert is metaphorically charged with images of all that threatens man. In the
"nothingness" of the desert, the insects or "knights" dominate human
horsemen in rags. Alien to human consciousness, the insect, as in *La
Voie royale,* suffers comparison with nothing other than insects or
crustaceans.[21] Other weighted symbols contribute to the sense of void.

Although of water images only references to the "crayfish" and dessi-
cated fishbones remain, a reminder of imprisonment is provided by
"windowless streets" and in the only elements distinguishable from
the sky, "the walls."

Even before he has consciously formulated his disappointment, Berger recapitulates the response of each of Malraux's previous heroes
when faced with the absurdity of his position. Just as Perken's gangrene and Garine's fever portend their defeat, Vincent's "increasingly
painful bout of dysentery" (p. 54:70) represents his nascent awareness
that a philosophy of engagement in meaningful political action cannot alone be sufficient to the problem of destiny.

When Vincent is nearly killed by a madman whom he is restrained
from resisting because of the traditional Islamic veneration of the in-
sane, one more sign of the defeat of the European's attempt to leave a
scar on the map, Vincent capitulates completely to his symbolic sickness: "illness had laid him low the minute he had lost all faith in the
mission" (p. 56:73). He decides therefore to return to Marseilles, dis-
abused and disillusioned by an adventure too sterile to command his
energies and respect: an adventure symptomatic of all adventure.[22]

THE "RETOUR SUR TERRE"
AT MARSEILLES

In Marseilles, far from the site of his folly, Vincent discovers, as
will his son at Chartres, visions of a quality fundamental in man
which is capable of combating the debilitating experiences of the
Middle East. Disembarking at the Mediterranean port in the late af-
ternoon of a summer day, he is at first too marked by his recent illness, physical and metaphysical, to notice the people around him.
Clothes glide along as if no corporeality substantiates them; the
women are nothing but shadows: "Through the smiling blue haze,
panama and straw hats, fine-checked trousers and strange female
shapes (*silhouettes*) glided past" (p. 58:75). Moving toward the Cane-
bière, Vincent is still motivated by a fundamental antagonism toward

social man, once again manifested through the traditional pessimistic images of the mask and sickness: "In all this crowd . . . not a single face with an expression on it. . . . And the intimacy of these women . . . gave every face he could see the blank, fixed look of madmen's faces" (p. 58:76).

Only upon retiring to his hotel room does the meaning of these street scenes begin to reach him:

> Through the open window behind the closed shutters came the hub-bub of the summer-time Canebière, the cries of the newspaper-sellers, the metallic din of the trams—and strange tunes which were a cross between a waltz and a gypsy ballad, like the songs of a procession winding past, stopping and starting up again: he had never heard a tango. . . . In Afghanistan, how many times had he dreamt of the first thing he wanted to see again! (pp. 58–59:76)

In the street once again, Vincent gathers from the reflections in the shop windows an even more important insight into the reality of the people around him: "Large mirrors reflected the ladies looking into them. My father now had time to scrutinize these ladies and . . . the exposed faces, gave Europe a touching innocence. What stamped these faces was not nakedness, but work, worry, laughter—life. Un-veiled" (p. 59:77).

Still unable to explain his discovery, Vincent can only compare his sensations to those of the terrorist who has killed for the first time,[23] whose temporary separation from the rest of humanity offers a unique vantage point for viewing and comprehending his fellow men. For Vincent, this vantage point produces an apperception of mankind from its earliest origins to the present culmination of its hopes and fears, what Malraux was to label the "unity of the world after a season in hell." [24] In a burst of communal feeling whose figurative language contrasts radically with the aridity of the Enver Pasha episode, Vincent catches a glimpse of this unity of all men of all epochs:

> Feeling like a castaway on the bank of either nothingness or eternity, he looked at its troubled waters (*la confuse coulée*)—as divorced from it as from those who had passed by, with their forgotten suffer-

ings and lost legends, in the streets of the early Bactrian and Babylonian dynasties, or in the oases overlooked by the Towers of Silence.
Through the strains of music and the smell of warm bread, house-
wives were hurrying along, shopping-bags on their arms; a
paint-shop put up its multicolored shutters on which a last sunbeam
lingered . . .—on earth, towards the end of the second millennium
of the Christian era. . . . (p. 60:78–79)

The central comparison between small French merchants and citizens
of the great Babylonian and Bactrian empires broadens the scope of
the scene and would appear to reduce the individual to insignificant,
ordinarily pessimistic proportions. This negative weight is reinforced
by the terms *nothingness, eternity,* and *troubled waters,* and by the
phrase "the second millennium of the Christian era," which conveys
the individual's ephemerality in the eras of the earth. Yet between
these two expressions of eternity, common man carries on unper-
turbed by the immensity of history precisely because this history is
also the history of Man.[25] With this discovery, Vincent "felt released
. . . with a rapturous liberty which was indistinguishable from li-
cence" (p. 61:79). He must, however, expand and deepen this initial
recognition of the tension between the finitude and the grandeur of
Man before transforming his experience into true consciousness.

THE SUICIDE OF DIETRICH

Five days after Vincent's return from the Middle East, his father
takes his life. The force of this episode arises largely from the carefully prepared character of Dietrich, whose every decision is premedi-
tated as if it were his last.[26] His death "that was like his life" (p.
67:90), as deliberate as any of his other decisions,[27] clearly exemplifies Nietzschean redemption.[28] Only two days before his death, Dietrich had told Walter, "Whatever happens, if I had to live another
life again, I should want none other than Dietrich Berger's" (p.
65:87). As Walter later explains to Vincent, "Suicide was implied by
his 'whatever happens'" (p. 65:87).

Vincent, unable to appreciate the redemptive side of his father's death, feels only anguish that "the millennia have not been long enough for man to learn how to look on death" (p. 30:38–39). Although the apparent inexplicability and deliberateness of the death seem to him an accusation of the nature of life itself, Vincent is saved from a paralyzing pessimism by recalling his discovery in Marseilles that "man is more than his secrets" (p. 67:90). In a passage whose rich imagery strongly contrasts with the purely formal dialogue concerning Dietrich's death and motives, Vincent recapitulates his earlier maturation from profound and pessimistic despair to an intoxicating confrontation with the mystery of life.

Entering the room, Vincent immediately senses death in the disorder of the bed and its "hollow . . . like the hollows sleepers always make," the negative form of the living man. Even the electric light cannot combat animated death: "The electric light was still on, as if no one—not even himself—dared to scare death away by drawing the curtains" (p. 68:90). The presence of death is immediately reinforced by Malraux's most haunting and consistent objective correlative of submission and death, the insect:

> An ashtray lay on the bedside table; inside it were three cigarette-ends; my grandfather had been smoking, either before taking the veronal or before falling asleep. An ant was scuttling along the rim of the ashtray. It continued on a straight course, then climbed on to the revolver lying there. (p. 68:91)

The insect's route is far from arbitrary. Moving along the circular perimeter of the ashtray, it triply associates death with the absurd. The circle has consistently referred to imprisonment in Malraux's work; ashes traditionally symbolize death; and the ashtray is vividly, if hypothetically, linked to Dietrich's last moments. Quitting the ashtray, the ant continues "on a straight course" to the instrument of death, the revolver.

Vincent's next impression, "the feeble (*indifférent*) sound of the travelling-clock," reinforces the anguish of mortality through awareness of time passing.[29] The merciless march of time underlined by the adjective "indifférent" reminds one that life is only a short sojourn; the clock is, after all, a "pendulette de voyage."

A return to the insect metaphor recalls Perken's comparison of man's submission to destiny with the termites' submission to the order of their hill: [30] "Mechanical and alive like this ticking, the insect social order was pullulating over the face of the earth" (p. 68:91). The menacing presence of destiny, submission to death, continues far beyond the confines of this curtained darkness.

And yet the dominant presence of death is gradually countered by a positive awareness of the human potential for liberty. The dire vision of universal submission within the insect communities suddenly sinks "below the mysterious liberty of man" (p. 68:91). Although "Death was in the room . . . in the vague traces left behind by the men who remove bodies" (p. 68:91), life outside continues irrepressibly: "From the living world outside came . . . early morning birdsong, men's voices." Time and place expand as in the Chartres episode, suggesting a universality and permanence of man: "At this moment donkey caravans were making their way towards Kabul, towards Samarkand, their rattle and clatter drowned in the lassitude of Islam" (p. 68:91).

Two short ungrammatical and elliptical exclamations, "The human adventure, the world," suddenly enlighten Vincent with the understanding that though the world and destiny are inalterable, man can actively modify his response to his fate. "Gradually possessed by an unknown sensation, as he had once been at night in the highlands of Asia, by the divine presence" (pp. 68–69:91–92), a prophetic reconciliation with the world and a renewed interest in man, Vincent is reminded of his liberating "return to earth" in Marseilles: "In the same way, he now felt the whole of his life was disordered (*insolite*); and suddenly he felt delivered from it—strangely unfamiliar with the world and astonished by it" (p. 69:92).

Having intuitively rediscovered an as yet only vaguely discernible secret of life, Vincent possesses the courage to draw the curtains. Ironically, it is only with this act that one fully realizes the imprisoning

quality of the room. Vincent had earlier labeled everything beyond
the curtains "the living world outside." He draws them apart only to
discover that the room is still cut off from the outside by a "huge iron
doorway." Death is still manifest through the insistent prison; Vincent is able, however, to glimpse "on the other side . . . the bright
green of early summer" (p. 69:92).

The final paragraph completes Vincent's enlightenment. No longer
menacing, destiny, like life itself, is revealed as an adventure; mankind has the courage and the permanence to transcend individual destiny:

> Like a man's fate, the whole of life was an adventure. He looked at
> the infinite repetitions of this commonplace countryside, listened to
> the prolonged rustlings of Reichback as it came to life, just as in his
> youth he used to gaze beyond the constellations at smaller and
> smaller stars until his sight failed. And the mere presence of the peo-
> ple passing hastily by in the morning sunshine, as alike and as differ-
> ent as leaves, seemed to yield a secret that did not spring only from
> the death which still lurked behind him, a secret that was far less the
> secret of death than of life—a secret that would have been just as
> impressive if man had been immortal. (pp. 69–70:92–93)

Although Vincent cannot yet precisely identify this secret, obscured
within a confused flow of emotion, intuition, and logic, he suggests it
to be Man himself. Death, stars, and constellations, formerly overpowering images of destiny, are here counterbalanced by earth and man,
possessing infinite variety and resourcefulness. By concentrating on
the variety and vitality of *paysan* and *paysage* alike, Vincent succeeds
for the first time in putting death behind him.

Once again in this third episode, Malraux effects a startling confrontation between major images of destiny and a new image of life.
In the prison of this tiny, dark room Vincent manages to discover an
image durable enough to defy the imperious power of destiny, the
image of Man.

NIETZSCHE'S "CHANT SUBLIME"

As with Perken, Garine, and so many of the prisoners at Chartres, Nietzsche's sickness represents a hyperbole of man's submission to destiny. The fact that his particular ailment is emotional and arises from an unsuccessful confrontation with the social and physical world increases enormously its metaphysical implications. Walter agrees to assist Overbeck and Miescher in taking the philosopher back to Basel on the train. This train ride, itself an allusion to the voyage of life, provides a symbolic framework within which the image of the prison appears in triple strength. First the men are crowded into a cramped third-class compartment. This claustrophobic constriction increases as the train enters the Saint Gothard tunnel, an endless cavern of darkness recalling Attignies's experience in *L'Espoir:* [31]

> The train entered the St. Gothard tunnel. . . . In those days it took thirty-five minutes to go through—thirty-five minutes—and the carriages, the third-class ones at any rate, had no lighting. Swaying about in the dark, the smell of soot, the feeling that the journey would never end. . . . Supposing a crisis occurred in this darkness? (p. 72:95–96)

A third significant image of imprisonment and destiny describes a peasant girl's large wicker basket out of which a hen keeps trying to poke its head (p. 71:95). In the darkness of the tunnel, the only sounds are the clicking of the wheels and the hen's beak "pecking at the wicker-work" (p. 72:96). Nietzsche is forced to contemplate another being trapped against its will in a cell within the cell of the train compartment.

Another of Malraux's most consistent images reinforces this vision of the human condition: "His voice, punctuated by the raindrops falling from the tiles, was shaking with the scorn that is to be found in certain forms of pity" (p. 72:96). The drops of water which punctuate the philosopher's sentences orchestrate the dissolution of the human will in the face of destiny.

This compendium of negative themes forms a composite image of man's condition that threatens to overpower man entirely. As in the episodes of the prison camp, the desert, and the dead man's room, Malraux has consummately interplayed literal physical elements fraught with significance from their earlier imagistic use. The context of this weighted symbolism insists on Nietzsche's poem, *Venise,* as a metaphor for the possibility and necessity of human creation in the face of destiny. Walter exclaims:

> This song . . . well, by God, it was sublime. . . . It was life—I merely say: "It was life." . . . the song was as strong as life itself. . . . In the prison which Pascal describes, men manage to drag out of themselves an answer which . . . cloaks those who are worthy of it with immortality. . . . Sometimes—the millennia of the starlit sky seemed as completely wiped out by man as our own petty destinies are wiped out by the starlit sky. . . . certain works can withstand the intoxication provoked by the contemplation of our dead, of the starlit sky, of history. (pp. 72–74:96, 98)

Walter's statement makes explicit both the symbols of destiny surrounding Nietzsche and the nature of his response to it: "The greatest mystery is not that we have been flung at random between the profusion of the earth and the galaxy of the stars, but that in this prison we can fashion images of ourselves sufficiently powerful to deny our nothingness" (p. 74:98–99). The fourth of Berger's purely intuitional discoveries thus reworks both Kassner's and the Chartres prisons into the coherent proposition of man and art as an answer to destiny. As in those earlier prisons, the accumulated insights of negatively charged symbols and images celebrate creativity as a form of salvation.

THE COLLOQUY AND THE WALNUT TREES
OF THE ALTENBURG

Of the many forms of destiny in *Les Noyers,* Mollberg's testimony before the Altenburg colloquy constitutes in explicit terms the most potentially devastating, though finally and paradoxically, the least destructive. This, the novel's sole deliberate attempt intellectually to destroy the notion of man, fails to convince Vincent, both because of his limited faith in intellectuals [32] and because of the strength of his own intuitional experiences.

The colloquy explores the question "What is man?" as rephrased by Mollberg, the pessimistic ethnologist:

> Is there any meaning to the idea of man? In other words: from beliefs, myths, and above all the multiplicity of mental structures, can one isolate a single permanent factor which is valid throughout the world, valid throughout history, on which to build one's conception of man? (p. 98:130)

He rapidly eliminates any ethnological definition of man by reviewing the world's notions of destiny, birth, death, and God:

> No need to collect a mass of facts. We have just considered societies which are ignorant: the first, of our conception of fate; the second, of our conception of birth; the third, of our conception of exchange; the last, of our conception of death. That's enough. Between the men we have just mentionned, and the Greek, or the Gothic man—or anybody else—and ourselves, what is there in common? (p. 104:138)

Mollberg terminates the colloquy with two different metaphors which reduce man to his most appalling form of destiny. He first postulates man's "permanence du néant" in the following terms: "Since at the back of man—always assuming the word has any meaning— . . . what do we begin to see appearing? A kind of ant" (p. 98:130). At the end of his talk he returns to his original metaphor: "I'm the most qualified commentator on Africa in the world . . . there's no better way of concentrating on man than looking at ant-hills" (pp. 113–14:149). Mollberg's metaphor is more apt than he perhaps realizes; his reduction of man to the level of the insect allows the concept of German supremacy [33] and opens the way for a reign of Fascism which threatens Europe with submission as irrevocable as that of insects to light. It inaugurates the era of death, the "large insect" which recalls the invasion of the scorpions in *Royaume farfelu*.

Not content with simply reducing man to the level of the insect,

Mollberg sees him as prisoner as well: "When man stopped being a prisoner in the cosmos, he inevitably encountered death . . . conceiving himself as mortal. He therefore began to struggle against death" (p. 103:136–37). This Pascalian picture of the metaphysical prisoner demonstrates how thoroughly Mollberg succumbs to the tide of destiny that has beset Malraux's protagonists from his earliest writings.

The entire thesis, a reasoned exposition of destiny more withering than any Vincent has yet encountered, appears to destroy any hope for a new vision of man with which to confront death. Mollberg's pessimism is heightened by several of Malraux's most tested correlatives of the human condition. Supporting both Mollberg's appearance [34] and message, the hall is invaded by flies, which alone among the audience seem to possess the possibility not only of movement (p. 97:129) but also of sound (p. 102:134).

Mollberg's language is rich in metaphors which, like the invocation of ants, contribute to the explicit sense of destiny in his talk. Repeated references to raindrops punctuate his discourse as they did Nietzsche's poem: "the summer rain beating on the stained-glass window" (p. 83:111; cf. p. 97:129) envelops the colloquy. "Curiously in keeping" with the meteorological situation (p. 98:130), Mollberg chooses a prominent metaphor of water:

> Every mental structure considers as absolute and unassailable any particular sign which directs life, and without which man could neither think nor act. . . . It is to man what the aquarium is to the fish swimming inside it. It does not enter his mind. It has nothing to do with the search for truth. It seizes and possesses man, while he never possesses it entirely. So much so . . . that men are, perhaps, more thoroughly defined and classified by their form of fatalism than by anything else. . . . It's not easy for a fish to see its own aquarium. (pp. 104–5:138–39)

This passage climaxes Malraux's previous use of water imagery as a metaphor of the confusing forces which so surround man that they dissolve the fiber of mental processes.

The familiar metaphor of sickness also serves to reinforce Mollberg's thesis. To describe a tribe in which the functions of the king depend upon the phases of the moon, Mollberg thrice relies upon metaphors of sickness to convey the fatalistic attitude of the court:

> They knew their fate as surely as a uraemia-specialist or cancer-specialist knows the outcome of uraemia and cancer; it was governed by the heavens just as we are by our germs. Nearly all the state officials followed them to their death. They died as a result of the king's death as we die as a result of a blood-clot. (p. 100:132)

But imagery can be a double-edged sword, and the image of sickness is just as devastating when applied to Mollberg as when applied to man. Although Mollberg's speech appears to deal a death blow to the notion of man when he endorses the concept of German supremacy, it is he who is compared directly to a sick man. He affirms the *echtdeutsch* theory "with the suppressed fury of an incurable to whom one has incautiously mentioned his disease" (p. 112:148). This metaphoric attack may be viewed as the first of several elements which begin to undermine Mollberg's unmitigated cynicism.

Seconding this inversion of the sickness image, two counterarguments and a powerful positive image begin to revive Vincent's new-found faith in his confrontations with Man. Despite Mollberg's apparently conclusive denial of any universal characteristic which validates a notion of man, Rabaud and Berger together propose the notion of man's permanence in art. Each successively refines the other's premises until their joint effort produces the only possible intellectual response to Mollberg.

To the question of the permanence of man, Rabaud first answers that only "the great artist . . . demonstrates how the continuity of man is identified with himself." Artists alone have "that great gift, that divine quality, of finding in the depths of themselves . . . the means of releasing ourselves from the bonds of space, time and death" (p. 84:112–13)—clearly the intellectually formulated equivalent of Kassner's and Nietzsche's experiences. To demonstrate that art reveals not individual psychology but rather man's fundamental resili-

ence in the face of his destiny, Rabaud resorts to the same image
which Mollberg had employed to illustrate man's submission:

> I once had occasion to visit a friend on his release for prison. . . . I
> wanted to ask him what he could have read, I mean, what stood up
> to prison atmosphere, what kept alive inside there. . . . Three books
> . . . hold their own against prison life. . . . *Robinson Crusoe, Don
> Quixote, The Idiot.* . . . In all three cases . . . we have, in the first
> place, a man set apart from his fellow men . . . by his own nature,
> by . . . innocence. The three isolated heroes of the world-novel! . . .
> The encounter of each of these three with life, the account of his
> struggle to put an end to his isolation, to get back to his fellow
> men. (pp. 89–90:119–20)

Thus Rabaud instinctively resorts to the most encompassing image of
the human condition to situate the discovery of the fundamental and
durable in man.

Vincent develops Rabaud's notion of art from a fraternal vision of
reunion to the possibility of reordering the world:

> Our fiction . . . implies an analysis of man. But it's clear that this
> analysis by itself would not be an art. In order to become one, it has
> to be matched with the awareness we have of our destiny. . . . Man
> knows the world is not on the human scale, and he wishes it were.
> And when he rebuilds it, it's on that scale that he does so. . . . To
> me our art seems to be a rectification of the world, a means of escap-
> ing from man's estate. . . . Representing fatality is . . . almost pos-
> sessing it. The mere fact of being able to represent it, conceive it, re-
> lease it from real fate, from the merciless divine scale, reduces it to
> the human scale. Fundamentally, our art is a humanisation of the
> world. (pp. 95–97:127–28)

Man's ability to face his destiny and wrest a response from it on his
own terms finally results in a rejection of Mollberg's nihilism: "Something eternal lives in man," argues Rabaud, "in thinking man—
something that I shall call his divine quality: it's his ability to call
the world in question" (pp. 111–12:147).

The colloquy, however, can reach no conclusion; Mollberg refuses to budge from his philosophical posture, as his final comparison of human society with an anthill makes clear. Intellect has battled intellect to a standstill; the colloquy ends with Walter's dolefully echoing the original question: "Is there any factor on which we can base the notion of man?" (p. 114:150).

Vincent leaves the colloquy and sets out across the fields toward a pair of stately walnut trees. These trees, probably Malraux's most discussed but least understood image,[35] will provide a series of intricate intuitive revelations which ultimately refute Mollberg's desolate vision of man.

Vincent's first impression fixes a harmony between earth and sky: the blue chicory of the fields mirrors "a sky now as clear (*transparent*) as the sky at high altitudes—in which fleeting (*éphémères*) clouds were drifting" (p. 114:150). For the first time, Malraux presents a sky neither terrible nor imposing, but as transparent, knowable, and changing as man himself, which inspires in Vincent not anguish but a serene calm: "Everything growing out of the earth was cradled in a soft radiance, bathed in the dust of the gathering twilight" (p. 114:150).

Increasingly conscious of a harmony between earth and heaven, Vincent begins to sense an analogous adjustment between the anguish of mortality and a faith in Man's permanence: "Idle thoughts, orchards eternally reborn which the same fears kindle like this evening's sun (*Vaine pensée, vergers aux inépuisables renaissances, que toujours la même angoisse éclaire comme un même soleil*)" (p. 114:151). *Inépuisables renaissances* counters the weight of *vaine pensée* and *angoisse;* this adjustment of opposites, like the sun and rain in the following passage, hearkens back to the similar discoveries of life's secret in Marseilles and at Reichbach:

Thoughts of long ago, thoughts of Asia, thoughts of this rainy, sunny summer day, so accidental, so rare—like the white race of men in Marseilles evening, like the race of men outside the window of the dead man's room, the overwhelming, commonplace mystery of life in the restless light of dawn. (pp. 114–15:151)

The two walnut trees which Vincent encounters immediately reinforce the harmonies intuited beneath apparent chaos and become
symbols not only of that harmony but of the creativity which reveals
it: "This wood . . . created at the same time an impression of free
will and of endless metamorphosis" (p. 115:151); that is, the possibility of the reconciliation of man's creative free will and the recognition of his inevitable submission to death. This series of adjusted opposites continues with the confrontation of man's creations with
nature's:

> Between them the hills rolled down to the Rhine; they framed Stras-
> bourg Cathedral far off in the smiling twilight, as so many other
> trunks framed other cathedrals in the meadows of the West. And
> that tower standing erect like a cripple at prayer, all the human pa-
> tience and labour transformed into waves of vines reaching right
> down to the river, were only an evening decoration round the vener-
> able thrust of living wood. (p. 115:152–53)

Negatively charged expressions ("a cripple at prayer [oraison am-
puté] " and "waves of vines," negative in light of Malraux's consistently pessimistic water imagery) counter positive ones ("the smiling
twilight," "patience," and "living wood"). Berger does not attempt to
dominate the elements of destiny, but discovers rather a possible harmony with them and among them.

The final polarity in this series of contrasts clarifies further this harmony: "The tortured wood of these walnut trees flourished with life
everlasting in their polished leaves under the sky . . . in all their venerable bulk above the wide circle of young shoots and dead nuts of
winter" (p. 116:152). An established symbol of destiny and imprisonment, the circle motif encompasses the process of death (the dead nuts
of winter) but simultaneously evokes the possibility of renascence (the
young shoots), the very process in which "life was attuned to death as
day is to night." [36]

This series of balanced antipodes in man's struggle with destiny
culminates in a vision of the walnut trees themselves as a recapitula-

tion of the creative process. Vincent considers the two trees as "two sturdy, gnarled growths which dragged (*arrachaient*) the strength out of the earth to display it in their boughs" (p. 115:152), echoing Walter's exclamation concerning Nietzsche: "Man's greatest mystery is that he succeeds, in the nothingness of the universe, in creating images strong enough to deny that nothingness" (p. 73:98–99). "This kindly statue which the strength of the earth carved for itself and which the sun at the level of the hills spread across the sufferings of humanity as far as the horizon" (p. 116:152–53) demonstrates the creation of images out of nothingness, of a monument to life drawn only from seed, soil, and water. The walnut trees thus symbolize that same process by which man achieves the "humanisation of the world."

Only with this understanding of the living creative force of the trees can the bankruptcy of Mollberg's metaphor of the logs be fully appreciated: "A civilization is not an ornament, but a structure. Look," Mollberg had claimed, "those two Gothic sculptures and that figurehead are of the same wood, as you know. But those forms are not shaped from fundamental walnut, but from logs of wood" (p. 111:146). Mollberg could discover no element unique to man but cells and other tissues common to all living organisms. Vincent discovers, in contemplating the walnut trees, however, that "between the statues and the logs there were the trees, and their design which was as mysterious as that of life itself" (p. 116:152). Between opposing definitions of man, there remain the visions of Chartres, Marseilles, and Reichbach, of a mysterious depth and permanence in man which no definition can account for or refute. Man's patience, his durability, his drive to "call the world in question," and his remarkable ability to achieve some harmony with the world all compose this mystery stronger than any logic.[37]

The walnut trees give the work its title because they constitute the only symbol which incorporates the three major discoveries of the novel: the discovery of Art as a humanization of the world, the possibility of harmony between man and the world, and finally, the discovery of a notion on which one can found a concept of man. The final episodes of the novel generalize and reinforce these discoveries.

THE RUSSIAN FRONT

Unable to comply with the sadistic rituals which replace justice within the German intelligence service,[38] Vincent is transferred to the front to protect a Professor Hoffmann arriving to unveil a particularly lethal gas to be employed against the Russians. As in the previous episodes, a series of metaphors and symbols present what appears at first to be an insurmountable image of destiny, but eventually furnish a fundamental revelation of Man.

Even as the project is announced, the presence of insects insists upon the ruthless inhumanity of the gas. The General staring vaguely out the window leads Vincent to wonder: "Was the General thinking about the flies, the weak points in his division or the consequences of what he was about to tell them?" (p. 126:168). As the General exposes his project, Vincent's speculations are at least partly confirmed by the associations between what the General delicately calls "this method of combat" and the insect: "Did the gas work chemically, or by means of bacilli, or simply by restricting the air supply of whoever it encircled? The sound of crickets could be heard. It was to them that the General seemed to be speaking" (p. 126:168–69).

Vincent observes an increasing dehumanization in the Professor and his surroundings. Hoffman has the face of a "dovecote" (p. 127:169), a laugh "like the great apes" (p. 130:173), and his son curiously resembles his bulldogs (p. 129:172). As Hoffmann extols the humanity of the fatal gas, the hotel room communicates a feeling of disintegration with its "rough texture of old walls under their recent coating of lime, a world of lizards (*lézardes*), dry-rot and mouse-holes. The Professor would be fighting the bed-bugs all night long" (p. 130:173).[39] Captain Wurtz shakes "his round, snub-nosed head, as though bothered by invisible flies" (p. 135:180). The only insect actually present is Hoffmann himself, elaborating the possibilities of destruction, moving in his "ant's crawl" (p. 136:180), while he consumes a sausage with which he is "beating time to humanity's funeral march" (p. 132:176). The outside world reflects the new menace to mankind in a vocabulary rich with Pascalian anguish and dissolution: "All the stars were out, thick as nebulae. Some cavalry were gliding past (*glissaient*) in the depths of the night, dispelling the sadness forced into the heart by the monotonous presence of the encircling worlds" (p. 136:181).

Vincent, however, manages to sustain the conviction which he had gained in Marseilles and at the Altenburg priory. He twice senses outside the window a vast and indomitable strength in the very people Hoffman is preparing to destroy:

> My father felt himself hemmed in by Russia, not so much because of the gold and purple cupolas, but because of the old pavements of the bulging square . . . the invincible Russian past was the only thing alive in the evening and the breathless silence of the war . . . and my father was conscious of the depth of the Slav world extending as far as the Pacific. (pp. 131–32:175)

As Hoffmann continues to rave, "Beyond the window my father was still conscious of Russia and its sunflowers blooming in the night as far as Mongolia" (p. 133:177). Despite the disintegration and "encircling worlds" of the night, Vincent reexperiences a harmonious universe which refutes Hoffman's calculating nihilism: "My father looked up at the night sky, as though he had suddenly been made a miraculous, personal gift of the millions of nebulae" (p. 136:181). This rendering personal and immediate of the infinite vividly illustrates man's ability to effect "a rectification of the world."

On the day of the attack Vincent observes "the troops . . . drawn up in . . . a huge cavern streaked with light, a bar of sunlight lodged in every observation hole" (p. 137:183). The coincidence of the expressions "huge cavern" and "bar" leaves no doubt that the author has again symbolically situated his characters in a prison whose obscurity is "like the darkness in mines" (p. 141:188). The inhuman supplants the human; bottles of poison gas stand guard "in ranks like soldiers, they seemed . . . to have taken the place in battle of the German army" (p. 137:182). The metaphysical dimensions of the anguish within the prison are underscored by Malraux's most consistent symbol of mortality, sickness: "The soldiers' nervous suspense (*angoisse*) had subsided without disappearing, like an acute illness that had become a chronic one; during the last year each one had got used to the fact that his own fate did not depend on himself" (p. 139:184–85).

Nor is the familiar insect missing from this grim picture of destiny. Hoffmann, scheming the "humanitarian" destruction of mankind, "remained crouched over the observation hole like a great daddy-long-legs" (p. 145:192).

The concentration within this trench of the metaphors of destiny sets the stage for still another discovery of Man's permanence, patience, and courage. Just as he had instinctively felt the reassuring presence of the Russian people in the darkness of the previous night, "Listening in this live darkness (*cette obscurité vivante*), my father was conscious for the first time of the people of Germany. Or perhaps just of people: men. A voice close to the darkness of primitive man, like these silhouettes barely visible in the shadows" (p. 143:190). He discovers in these voices which compose "l'homme," "the low measured voice of people in face of a mystery" (p. 146:194). Vincent sees this fraction of the enduring human continuum ("so many voices . . . in the dark underground like the pulsating of blood" [p. 148:196]) victorious in their biblical battle with the Angel of Death:

> My father was reminded of the town in *The Thousand and One Nights,* where every human gesture . . . [was] arrested by the Angel of Death . . . He was here, quite close, in the container-heads. But the passage of time also leads so certainly to death, that the old dream of fate being arrested kept recurring as though it was the secret of the world, lurking in these men . . . as it had once lurked beneath the helms of Saladin's soldiers. In this mushroom-bed smell my father saw, for a split second, the petrified gestures of the mythologi-

cal blacksmiths under light for ever forgotten—a light scarcely dimmed by the passage of fleeting human wills. (pp. 149–50:198)

Vincent here effects a symptomatic rectification of the world not by changing the world but by reinterpreting the old myths of despair. In the vision of Death's arrest of time, he sees more the defeat of death than the demise of man, for in arresting time, the Angel of Death thwarts the process of aging which culminates in death. By analogy, Vincent arrives at an equally powerful vision, the death-defying vitality and endurance of the rough-hewn life within the trenches. Though individual lives and will are "fleeting (*éphémères*)," mankind as a whole stretches from an almost indefinable moment in the past to the present. This discovery is accompanied by yet another vision of enduring fraternity in the trench:

> The darkness was once again alive with voices, unconcerned voices, venerable voices, professional voices—as though only their professions lived on inside these impersonal, provisional men. Their pitch varied, but their tone remained the same, very old, enveloped in the past like the shadows in this trench—the same resignation, the same false note of authority, the same absurd opinions and the same experiences, the same inexhaustible cheerfulness, and these arguments consisting of protests that grew more and more violent, as though these voices in the dark had never even managed to individualize their anger. (p. 150:199)

This vision of collective and inexhaustible Man encompassing both weaknesses and strengths prepares Vincent to withstand the final onslaught of his destiny.

Metaphor elaborates the literal instrument of death which comes to represent the destiny of all men. A gradual expansion in time and space impresses Vincent as "the ceaseless, creeping advance of the gas . . . seemed bound to continue up to the ends of the earth" (p. 155:205). A temporal expansion follows closely: "It was still advancing with the twisting movements of a prehistoric saurian, as though it would never stop while it still remained on earth" (p. 156:207).

The lethal cloud is also significantly seen in terms of water, "swamping (*noyant*)" (p. 153:203) everything in its path. The rider-less horse charging the immaterial enemy emerges from the noxious cloud "as if from underwater" (p. 155:205) before being engulfed in the "milky background of the gas" (p. 155:206).

Viscosity is pervasive, creating "a marsh" (p. 158:209), "the depths of some foul mud" (p. 164:217–18). Men slide under this oozing, suffocating "marsh-bottom world" (p. 170:225).

Insects, too, permeate this death-ridden vista. In the area immediately affected by the gas, everything Vincent touches is "repulsive like tufts of dead hair, spiders' webs, dust-fuzz" (p. 164:217). The gas is so deadly that it overcomes the insects, hyperbolically destroying the familiar correlatives of death, itself a grim testimony of Hoffman's over-kill: "a swarm of dead bees had stuck like the grains on a head of corn" (p. 165:219), "an occasional spider dead in the centre of its web in which there sparkled a greenish dew" (p. 166:220). In the blackened, sticky grass "countless little spiders' webs, intact, sparkling with a poisonous dew; in the shimmering light . . . twinkled from one end of the field to the other, as though carpeting it with flowers" (p. 170:226).

The increasing number of enmired insects announces the soldiers' dehumanization. The distant Germans approaching Russian trenches through barbed wire appear mere "spots [which] squirm in and out of the wire network [and] kick about in it like spiders in an invisible web" (p. 160:213). They first emerge from the trenches in an unrecognizable form which Vincent, obsessed with death, involuntarily relates to the insect: "Some soldiers were coming back through the barbed-wire, moving with the same gait, like spiders. . . . a confused swarm round the soldiers who were carrying the white spots like ants carrying their eggs" (pp. 161–62:215). As the Germans return toward their lines, defying their orders, "my father saw only the death of men . . . from every point of the forest, men carrying other men, their ranks rebroken by the anthill confusion of their flight" (p. 177:234). Death forces upon these men the submission of the anthill, long a paramount correlative of defeat in Malraux's work.

Other familiar images deepen the perspective of despair. The cloud of gas rolling ineluctably toward the Russians takes on familiar contours; "uniformly thick and tall, like a wall" (p. 153:203). Galloping forward Vincent suddenly finds himself trapped "within the four dark-green walls of the trees" (p. 163:217); he is caught "between two walls of forest" (p. 165:219), a "barricade" (p. 166:220) in which a clearing is only "another open field walled in by the slimy trees" (p. 170:226).

These patterns produce a composite picture of human destiny whose scope far surpasses the immediate scene of death. Yet as in each previous episode, Vincent discovers that man can propose an answer to destiny. The first of two major revelations occurs as he contemplates the men around him, miners, gravediggers, farmers, barbers, "men like so many others, between all the dead men and all that had been killed" (p. 159:210), soon to meet their destinies, yet at one with the earth and sky:

> High above, the great flight of birds was sweeping on; and under-
> neath, the human species flattened on those livid fields, waiting for
> the pounding from the Russians, had the same complex harmony as a
> summer night, the harmony of distant cries, dreams, presences, of the
> penetrating smell of trees and cut corn, of restless sleep on the face
> of the earth under the immense, unstirring sky (*sous l'immense nuit
> immobile*). (p. 159:211)

No longer simply dwarfed by the vastness of his surroundings and the heavens, Vincent senses once again the "complex harmony" of man with the world despite the presence of correlatives of death, "livid fields," "restless sleep," and an "immense, unstirring sky."

Vincent's second revelation is directly inspired by the German soldiers, who instinctively transcend national and military structures in an attempt to save their "enemies" from a form of death surpassing their understanding. Though at first unable to comprehend the massive mutiny, Vincent comes to realize that men can confront such inhumanity only with that idea they believe to be as powerful—human faternity:

> My father saw only the death of men. And yet . . . he felt the dead
> blaze quicken with a secret life. . . . In the distance he could see
> . . . men carrying other men. . . . What these men were doing, my
> father now knew: not through a mental process but through the body
> under whose weight he kept sinking into the ground up to his calf.
> On the whole of the dark slope he could see their lives extending,
> stretching into the waste land, buried in the woods, compelled by the
> same solemn fatality as clouds on the highest mountains . . . they
> seemed to him to be fanning out under the dark trees as far as the
> Vistula and as far as the Baltic. (p. 177:234)

Once again, the juxtaposition of hopeful optimism with such powerful
expressions of destiny as "sinking," "waste land," and "solemn fatality" produces a unity with the world by forming an image out of the
holocaust which denies the anguish of death. Each pair of men is not
only greater than the sum of its parts,[40] it brings together one living
and one dead, reformulating Vincent's discovery of the circle of dead
walnuts and live shoots. Man transcends his destiny not by opposing
himself to the world and death but rather by finding a place for himself in the greater order of nature:

> From wasted day to wasted day I am increasingly obsessed by the
> mystery *which does not conflict* with the indeterminate aspect of my
> companions who sing while they hold out under the *infinity of the
> night sky*. Rather does it link it up, by a long-forgotten path, with
> the *nobility* which men do not know exists in themselves, with the
> *victorious* side *to the only animal that knows he has to die.* (pp.
> 189–90:250; italics mine)

This triumphant discovery is reinforced during the gassing by a series of images related to the alternative title, "La Lutte avec l'ange."
While the idea of gas as destiny dominates, action is related in terms
of biblical disasters: "scourge (*fléau*)" (p. 157:208), "these infernal
woods" (p. 167:222), "a biblical curse" (p. 177:234), "an unreturning
force like the force of the Creation" (p. 177:234); the devastating
coral cloud leaves behind "this valley of death" (p. 165:219). The rediscovery of the fraternity between living and dead, however, transforms the surroundings into "this valley of the Promised Land" (p.
173:230).

Vincent's final revelation also springs from this eternal union of life and death. He realizes that the comradeship he has just witnessed has little to do with pity:

It was something a good deal deeper, an urge in which pain and brotherhood were inseparably united, an urge that came from far back in the past. . . . All of a sudden there flashed through his mind the memory of Altenburg: opposite my father were some huge clumps of walnut trees. . . . What was even the earthly adventure behind that window of Reichbach, compared with this human apocalypse that had just seized him by the throat, compared to this spark that had illuminated the depths of the earth that teemed with monsters and buried gods. . . . A mystery that would not yield its secret but only its presence, a presence so simple and so absolute that it cast into nothingness all thought connected with it—in the same way no doubt as does the presence of death. (pp. 184–85:243–44)

For the last time, Vincent confronts the mystery of life, the mixture of anguish and fraternity, of life *and* death that he had encountered before the walnut trees of the Altenburg.

THE TANK TRAP

Although the final episode of the novel occurs in the context of another character and another war, it nonetheless conforms to the established structure of a pessimistic situation balanced by a reassuring revelation. Vincent's son [41] feels the full impact of destiny when he and two companions confront imminent death in a mined tank trap. Inexplicably and miraculously they escape to rediscover the meaning and joy of life. Taken purely in terms of its literal action, the scene, like the preceding episodes, apparently constitutes merely a dramatically narrow escape. As previously, however, the convergence of several highly charged images elevates Berger's response to the situation to a universal existential level.

The dominant imagistic element in this incident, as at Chartres and in Nietzsche's tunnel, is the prison, which, as earlier, comprises several levels of significance. The war itself is "like a prison" (p.

195:257), whose scope is expanded: "There is no word to describe what one feels when advancing on the enemy. . . . The whole world becomes an insensible (*indifférente*) menace" (p. 204:267).

Within the tank each man is isolated in his tower or prow. Deprived of sight, the driver must rely on the tiny circle of his "dimly luminous compass, which quivers, swerves, swings back, seems anxious to veer off the course but, with every heave on the steering-wheel, swings back again, like our life pointlessly and ceaselessly fighting against our fate (*débattue autour de son destin*)" (p. 209:273).

The tank trap itself constitutes a third level of imprisonment. Of all the dangers, the "most obsessive is the ditch. One does not talk about the mine any more than one talks about death" (p. 205:268). Enclosed in their tiny compartments and in turn encircled by the impenetrable walls of the trap, the crew can only wait in anguish for the death-dealing shells. The tank trap thus perfectly symbolizes man's obsession with the limits to his freedom and his submission to an overpowering destiny. Malraux again generalizes particular into symbol: "the world of ditches is a vast one" (p. 205:269). Berger's fear that "nothing remains of the old fellow feeling (*accord*) between man and earth" (p. 205:269) temporarily jeopardizes the faith in an ultimately harmonious universe that his father had achieved. When the tank actually plummets into the trap, Berger realizes "it is as if we were in one of those dungeons where daylight only comes in through an inaccessible trap-door" (p. 216:282).

Several other images contribute to the generalization of tank and trap into symbols. References to water and dissolution accompany the first sign of entrapment: "we are sliding (*glissons*) in panic on a surface which is giving way" (p. 209:273). Caught in the trap, the tank is powerless, "tail in the air like a Japanese fish" (p. 210:274), and "slips, collapses (*glisse, s'effondre*)" (p. 210:274) while the "waves of tanks are still moving on up there" (p. 216:282). Nor is the image of sickness absent: Berger fears that the tank "will meet the shell by turning over on itself like an epileptic cat" (p. 205:268).

Once again the coordination of different images [42] accompanying frequent dehumanizations of the tank crew (into birds, beasts, mummies, frogs, and stones) provides a coherent larger image of destiny.

Berger's escape from this death provides a new revelation: "The living darkness appears to me like a prodigious gift, a huge germination" (p. 218:284). This gift, the rediscovery of life, appears as if for the first time, as it did earlier to his father in Marseilles. Berger's encounter with destiny permits him to view the simplest aspects of his surroundings with the eyes of revelation:

> Everything that I look at this morning, I also see through the eyes of a stranger. . . . and it suddenly strikes me that man has emerged out of the depths of the past simply to invent a watering-can. . . . What is it in me that makes me amazed—my only feeling since waking has been one of surprise. (pp. 219–20:286–87)

The vision of man and the surprise of which Berger speaks reside in the budding realization of man's potential to be at one with his world, with the universe. Berger envisages man united in harmony with destiny:

> I can hear in this picturesque profusion the hum of the centuries buried almost as deep as last night's darkness: . . . these are the barns of the Gothic Age . . . the wells of the Bible. O life! how old you are! . . . There is nothing here that does not bear man's imprint. . . . the old race of men . . . seems to have risen, across the millennia, from the darkness we were in last night. (pp. 221–22: 287–88)

"Profusion" and the "old race of men" grow directly out of the language of a once-formidable destiny, darkness and night. Berger likewise notices "grindstones . . . gleaming in the sun, spiders' webs hang sparkling with dew; . . . for a long time I stare at a . . . flower . . . born of the earth" (p. 222:288). Confirming his freedom from a sense of metaphysical imprisoment, Berger can recall without anguish Pascal's vision of "a large number of men in chains," observing:

> How firmly a meditation of this kind can make men cling to their wretched share of happiness. I remember my father. Perhaps pain is

always the more powerful; perhaps the joy granted to the only animal that knows it is not eternal was poisoned from the very start.
But this morning I am all birth. I can still feel within me the invasion of the earthly darkness when we came out of the ditch, that germination in shadows deepened by the constellations in the gaps of
the drifting clouds; and just as I saw the thundering, teeming night
rise up out of the ditch, so now from that night there rises the miraculous revelation of day. . . . life . . . this morning for the first time,
has shown itself as powerful as the darkness and as powerful as
death. (pp. 222–23:290–91)

This remarkable passage brings together many previous antipodes
in the anguish which Malraux's work sought to conquer. Berger experiences anguish and joy, he can acknowledge both his mortality and
the eternal possibilities of birth, man's importance despite the terrible
immensity of the skies, the fearful destiny of night along with the assurance and revelation of the morning. For the first time vocabularies
of destiny and hope are reconciled; Berger and Malraux have learned
through art's rectification and humanization of the world that man
can be part of the movement of the universe. Thus Berger can ex-
claim: "I now know the meaning of the ancient myths about the
living snatched from the dead. I can scarcely remember what fear is
like: what I carry within me is the discovery of a simple, sacred secret. Thus, perhaps, did God look on the first man . . ." (p. 224:292).

Like Adam before his fall, Berger is at one with his world; he has
learned that "representing fatality . . . is almost possessing it; the
mere fact of being able to represent it, conceive it, release it from real
fate, from the merciless divine scale reduces it to the human scale"
(pp. 96–97:128). Malraux had discovered that art can transform
experience into consciousness, creating a new myth of man consen-
tient with life *and* death.

THE ATTAINMENT OF GRACE

There is day, also, and night in the universe:
The wise know this, declaring the day of Brahma
A thousand ages in span
And the night a thousand ages.
Day dawns, and all those lives that lay hidden asleep
Come forth and show themselves, mortally manifest:
Night falls, and all are dissolved
Into the sleeping germ of life. . . .
I am Being and non-Being, immortality and death . . .
—*Verses of the Bhagavad-Gita, cited in A, p. 195:287*

The conclusions of *Les Noyers* leave little doubt that, at least in his last three novels, Malraux was in the process of formulating a personal, decidedly Eastern philosophy, in which man could resolve his Western existential anguish through a total integration into the eternal life-death cycle of the universe. Any doubt as to the logical outcome of this evolving philosophy was finally dispelled with the publication of his *Antimémoires*. Here the tendencies previously dealt with largely through imagery are made explicit in a passage which directly precedes a readaptation of Berger's miraculous escape from the tank trap. Recalling his experiences in India, Malraux writes:

Man can experience the presence of universal Being in all beings, and of all beings in universal Being; he discovers then the *identity of all appearances, whether they be pleasure and pain, life and death,* outside himself and within Being; he can reach that essence in him-

self which transcends his transmigrated souls, and experience its identity with the essence of a world of endless returning, which he escapes through his ineffable communion with it. . . . Being,
conquered from *universal appearance and metamorphosis,* does not
part company with them, but often becomes inseparable from them
"like the two sides of a medal" to point the way to an inexhaustible
Absolute which even transcends Being itself. (*A*, p. 198:292; italics mine)

The phrase "like the two sides of a medal" directly recalls the description of Berger's rediscovery of man the morning following the
narrow escape from death in the tank: "peasant life . . . was attuned
to death as day is to night" (*A*, p. 219:321). Throughout *Les Noyers,*
Malraux's images build toward this conclusion. The walnut trees surrounded by both dead fruit and live shoots (*NA*, p. 116:152) and the
coupled living and dead forming a whole greater than the sum of its
parts (*NA*, pp. 176–85:223–44) lead to "the identity of all appearances whether they be . . . life and death" (*A*, p. 198:292). This
unity of life and death coupled with a sense of universal metamorphosis recalls the walnut trees' "endless metamorpohsis" (*NA*, p.
115:151), and ultimately results in a sense of man's identity with,
rather than opposition to, the world.

    References to Indian philosophy lead directly in *Antimémoires* to a
reworking of the tank episode in *Les Noyers;* [1] the verbatim transcription of the last pages of *Les Noyers* is immediately followed by
direct allusions to Eastern philosophy:

    That sinister night followed by that dew-drenched morning . . . the
    cycle of blood, rebirth and death was that of Vishnu and of Shiva
    . . . the real dialogue would not have been between the Bhagavad-
    Gita and the Gospel . . . but between the Majesty in the shadow of
    the cave and Pradé's pale, phosphorescent face, transfigured by the
    moon reflected through the periscope like the glimmer of death
    —between the civilizations for which death has a meaning and
    the men for whom life has none. (*A*, pp. 219–20:322–23)

To this explicit link between the *Noyers* cycle of life, death, and
renascence and specifically Buddhist thought, Malraux adds the fol-

lowing reflection on the relative importance of the "fraternité virile" experience in the tank and a larger, deeper discovery of the fundamental mystery of life:

> These feelings paled before the unity of the world after a season in hell: before the certitude that the world—much more than men —could not be otherwise. A conviction reinforced here by this religion intoxicated with the unreal, whose imprisoned *maya* would go on forever bringing back the same men, the same dreams and the same gods in its eternal cycles. (*A,* p. 220:323)

Malraux's reflections on *Les Noyers* in *Antimémoires* thus culminate in an explicit avowal of a calm vision of an eternal cycle of life and death into which man can successfully integrate himself. The difficulty of such a conclusion can be appreciated only by a recollection of his evolution through forty-five years, six novels, and several major essays.[2] Convinced of the fundamental absurdity of society, the novelist's heroes sought answers capable of denying their nothingness first in isolated, then in collective action. Ultimately the artist, rather than the activist, came to possess the only satisfying solution to his anguish, a vision of man totally integrated into a universe no longer alien. Thus Malraux's protagonists progressed from a purely problematic status to "the highest form of grace that life may accord, the only goal worthy of an entire life: la simple vision du sens." [3]

The evolution of this response was all the more hesitating and painful since its seed had lain dormant in his work from its inception.[4] As early as *La Tentation de l'Occident* Malraux had appreciated the appeal of what one is tempted to call an Eastern response to man's "fragmentary nature" (*TO,* p. 59:103), and yet was unable to accept its answer without first testing the alternative of individual and collective action, embarking upon the long, discouraging journey from the suffocating forests of *La Voie royale* to the prison camps of *Les Noyers.*[5]

A close textual analysis of Malraux's metaphoric language elucidates the early discouragement and final hope of his evolution. Only through a study of his insistently recurring image patterns does one realize the pervasiveness of the pessimism in the first three novels. Only through understanding Malraux's most obsessive correlatives of despair could the fundamental uncertainty of the message be discerned in *Le Temps du mépris* and in *L'Espoir*.

Without a prior understanding of the operation of tensive language in Malraux's work, the complex revelations and final acceptance of man's harmony with his universe in *Les Noyers* would have remained obscured. Without a thorough comprehension of the metaphors of despair as they were developed particularly in *La Voie royale* and *Les Conquérants,* their significance in *Les Noyers* in scenes of apparently positive impact was destined to remain unappreciated. Subsequently, the gradual opposition of tensive language to explicit statements in *Le Temps du mépris* and *L'Espoir* prepares one for the substantive rather than supportive use of metaphor in *Les Noyers*.

Thus it can be said that through his metaphoric language Malraux accomplishes the sober messages of both Garcia and Berger.[6] Through metaphor's ability to metamorphose the individual into the general and its postulation of an underlying order in the world, Malraux converts his heroes' adventures into universal statements about Man's fate. In this sense, Malraux has transformed his own experience into a general consciousness which is capable of rectifying and humanizing the world.

NOTES

METAPHOR AS A RECTIFICATION OF THE WORLD

1. Irving Howe, *Politics and the Novel* (New York: Horizon Press, 1957), p. 20. Cf. Lucien Goldmann, *Pour une sociologie du roman* (Paris: Gallimard, 1964), pp. 32–33.

2. Georg Lukács, *Théorie du roman* (Paris: Gonthier, 1963), pp. 37, 60.

3. *Ibid.,* p. 81. 4. *Ibid.,* pp. 54, 60.

5. *Ibid.,* pp. 79, 71. 6. *Ibid.,* p. 64.

7. *Ibid.,* pp. 67, 76. 8. *Ibid.,* p. 71.

9. I. A. Richards, *The Philosophy of Rhetoric* (New York: Oxford University Press, 1936), pp. 130, 131, 134.

10. C. Day Lewis, *The Poetic Image* (London: Jonathan Cape, 1947), p. 34.

11. *The Basic Writings of C. G. Jung* (New York: Modern Library, 1959), p. 290.

12. Stephen Ullmann, *Style in the French Novel* (Cambridge: The University Press, 1957), p. 259.

13. "Malraux's *Antimémoires,*" *Columbia Forum,* XI, No. 4 (Winter, 1968), 35.

14. For the sake of clarity, I shall borrow Richards's terminology, designating as *tenor* that term of the metaphor which is the subject of the "image" and which is to be enhanced in vividness, complexity, and breadth of implication. The term *vehicle* I shall use to signify that which serves to carry or embody the thought, the term usually explicitly stated, eliciting the implicit tenor. The qualities shared by the vehicle and tenor shall be referred to as the *base* of the metaphor.

15. Day Lewis, *The Poetic Image,* pp. 99–100.

16. We must bear in mind, as Malraux readily admits, that an artist's theories and his practice relate to each other only tenuously at best: "The relations between theory and practice in every kind of art often give scope to irony. Artists build theories round what they would like to do, but they do what they can" (*VS,* p. 117:115).

17. "Laclos," in *Scènes choisies* (Paris: Gallimard, 1946), p. 342. In his many various reviews and prefaces (see bibliography) Malraux has always accorded major consideration to style, to the "poetic power" of the author ("Préface," in Manes Sperber, *Qu'une larme dans l'océan* [Paris: Calmann-Levy, 1952], p. xix).

18. "Introduction à la psychologie de l'art," *Cahiers de la Pléiade,* No. 2 (April, 1947), pp. 23, 24; translation mine.

19. Gaëtan Picon, *Malraux par lui-même* (Paris: Editions du Seuil, 1953), p. 60; translation mine.

20. "Laclos," p. 340; translation mine.

21. "Lignes de force," *Preuves,* V. No. 49 (March, 1955), 12; translation mine.

22. *Ibid.,* p. 11; translation mine.

23. *Malraux par lui-même,* p. 38; translation mine.

24. Cf. *VS,* pp. 279, 461:277, 459; *MD,* p. 63.

25. See *VS,* p. 335:333.

THE IMPASSE OF LES CONQUÉRANTS

1. See Lucien Goldmann, *Pour une sociologie du roman* (Paris: Gallimard, 1964), p. 194.

2. Leon Trotsky, "La Révolution étranglée," *NRF,* XIX, No. 211 (April 1, 1931), 493–500 (translation mine).

3. See Goldmann's definition of the problematical character, *Pour une sociologie du roman,* p. 47, and cf. Georg Lukács, *Théorie du roman* (Paris: Gonthier, 1963), pp. 37, 54, 60–81. Goldmann insists (p. 23) that authentic values will not be present directly in the work but instead operate implicitly.

4. *Pour une sociologie du roman,* pp. 97, 98, 129.

5. The phrase "in the same way *(et de la même façon)*" does not occur in the Whale translation; it is my translation.

6. This parallel is unusually devloped in all three versions of the work: the original manuscript, from which a chapter was deleted and published separately (see bibliography); the Cahiers verts edition (1928); and the much-changed final Grasset edition.

7. Translation mine. This passage does not appear in the Whale translation (see p. 159).

8. Cf. "It is to be able to continue his action that he is risking his life, not for some future result. He doesn't only want the doctrine to be spread; he wants to be the one to spread it. . . . He certainly doesn't doubt the value of Marxism, he simply never thinks about it." "Fragment des Conquérants," *Bifur,* No. 4 (December 31, 1929), p. 11; translation mine.

9. *Ibid.,* p. 8.   10. *Ibid.,* p. 4.   11. *Ibid.,* p. 6.

12. *Ibid.,* p. 8.   13. *Ibid.,* p. 12.

14. Rensky, too, employs the Party-Church parallel: "The Kuomintang . . . is reorganizing itself at Canton, from defeat to defeat or from victory to victory, much as budding Protestantism reorganized itself at Geneva" (p. 8:Cahiers verts ed., p. 19; translation mine).

15. Cf. p. 81:106.   16. See *TO,* pp. 19–22:40–45.

17. See *TO,* pp. 103–4:176–77.

18. Hong perfectly symbolizes this situation: educated as a Christian, he learned only enough about his own dignity to become the most fanatic of revolutionary terrorists.

19. For a discussion of the clash between militancy and individualism, see Jean-Paul Sartre, "Préface," in Roger Stéphane, *Portrait de l'aventurier* (Paris: Bernard Grasset, 1965), pp. 11–30.

20. See *TO,* letter No. 8, "A.D. to Ling" (pp. 49–53:85–95); especially, "By accepting the notion of the subconscious, and by having become fascinated with it, Europe has deprived herself of her best weapons. The absurd . . . is never completely hidden, and we watch it prepare its most seductive games with the wholehearted assent of our will. If it is possible to judge others on the basis of their actions alone, we can't do the same for ourselves; the real universe, harmonious and controlled, is only that place inhabited by other men. Our own is a dream world" (p. 49:86).

21. The reference to Malraux's *Lunes en papier* is worth noting, especially in the context of Goldmann's interpretation of that earlier work as particularly antibourgeois. (See Goldmann, *Pour une sociologie du roman,* p. 72.) A.D. defines the part of comedy in Western imagination as being not only inevitable but unoriginal as well: "Have you a taste for the burlesque? Go to the cinema. Its action enveloped in silence and its accelerated tempo are perfectly suited to stir our imaginations. Observe the audience leaving when the film is over; you will recognize in their mannerisms those of the characters they have just been watching. . . . Hidden behind the foreheads of Europeans, my friend, are uncut phonograph records. Certain events, which affect our sensibilities strongly, engrave themselves there. Incited either by desire or idleness, the beast begins its tragicomic melody, a melody that will be only barely embellished by our culture, which at times will give us the comfortable feeling of being haunted by the ghosts of old mistresses. . . . Pitiable actors who don't want to stop playing our glorious roles, we are, in our own eyes creatures in whom is dormant an unsophisticated and jumbled procession of the possibilities of act and dream" (*TO,* pp. 52–53:88, 89, 92).

22. This passage is found in neither the Cahiers verts edition nor the Whale translation.

23. The narrator tells us that "Garine had named him Gnafron" (p. 30:39). See André Vandegans, *La Jeunesse littéraire d'André Malraux* (Paris: Jean-Jacques Pauvert, 1964), p. 198, for an explanation of this character.

24. This passage is not included in the Cahiers verts edition or the Whale translation.

25. There is yet another, though nonimagistic, illustration of this tendency, when the citizens of Canton parade through the streets in a ritual of hatred against the English. Dressed in festive costumes, they carry a huge canvas house on which is painted "Mort aux Anglais" and "Mort à ces brigands d'Anglais" (pp. 139–40:192–93). Once again, hatred takes a ritualistic form, and when the cortege has passed from sight, it is hidden by "le coin de la rue comme par un portant de théâtre." (The Whale translation omits the comparison.)

26. Since Malraux argues (see above, p. 6) that the source of much of an author's imagery is the subconscious, it is interesting to note in passing that much of Garine's biography, particularly the two sentences in question here, coincides with details in Malraux's life. Clara, Malraux's first wife, reports that they lost everything on the stock market (*Le Bruit de nos pas: Nos vingt ans* [Paris: Bernard Grasset, 1966], p. 88), and that "he takes me to the races —we both deeply love betting" (*Le Bruit de nos pas: Apprendre à vivre* [Paris: Bernard Grasset, 1966], p. 274).

27. Garine, like many of Malraux's future characters, combines the quest for the exotic with an erotic urge (the narrator surprises him with two prostitutes). Eroticism, as I shall demonstrate in the next chapter, also serves as a pretext for self-discovery.

28. See pp. 47, 80, 88, 153, 161, 170–71, 190, 206–7, 213, 224–25, 230, 232–33, 237, 240–41, and 242–43 in Grasset edition.

29. *Pensées* (Baltimore: Penguin, 1966), p. 67 (Pensée No. 136).

30. See Lucien Goldmann's analysis of Garine's predicament (*Pour une sociologie du roman*, pp. 107, 122–23). Cf. Joseph Hoffmann, *L'Humanisme de Malraux* (Paris: Librarie Klincksieck, 1963), p. 124, and Gerda Blumenthal, *André Malraux: The Conquest of Dread* (Baltimore: Johns Hopkins Press, 1960), p. 8. In *Antimémoires* Malraux develops the image of sickness into an explicit statement about the human condition: "The human condition is the condition of creaturehood, which dictates man's destiny as mortal illness dictates the destiny of the individual. To destroy this condition is to destroy life—to kill" (p. 401:587).

31. Nicolaieff has another explanation of Garine's illness: "Human, all too human. . . . This is what neglected maladies lead to. . . . He is not a Communist. That is it. Of course, it does not matter to me; but all the same . . . communism has no room for those who want to be themselves first, and to lead an independent life. . . . Individualism is a *bourgeois* malady" (p. 161:225–26).

32. "Fragment des Conquérants," p. 8. Cf. Goldmann, *Pour une sociologie du roman*, pp. 105–6.

33. *Lunes en papier* (Geneva: Skira, 1943), p. 180; *Royaume farfelu* (Geneva: Skira, 1943), pp. 139, 150.

34. For example, ". . . a bare wall of Chinese mountain, muddy, dotted with patches of short grass, rapidly growing invisible as night approaches, and swarming with mosquitoes, just as it did three thousand years ago" (p. 47:55).

35. "Jeune Chine," *NRF*, XX, No. 22 (January, 1932), 5.

36. See *VR*, p. 142:158.

37. The ephemeral quality suggested by the moth is not only borne out in the scene of the execution of the spies (see below, pp. 26–27) but is also reinforced in *Antimémoires* when Malraux notes, apropos of the Orient, "a geological rhythm in which man flitted past like a butterfly" (p. 51:79).

38. I take issue with Frohock's interpretation of this scene. See *André Malraux and the Tragic Imagination* (Stanford: Stanford University Press, 1952), p. 41.

39. I take issue with Hartman's interpretation of this scene. See *André Malraux* (London: Bowes and Bowes, 1960), p. 34.

40. This alterity of the hand will, as we shall see, recur in *Le Temps du mépris*, pp. 74, 134:82–85, 97.

41. "André Malraux nous parle de son oeuvre," *Monde*, III, No. 124 (October 18, 1930), 4. Cf. *C*, pp. 17–18:22.

42. From Malraux's marginal notations in Gaëtan Picon, *Malraux par lui-même* (Paris: Editions du Seuil, 1953), p. 78.

43. Sartre, "Préface," p. 24.   44. *Ibid.*, pp. 20, 26–27.

45. Marginal notations to Picon, *Malraux par lui-même*, p. 78. See also Goldmann, *Pour une sociologie du roman*, p. 195.

46. "Malraux, "Lettre à M. van Hecke," *Variétés*, II, No. 4 (August 15, 1929), 307. Malraux suggests Garine's and Perken's parentage in other terms as well: "In comparison with *Puissance du désert*, the essential element of *La Voie royale* is to translate, by means of an extremely violent theme, man's fundamental solitude in the face of death—this work being only the prologue of the collective struggles which are to follow" ("André Malraux nous parle de son oeuvre," p. 4).

47. "André Malraux nous parle de son oeuvre," p. 4.

THE ROYAL WAY TO THE SELF

1. Malraux defined eroticism in his essay on Laclos: "There is eroticism in a book when the idea of constraint is suggested in scenes of physical love" ("Laclos," in *Scènes choisies* [Paris: Gallimard, 1946], p. 340; translation mine).

2. For a different approach to the theme of eroticism in Malraux's work,

see Brian T. Fitch's excellent study, *Les Deux univers romanesques d'André Malraux* (Paris: Minard, 1964). Fitch develops the theme of "the stranger in the mirror" (pp. 29 ff.), and establishes what he sees as "a link between his [Malraux's] creation and the initial problem of alienation. . . . The creation of this universe represents Malraux's wager for an exterior world and against the interior being. . . . Such an attitude eliminates the threat of interior alienation by reducing man to what he is for others, and, in so doing, such an attitude removes at the same time the danger of being alienated from the world, for, since his existence can be defined only by his situation in the world, man and the world become one" (p. 85; translation mine). See also René Girard, "The Role of Eroticism in Malraux's Fiction," *Yale French Studies*, No. 11, pp. 49–55. Girard notes that "in eroticism, the absurd is present when the hero learns that he can no longer interpret as omnipotence a solitude which has been violated but not conquered" (p. 51).

3. The entire passage reads: "One of the most important single elements of our lives: that awareness we have of ourselves which is so veiled, so opposed to reason that any attempt of the mind to understand it only makes it disappear. Nothing definite, nothing that allows us to define ourselves; only a sort of latent power. . . . Pitiable actors who don't want to stop playing our glorious roles, we are, in our own eyes, creatures in whom is dormant an unsophisticated and jumbled procession of the possibilities of act and dream" (*TO*, p. 52:91–92).

4. See *TO*, pp. 43–45:78, 80–82: "A woman affects a man by proposing to him the emotions he needs or desires. . . . It seems that you take her hand to place it on your shoulder: she interests you because she touches you, but it is you who strive to allow her to touch you. In so far as you attempt to understand her, you assume her identity. . . . The Western concept of love gathers its force and complexity from the necessity you feel to identify yourselves, voluntarily or not, with the woman you love."

5. Cf. Hoffmann's discussion of eroticism: "Eroticism should be understood as an attempt to escape from solitude—not from psychological solitude but from the essential solitude which makes one prisoner of himself. In the erotic act, man will attempt to make the two normally conflicting images of himself coincide; the absolute affirmation that he is for himself and the sum of actions he is for others: interiority and exteriority. Acting in the erotic act, man will know himself as source of his acts and simultaneously, imagining himself to be his partner, he will know himself as he is known: in terms of his action" (*L'Humanisme de Malraux* [Paris: Librarie Klincksieck, 1963], p. 171; translation mine).

6. "Préface à L'Amant de Lady Chatterley" (Paris: Gallimard, 1932), pp. iii, v.

7. *Ibid.,* p. iii.

8. In a sudden outburst of rage at his feeling of enclosure in a fixed static

system, Claude cries out, "To wrench one's dreams clear of the inert world that shackled them!" (p. 44:54–55). The relevance of this last image to the prison will be rendered explicit in *Les Noyers de l'Altenburg* (pp. 73–74:97–98). It is noteworthy that Claude's fleeting suggestion that art constitutes a response to the problem of destiny, which will become Malraux's final proposal in his quest for an answer to the Absurd, is enunciated in this first novel, but immediately abandoned. Although art objects constitute the immediate objective of the expedition, Claude's real interest seems to lie elsewhere.

9. The forest's imprisoning power is captured by Malraux-Clappique in Mayrena's scenario in *Antimémoires:* "One must convey the impression of penetration. It's nothing but endless leaves among endless treetrunks, but the shots must be closer and closer together, because after three days you get the feeling that the forest is closing in. . . . One goes back into the forest as if one were going underground" (p. 276:406–7).

10. See p. 44:55: " 'Adventure, as they call it,' he reflected, 'isn't an evasion, but a quest.' "

11. See *TM,* p. 41:50.

12. Pascal, *Pensées* (Baltimore: Penguin, 1966), p. 89 (Pensée No. 136). Italics mine.

13. Cf. Pascal's image of a large number of men in chains, *ibid.,* p. 165 (Pensée No. 434), which will be central to *La Condition humaine* and *Les Noyers de l'Altenburg.*

14. Pascal, *Pensées,* p. 67 (Pensée No. 136).

15. See Hoffmann, *L'Humanisme de Malraux,* pp. 77–78.

16. The metaphor of sickness also describes such social conventions as Claude's parents' marriage ("they . . . settled down to a tacit antipathy, much as chronic invalids learn to put up with illness" [p. 18:27]); Claude's and Perken's friendship (" 'And don't you worry about the situations in which such friendships may involve you?' 'Must I fight shy of love because of syphilis?' " [p. 71:84]); and Sarah's discovery of her hatred of Perken ("Then all the hopes she'd cherished as a girl began, like a dose of syphilis caught in early youth, to eat away her life" [p. 72:85]).

17. "Un quart d'heure avec M. André Malraux," *Candide,* VII, No. 48 (November 1, 1930), 3. The association of insects with the forests of Cambodia was still very powerful at the time of writing *Antimémoires.* In composing his scenario of Mayrena, whose legend is, in part, the origin of *La Voie royale,* Malraux-Clappique fills the proposed work with spiders, leeches, and bugs: "Inside there, everything pullulates . . . right from the beginning there must be insects. The thatched villages look like wood lice. The camera must zoom down on leeches . . . the skull swarming with insects. The tiger is the lord of all insects. . . . Drought is not always spiders. Sometimes it is scorpions. . . . The dripping forest, the insects, the giant spiders' webs, the

green night: the camera must render all this, by smothered images" (pp. 276, 278, 300:407, 410, 442).

18. Of the 941 images in *La Voie royale,* no less than 42 deal specifically with insects, and in another 36 less direct references can be found. (This latter category of nonmetaphorical references is significant, since the author's equation of insects, horror, and death is so firmly established by the imagery that any subsequent reference to insects is contaminated by the imagistic equation and operates as an objective correlative of that horror.) This total of 78 makes the insect, image by far the most prevalent. See Gerda Blumenthal, *André Malraux: The Conquest of Dread* (Baltimore: Johns Hopkins Press, 1960), p. vii.

19. Cf. "Black ants . . . as big as wasps" (p. 88:102).

20. Pascal, *Pensées,* p. 90 (Pensée No. 199).   21. *Ibid.*

22. Hence Perken's interest in the tribes called "insoumis."

23. The intimate relationship between the roles of death and eros in the insect image is stressed in *Antimémoires:* "Drought near a village means there are many adulterers. Adultery is when a spider has dropped on to the bed . . . not always spiders. Sometimes it is scorpions" (pp. 277–78:408, 410).

24. See *TO,* pp. 49–53:85–95.

25. Albert Sonnenfeld has effectively analyzed the symbolism of this circular prison: "In addition to being the emblematic figuration of time itself, Grabot's dehumanized circular movement conveys his enslavement to the teeming jungle, the enemy of the individual, and his return to the world of ordinary passive mortals (*les soumis*) who spend their lives in futile mechanized toil. And because of its function in primitive religions as a positive symbol of the cyclical renewal of the seasons, the circle taunts Perken with the proof of his own impotence: renewal and rebirth are the very powers which seem to be denied to man" ("Malraux and the Tyranny of Time: The Circle and the Gesture," *Romanic Review,* LIV, No. 3 [October, 1963], 200).

26. Pascal, *Pensées,* pp. 67–72, 149–55 (Pensées Nos. 132–39, 418–26).

27. As he lies dying, Perken recalls this earlier conversation and the full realization of the stakes: "It seems to me that I shall stake myself, all that I am on the moment of my death" (pp. 245–46:264).

28. Cf. "He probably went there on their account, and now he's playing some game of his own" (p. 78:92); and "He's never given a thought to anything except himself, or, more exactly, the side of his character which makes him a man apart; he's set on it as other men are set on gambling or authority" (p. 125:142).

29. Cf. pp. 26, 70:36, 83.

30. This ambiguity is strengthened by the fact that, as Perken dies, blood

flows onto his chin, "like the blood that had trickled from the bullet in the gaur's head" (p. 247:266).

31. *Lunes en papier,* p. 180.

32. Later, Perken, wounded and about to make love to a native girl, realizes that he is shaking "as a gambler trembles" (p. 212:230).

33. *TO,* p. 53:94.

34. The notion of *déchéance* is effectively generalized by a system of references to decomposition; see, e.g., pp. 217–18:235–36.

35. Cf. Jean-Paul Sartre, *La Nausée* (Paris: Livre de poche, 1938), pp. 141–43.

36. In Clappique's scenario in *Antimémoires* (p. 320:470), the insect plays a hauntingly significant role in the scene of the Westerner's ultimate defeat: "When an insect passes, the sound is cut off."

THE IMPRISONING OBSESSION OF THE HUMAN CONDITION

1. Lucien Goldmann, *Pour une sociologie du roman* (Paris: Gallimard, 1964), pp. 177–86.

2. Cf. "Sensitive to the very tip of the blade, he felt the body rebound up towards him. . . . A current of unbearable anguish passed between the corpse and himself, through the dagger, his stiffened arm . . . to his convulsive heart . . . the blood that continued to flow from his left arm seemed to be that of the man on the bed. . . . Nothing living must venture into the wild region where he was thrown" (p. 6:14–15).

3. Pascal, *Pensées* (Baltimore: Penguin, 1966), p. 89 (Pensée No. 199).

4. Cf. "What good is a soul if there is neither God nor Christ?" (pp. 63–64:78).

5. Ferral will rely on erotic imagery to convey his most basic attitudes. He sees commercial enterprise in sexual terms: his consortium of concessions is described as "sister societies engaged in living by profitable incests" (p. 84:106).

6. Cf. "It was from his need to imagine himself in her place as soon as he began to touch her body that he derived his acute feeling of possession" (p. 213:255).

7. "Un chapitre inédit de *La Condition humaine* par André Malraux, prix Goncourt 1933," *Marianne,* II, No. 60 (December 13, 1933), 4.

8. See above, p. 63. See also R. D. Laing, *The Divided Self* (Baltimore: Penguin, 1966), pp. 37, 39, 41–42, 65.

9. Goldmann, *Pour une sociologie du roman,* p. 186.

10. It should be noted that Malraux never formulated or directly accepted Marxist doctrine in his work. It remains always at the level of a vague context of action, and of the possibility of ennobling man. See Gaëtan Picon, *Malraux par lui-même* (Paris: Editions du Seuil, 1953), pp. 31, 32. Sartre

notes that "since action is a link between men, they will attempt to escape from their isolation through action. Through action, one becomes different, escapes from oneself, and changes oneself while changing the world" ("Préface," in Roger Stéphane, *Portrait de l'aventurier* [Paris: Bernard Grasset, 1965], p. 17; translation mine).

11. "D'une jeunesse européenne," *Ecrits,* ed. André Chamson, "Les Cahiers verts" (Paris: Bernard Grasset, 1927), pp. 141–44 (translation mine).

12. In *Les Voix du silence* (p. 630:628), Malraux relates this incident to the problem of self-awareness: "That part of man's nature which yearns for transcendence and for immortality is familiar to us. We know, too, that a man's consciousness of himself functions through channels other than those of his awareness of the outside world; every man's self is a tissue of fantastic dreams. I have written elsewhere of the man who fails to recognize his own voice on the gramophone because he is hearing it for the first time through his ears and not through his throat; and because our throat alone transmits to us our inner voice, I called this book *La Condition Humaine.*"

13. Cf. *TO*, pp. 120–21:202–3: "With calm distress we are becoming conscious of the profound opposition between our acts and our inner lives. The intensity of the latter cannot belong to the mind; sensing this, the mind revolves emptily, beautiful machine soiled by bloodstains. . . . For this inner life is also the most primitive, and its power, which exhibits the arbitrariness of the intellect, cannot save us from mind. . . . In order to destroy God, and after having destroyed Him, Western intellect has abolished all which might have stood in the path of Man; having reached the limit of its efforts, it finds only death. . . . It discovers that it can no longer be enamored of the vision it has at last achieved. Never has there been as disquieting a discovery. . . . There is no ideal to which we can sacrifice ourselves, for all we know is lies, we who have no idea what truth is."

14. The problem of the voice is reinforced by Kyo's "two faces." Under the swinging lamp in Hemmelrich's shop, Tchen sees "Kyo's two faces" (p. 11:21), and later, looking at himself in May's mirror, Kyo himself is aware of his "half-breed . . . face (*masque*) so Japanese" (p. 47:61).

15. It should be noted in passing that Katow had once tortured his wife, but had "outgrown" this tendency.

16. *CH,* p. 285:342.

17. That Kyo's life depends on Clappique's gambling is only fair, though ironic, since, as Clappique learns later from Koenig, "Kyo had . . . made him risk his life (*lui avait fait jouer sa vie*) without telling him" (p. 268:319).

18. Concerned for his wife and child, Hemmelrich had refused the terrorists his hospitality, and becomes "obsessed by Tchen as by a friend *in the throes of death,* and seeking . . . whether the feeling uppermost in him was shame, fraternity or an atrocious craving" (p. 178:217). The image is particularly rich, equating Hemmelrich's inability to alleviate his son's agony with

his failure to aid Tchen, while he simultaneously views Tchen's terrorist activities with a mixture of fear and desire for participation.

19. In the "hôtel des sensations interdites," "Chapitre inédit de *la Condition humaine*," Clappique's hand trembles "comme celle d'une malade" (p. 4) as he continues to avoid through sexual diversion any action which might commit him.

20. See above, pp. 34–35.

21. When Tchen arrives at Hemmelrich's there is another association of insect and death: "He went to look at the cricket asleep in its tiny cage; Tchen might have his reasons for keeping quiet. The latter watched the motion of the light, which enabled him to keep from thinking: the tremulous cry of the cricket awakened by Katow's approach mingled with the last vibrations of the shadow on the faces. Always that obsession of the hardness of flesh, that desire to press his arm violently against the nearest object. Words could do nothing but disturb the familiarity with death which had established itself in his being" (pp. 12–13:22).

22. *VR*, p. 142:158.   23. Cf. *TO*, p. 86:147–48; *VR*, p. 93:108.

24. Pascal, *Pensées*, p. 89 (Pensée, No. 199).   25. *Ibid.*

26. We have already seen how Ferral's need to dominate and impose himself by an overriding eroticism is revealed as another imprisoning obsession: "The difficulties which beset his present life drove him into (*l'enfermaient dans*) eroticism" (p. 114:139). As with Perken, this enslavement to a single form of human interchange turns love into war, isolating him from meaningful communication with others.

27. Clappique senses, as do Garine and Claude before him, the solution of art, but fails to profit from it because he is too separated from himself: "You must introduce the means of art into life . . . not in order to make art . . . but to make more life" (p. 295:352). Cf. Clappique's discussion of art with Kama, pp. 186–89:226–29.

28. Gerda Blumenthal, *André Malraux: The Conquest of Dread* (Baltimore: Johns Hopkins Press, 1960), p. 26, relates the gambling motif to the imprisoning-circle motif: "Malraux renders this magic metamorphosis in the gambling scene by means of a profound symbol: the spinning ball that magnetizes the eyes of the Frenchman Clappique and the other gamblers amidst the noisy, frenzied night-life of Shanghai. It symbolizes all at once fate's all-devouring cycle which is as immutable within itself as it seems capricious to the victim which it crushes, the victim's march in his prison cell and, finally, the carnival dance into which he transforms his march in a state of willful delusion, seeing himself transfigured in its course into a sacrificial godhead."

29. See note 17.

30. Clappique's return forecasts the return of Malraux's novelistic universe, for it had become clear that exoticism in general was but another form of es-

cape. Malraux's subsequent protagonists would have to find their solutions closer to home.

31. Pascal, *Pensées,* p. 165 (Pensée No. 434).
32. *Portrait de l'aventurier* (Paris: Bernard Grasset, 1965), pp. 123–24.
33. See p. 334:399–400.

LE TEMPS DU MÉPRIS RECAPTURED

1. André Malraux, "L'Attitude de l'artiste," *Commune,* No. 15 (November, 1934), p. 169.
2. Lucien Goldmann, *Pour une sociologie du roman* (Paris: Gallimard, 1964), p. 195; Georg Lukács, *Théorie du roman* (Paris: Gonthier, 1963), pp. 37, 60.
3. Goldmann, *Pour une sociologie du roman,* pp. 195–97.
4. Goldmann argues, in fact, that the primordial significance of death is actually missing from *Le Temps du mépris* because of Kassner's involvement in a set of values which transcend the individual. *Ibid.,* pp. 201–2.
5. *NA,* pp. 111–12:147.
6. Irving Howe, *Politics and the Novel* (New York: Horizon Press, 1957), p. 160. He adds, "The growth of ideology, I would suggest, is closely related to the accumulation of social pressures. It is when men no longer feel that they have adequate choices in their styles of life, when they conclude that there are no longer possibilities for honorable manoeuvrer and compromise, when they decide that the time has come for 'ultimate' social loyalties and political decisions." Roger Stéphane has suggested that, aware of this "hardening of commitment," Malraux was already attempting to refute the Marxist assumptions of the work (*Portrait de l'aventurier* [Paris: Bernard Grasset, 1965], p. 230).
7. Pascal, *Pensées* (Baltimore: Penguin, 1966), p. 165 (Pensée No. 434).
8. *Ibid.,* p. 89 (Pensée No. 199). One cannot help hearing two of Pascal's most awesome and awful cries, "What is man in the infinite?" (p. 89, Pensée No. 199) and "the eternal silence of these infinite spaces fills me with dread" (p. 95, Pensée No. 201).
9. *Ibid.,* p. 89.   10. *CH,* p. 278:333.
11. See *TM,* p. 27:35.
12. Quoted in Gaëtan Picon, *Malraux par lui-même* (Paris: Editions du Seuil, 1953), p. 91.
13. André Malraux, "Pour Thaelmann," in *Pour Thaelmann* (Paris: Editions Universelles, 1935), p. 17.
14. Cf. "D'you see all those damn-fool insects making for our lamp, obeying the call of the light? The termites, too, obey the law of the anthill. I . . . *I will not obey*" (*VR,* p. 142:158).

15. See *TO*, p. 86:147–48; *VR*, p. 93:108; *CH*, p. 281:337.
16. Pascal, *Pensées*, pp. 66–72 (Pensées Nos. 132–39).
17. *Ibid.*, p. 67.
18. Montaigne, *Les Essais* (Paris: Gallimard, 1962), I, 29–30.
19. *NA*, pp. 73–74:98–99.   20. *Ibid.*, p. 96:128.
21. Despite this purification, Kassner still cannot believe that his liberation is real. This doubt, a link with the prison, is communicated in several metaphors of water and dissolution. Thus, the agent who accompanies Kassner in the car becomes "the walrus" (pp. 106, 107, 108, 110, 112, 113:115, 117, 118, 120, 121, 122, 123), and Kassner is afraid that his new freedom may suddenly dissolve into the pool of his cell: "The other faces . . . were transformed into mobile, vulnerable, unstable images, ready to dissolve in the multicolored air. . . . His mind alone felt menaced: his body was free. Perhaps the walrus would presently dissolve, the auto disappear, and he would find himself back in his cell" (pp. 107–8:116–17). But this feeling continues to be countered by the sensation of light.
22. See "Pour Thaelmann."
23. E.g., "L'Attitude de l'artiste," *Commune*, No. 15 (November, 1934), pp. 166–74; "L'Oeuvre d'art," *Commune*, No. 23 (July, 1935), pp. 1264–66; "Réponse au 64," *Commune*, No. 27 (December, 1935), pp. 410–16.
24. "Sur l'héritage culturel," *Commune*, No. 37 (September, 1936), pp. 1–2.
25. *Ibid.*, p. 9.
26. Albert Camus, *The Rebel* (New York: Vintage, 1958), pp. 267–68.
27. This rediscovery of the earth grows partly out of Malraux's near-fatal flight over the Sahara (see "A la découverte de la capitale mystérieuse de la reine de Saba," *L'Intransigeant*, Vol. LV [May 3–13, 1934]), and will be reviewed in the discussion of *NA*.
28. Malraux, *La Psychologie de l'art: La Monnaie de l'absolu* (Geneva: Skira, 1949), p. 216; translation mine.
29. "L'Oeuvre d'art," *Commune*, No. 23 (July, 1935), pp. 1265–66.
30. In Kassner's visions, one of the images that returns regularly is that of "a vulture shut up with him in a cage, which with relentless blows of its pick-shaped beak was tearing off pieces of his flesh" (pp. 44, 50, 67:53, 60, 77) while Kassner is powerless: "There was nothing—nothing but the enormous rock on every side and that other night, the dead night" (p. 50:60). Kassner on his rock, submitting to the vulture, becomes a modern Prometheus whom Malraux several times equated to the primordial artist: "When the first artist reappears in the ruins of the last ghost town in the West or in Russia . . . he will take up again the old language of the discovery of fire" ("Sur la liberté de la culture," in Pierre Boisdeffre, *André Mal-*

raux [Paris: Editions Universitaires, 1960], pp. 145–46; translation mine).

31. "Sur l'héritage culturel," p. 9. See also *E,* p. 348.

THE TENSION OF HOPE IN L'ESPOIR

1. The pattern comparing the Party and the Church so prominent in several earlier novels is not developed sufficiently in *L'Espoir* to merit treatment in this chapter.

2. Irving Howe, *Politics and the Novel* (New York: Horizon Press, 1957), pp. 20–21; italics mine.

3. *TO,* p. 59:103.

4. Pascal, *Pensées* (Baltimore: Penguin, 1966), p. 89 (Pensée No. 199).

5. See also pp. 123, 187, 196, 222, 330, 392, 393:133, 196, 205, 231, 340, 400, 401; the passing reflection, "There was a sudden silence again, as if the elements were stronger than the war, as if the peace which fell from the winter sky, no longer muffled by the snowflakes, had imposed itself upon the battle" (p. 385:393); and René Girard, "L'Homme et le cosmos dans *L'Espoir* et *Les Noyers de l'Altenburg* d'André Malraux," *PMLA,* LXVIII, No. 1 (March, 1953), 49–55.

6. For other factors contributing to this sensation of the oceanesque, see pp. 236, 265:246, 276.

7. See above, p. 96.

8. In their turn the *milicianos* push forward in "another wave" (p. 20:28). Cf. the "first wave of Italians" (p. 379:387).

9. Since the movements of the armies are so consistently described in terms of waves, oceans, and floods, it is only natural that the wounded and dying should appear as fish out of water. An injured Fascist lies "puffing and blowing like a fish out of its element" (p. 72:80), while elsewhere a wounded Republican "was opening and shutting his mouth like a suffocating fish" (p. 383:391). In the descent from the mountain, a feverish Mireaux "fancied himself struggling to keep afloat in scalding water" (p. 417:424). The most concentrated use of such images occurs during Manuel's visit to Barca in the San Carla Hospital. The sickroom is full of "spectral forms" and gradually becomes "this cavern of sea-green gloom (*cet aquarium*)" (p. 78:86). Cf. pp. 80, 82, 84:88, 90, 91. See also Yvonne Moser, *L'Essai de la constitution d'un monde dans l'oeuvre d'André Malraux* (Aarau, Switzerland: H. R. Sauerländer, 1959), pp. 46–47.

10. Cf. "Bustling passers-by were walking one behind the other . . . tonight it seemed as if their activity had no purpose. Tchen looked at all those shadows flowing noiselessly towards the river, with an inexplicable and constant movement; was not Destiny itself the force that was pushing them to-

wards the end of the avenue where the archway on the edge of the shadowy river . . . was like the very gates of death?" (*CH*, p. 233:278).

11. See pp. 202–3:212–13.

12. E.g., tanks which are personified (pp. 201, 310–11:210, 320–21); planes which become birds of prey when attacking (pp. 123–24:133–34) and less threatening fowl when hit (pp. 373:381); trucks which have minds of their own (pp. 50–52:58–60); and a "living" battering ram (pp. 32–33:41–42). In the face of this type of animation, soldiers become correspondingly dehumanized.

13. Cf. *VS*, p. 541:539.

14. *Saturn: An Essay on Goya* (London: Phaidon, 1957), p. 82:82.

15. Malraux, "Esquisse d'une psychologie du cinéma," in *Scènes choisies* (Paris: Gallimard, 1964), p. 327.

16. *Saturn*, p. 93:92.   17. *Ibid.*, p. 111:111.

18. This is the only example of a gambling allusion in this work.

19. *Saturn*, p. 123:122.

20. Cf. "Meditation on death is in no way similar to the fear of being killed" (Malraux's marginal notes in Gaëtan Picon, *Malraux par lui-même* [Paris: Editions du Seuil, 1953], p. 70; translation mine).

21. There are eighty-six theater or theater-related images as compared with fifty-eight water and forty-five insect images.

22. Cf. "Etre un homme, c'est réduire sa part de comédie," *Monde*, VIII, No. 342 (June 27, 1935), 8.

23. Ximenes also considers the tendency of the Anarchists and Communists to call their leaders "comrade" part of their "heroic" behavior (see p. 149:158).

24. Puig's motives, even after the second and successful attempt, are questioned as too egotistical: "Puig felt envious of his dead comrades' fate" (p. 22:30). Histrionic references describe his attack on the guns: "Puig watched the gun crews . . . looming larger and larger, like close-ups on a screen" (p. 22:30).

25. Given this basic attitude of the unreality of war, it is natural that entire attacks should at times appear as games. Cf. pp. 84, 108, 249, 261, 398:92, 116, 259, 270, 405.

26. One possible source for this image is Malraux's interest in filming *L'Espoir*.

27. In the discussion leading up to Garcia's statement, Manuel remarks, "I'm through with music. . . . I think a new life started for me with the war—as definitely as the first time I slept with a woman" (p. 428:435). This is one of the few remnants of the erotic theme to be found in *L'Espoir*. Cf. p. 143:152.

28. E.g., "Manuel did not question the rightness of his decision; he had

done what he had done, so be it! Any problem of that kind should, he held, be settled either by modifying his conduct (and there could be no question of doing that) or else by simply refusing to consider it" (pp. 348–49:358).

29. Heinrich notes: "We are engaged in changing the conditions of this war. . . . Surely you don't believe you can change things without being changed yourself? From the day you take a commission in the army of the proletariat, your soul is no longer your own" (p. 350:360). Cf. Max Scheler (cited in Howe, *Politics and the Novel,* p. 9), "True tragedy arises when the idea of justice appears to be leading to the destruction of higher values."

30. See Everett W. Knight, *Literature Considered as Philosophy: The French Example* (London: Routledge & Kegan Paul, 1957), p. 135.

31. I am indebted to George Holoch for his remarkable discussion of this point in an as yet unpublished paper.

THE DISCOVERY OF TRANSCENDENCE
IN LES NOYERS DE L'ALTENBURG

1. See above, pp. 49, 86–87, 113.

2. See *C,* pp. 52–56:62–67; *VR,* pp. 43–44:54.

3. Malraux defined destiny as follows: "We know only too well what that word 'destiny' implies: the mortal element in all that is doomed to die . . . destiny is not death; it consists of all that forces on us the awareness of our human predicament . . . destiny means something deeper than misfortune" (*VS,* p. 630:628).

4. Malraux refers some twenty years later to the Nazi prisons as "this organized brutalization," and he adds, "The supreme objective was that the prisoners, in their own eyes, should lose their identity as human beings" (*A,* pp. 398–99:584–85).

5. Paul Baumgartner, "Solitude and Involvement: Two Aspects of Tragedy in Malraux's Novels," *French Review,* XXXVIII, No. 6 (May, 1965), 773.

6. Cf. *TO,* p. 86:147–48; *VR,* p. 94:108–9.

7. *Saturn: An Essay on Goya* (London: Phaidon, 1957), p. 123:122.

8. *JE,* p. 138; cf. *TO,* p. 97:166.

9. Reminiscing on his fellow prisoners in similar camps during World War II, Malraux evokes this mystical will to resist: "Yet even among the dying there remained enough humanity to divine that the will to live was not animal, but obscurely sacred. The mystery of the human condition manifested itself there. . . . The wretched . . . had not lost . . . the profound but vague idea of man for which they had fought, and which now became clear: man was what 'they' were trying to take from them" (*A,* p. 400:587).

10. The word "obsessed," recalling the first sentence of *La Voie royale,* suggests the permanence of Malraux's quest for the means of knowing others

11. "N'était-ce donc que cela?" *Liberté de l'esprit,* Nos. 3, 4, and 5 (May–June, 1949), pp. 86–87; translation mine.

12. Malraux supplements this recognition of the absurd in his essay on T. E. Lawrence (*ibid.,* p. 86): "Man is absurd because he is master neither of time, nor of his own anguish, nor of Evil; the world is absurd because it implies Evil, and Evil is the sin of the world" (translation mine).

13. See above, pp. 118–19.

14. Lucien Goldmann, *Pour une sociologie du roman* (Paris: Gallimard, 1964), p. 246. He continues, "The only permanent reality . . . the human condition which is the aspiration toward dignity and meaning."

15. *Ibid.,* pp. 255–56.

16. Baumgartner, "Solitude and Involvement, p. 773.

17. The alternative title of the work, "Jacob Wrestling (*La Lutte avec l'Ange*)," suggests that each of these episodes may be seen in terms of Jacob's struggle with the Angel of Death (Genesis 32:24–32). The protagonist, whether Vincent or his narrator-son (structurally they are identical), must come to grips in each episode with an experience which seeks to deny or destroy man, and wrest from that experience images of man's humanity or permanence. Jacob thus conforms to Malraux's definition of the artist: he succeeds in discovering and preserving what is best in Man.

18. Goldmann, *Pour une sociologie du roman,* p. 256.

19. Jean-Paul Sartre ("Préface," in Roger Stéphane, *Portrait de l'aventurier* [Paris: Bernard Grasset, 1965], pp. 27–30) supports Malraux's thesis.

20. See pp. 47, 51:62, 65.   21. See above, pp. 45–46.

22. N.B. the parallels with T. E. Lawrence. See "N'était-ce donc que cela?" and *A,* p. 64:98.

23. Like Tchen, one of the Anarchists in the newspaper story Vincent happens upon says, "The identity of the victim is of no importance! But afterwards, something unforeseen happens: everything is different, the most ordinary things, streets, for instance, dogs . . ." (*NA,* p. 60:78). The terrorist's act separates him from what he discovers to be an inferior breed, the "puceaux" who have never killed; Vincent's return to earth separates him as violently, but in order that he may rediscover the eternal quality of patience.

24. *A,* p. 220:323.

25. Malraux would seem to approve these conclusions in his later discussion of the *retour sur terre* phenomenon: "The sense of 'coming back to earth' which has played a big part in my life and which I have often tried to express. . . . It is the feeling that any man experiences when he comes back to his own civilization after being bound up with another, that of the hero of *Altenburg* on his return from Afghanistan . . . but if the wonderment seems the same, death is more foreign to us than foreign parts—especially when it is bound up with the elements . . . *the forces of nature stir up inside us*

the entire past of humanity. . . . People still existed. They had gone on living while I had descended to the blind kingdom. There were those who were happy to be together, in semifriendship and semiwarmth, and no doubt those who sought, whether patiently or forcefully, to extract a little more consideration from their companions; and at ground level all those tired feet, and under tables a few hands with their fingers intertwined. Life. On the human stage the sweet drama of evening was about to begin, the women round the shopwindows fragrant with the perfume of leisure. Shall I not come back at such a time—to see the life of men well up little by little, as steam and drops of moisture cloud over an iced glass—when I am really killed?" (*A*, pp. 64–65:98–100; italics mine).

26. When he disagrees with the local priest over a minor point in the observance of Lent, Dietrich first travels to Rome to protest personally to the Pope. Unsuccessful, he returns to spend the rest of his life following the service from outside the Church. Despite his anti-Semitism, he offers space to the local synagogue; hating animals, he offers sanctuary to a traveling circus.

27. Dietrich's careful preparations, the massive dose of strychnine, and the revolver under his pillow prove that it could not be said of him, as it was of Mayrena, "Every suicide's egged on by a phantom self of his own making; when he kills himself he does it with an eye to survival. Personally, I'd hate to let God make a fool of me" (*VR*, p. 12:20).

28. Friedrich Nietzsche, *Thus Spake Zarathustra* (Baltimore: Penguin, 1964), pp. 161–63, 216, 326.

29. Cf. *VR*, p. 42:53.   30. *Ibid.*, p. 142:158.

31. See above, pp. 104–5.   32. Cf. pp. 83, 94:111, 126; *A*, p. 22:41.

33. Mollberg's Spenglerian thesis leads Stieglitz to the idea of the supremacy of the German race (pp. 112–13:147–48).

34. Mollberg's appearance definitely suggests the Satanic, with his "smooth skull and remarkably pointed ears that reminded one of a vampire" (p. 97:129). Also, "The evenness of his teeth (false ones perhaps) was curiously in keeping with the mechanical precision of his speech" (p. 98:130), a phrase which recalls the mechanical activity of the insects in the suicide scene (p. 68:91).

35. Cf. Joseph Frank, "André Malraux: The Image of Man," in *Malraux,* ed. R. W. B. Lewis (Englewood Cliffs: Prentice-Hall, 1964), p. 82; Wilbur M. Frohock, *André Malraux and the Tragic Imagination* (Stanford: Stanford University Press, 1952), p. 133; Gerda Blumenthal, *André Malraux: The Conquest of Dread* (Baltimore: Johns Hopkins Press, 1960), p. 108; Rima Dell Reck, "Malraux's Transitional Novel: *Les Noyers de l'Altenburg*," *French Review*, XXXIV, No. 6 (May, 1961), 541–42.

36. *A*, p. 219:321. Cf. Leon Roudiez, "Schème et vocabulaire chez Malraux," *French Review*, XLI, No. 3 (December, 1967), 317, and Goldmann, *Pour une sociologie du roman*, pp. 263–64.

37. This ability to harmonize with the universe depends on man's capacity to perceive the world on his own scale. Walter's statues as logs become a metaphor for the void of a mind bent on submission, and as trees an image of man's permanence in a mind which conceives of man's dominion of the forms about him: "Our attitude towards an object varies according to the function we assign to it; wood can mean a tree, a fetish or a plank. The depiction of living forms begins not so much with the artist's submission to his model as with his domination of the model—with the expressive sign. . . . For the visible world is not only a profusion of forms, it is a profusion of significances; yet as a whole it signifies nothing, for it signifies everything. Life is stronger than man by reason of its multiplicity and total independence of his will, and because what we regard both as chaos and as fatality are implicit in it; but taken individually, each form of life is weaker than man, since no living form in itself *signifies* life" (*VS*, p. 324:322).

38. Cf. Garine's encounters with the ritual of justice. See above, pp. 14–17.

39. "Lézardes" is incorrectly translated. It means "cracks."

40. Baumgartner, "Solitude and Involvement," p. 773.

41. The breadth of vision and transcendence of national boundaries achieved by the creation of a two-generational Alsatian hero should be immediately obvious.

42. From the moment they enter the ditch, Bonneau screams hysterically; Berger notices that "his theatrical, terrified face has assumed a horribly innocent expression in the presence of death" (p. 212:276). Cf. Kassner's pilot, *TM*, pp. 129–30:139–40.

THE ATTAINMENT OF GRACE

1. That Malraux was thinking of *Les Noyers* as he wrote about Indian philosophy is evidenced by the phrase "but the Hindu multitudes, for whom death gives a meaning to life, made me think with bitterness of the men of our own land for whom death has no meaning" (*A*, p. 199:293), and the immediate movement without transition from the scene in Bombay to a readaptation of the tank scene.

2. Violet Horvath suggests that Malraux was coming to the same conclusion in *Les Voix du silence* and *La Psychologie de l'art*. See "André Malraux: The Human Adventure" (Unpublished dissertation, Columbia University, 1967), pp. 39–40.

3. Georg Lukács, *Théorie du roman* (Paris: Gonthier, 1963), p. 76.

4. Horvath's discussion of *Lunes en papier* and *Royaume farfelu* makes a case for an inchoate vision of the life-cycle process in these early works ("André Malraux: The Human Adventure," pp. 73–84).

5. In 1926 Malraux admitted, "The notion of man that we have inherited from Christianity was founded on the exalted conscience of our fundamental

chaos; such chaos does not exist for the Far East, where man is a locus rather than a means of action. . . . It seems that to escape from the rhythm of our civilization and to regard it with curiosity is to condemn it." But he nevertheless refused the consequences of his discovery: "But such a condemnation is impossible; our civilization is governed by our needs, whether they are lowly or not. . . . Can Asia teach us anything? I don't believe so. Rather she can bring to us a particular discovery of what we are. One of the strictest laws of our minds is that temptations overcome are transformed into knowledge" ("André Malraux et l'Orient," *Les Nouvelles littéraires*, V, No. 198 [July 31, 1926], 2; translation mine).

   6. See *E*, p. 338:348; *NA*, p. 96:128.

SELECTED BIBLIOGRAPHY

I. WORKS BY ANDRÉ MALRAUX IN CHRONOLOGICAL ORDER

A. Fiction

Lunes en papier. Paris: Editions de la Galerie Simon, 1921. Reprinted in *Oeuvres Complètes d'André Malraux*. Geneva: Skira, 1943.

"Les Hérissons apprivoisés—Journal d'un pompier du Jeu de Massacre— publié après la mort de l'auteur, avec des Notes, par le sieur des Etourneaux," *Signaux de France et de Belgique*, I, No. 4 (August 1, 1921), 171–77.

"Divertissement" and "Triomphe," *Accords*, Nos. 3–4 (October–November, 1924), pp. 56–61. (Excerpts from the unpublished "Ecrit pour une idole à trompe".)

"L'Expédition d'Ispahan," *L'Indochine*, I, No. 42 (August 6, 1925), 8. (Written under pseudonym Maurice Sainte-Rose.)

"Ecrit pour un ours en peluche," *900*, No. 4 (Summer, 1927), pp. 114–24.

"Voyage aux îles fortunés," *Commerce*, XII (Summer, 1927), 93–131.

Royaume farfelu. Paris: Gallimard, 1928. Reprinted in *Oeuvres Complètes d'André Malraux*. Geneva: Skira, 1943.

Les Conquérants. Paris: Bernard Grasset, 1928. (*The Conquerors*. Trans. W. S. Whale. Boston: Beacon Press, 1929.)

"Fragment inédit des *Conquérants*," *Bifur*, No. 4 (December 31, 1929), pp. 5–15.

La Voie royale. Paris: Bernard Grasset, 1930. (*The Royal Way*. Trans. Stuart Gilbert. New York: Vintage Books, 1935.)

La Condition humaine. Paris: Gallimard, 1933. Revised 1946. (*Man's Fate*. Trans. Haakon Chevalier. New York: Vintage Books, 1968.)

"Un chapître inédit de *La Condition humaine* par André Malraux, prix Goncourt 1933," *Marianne*, II, No. 60 (December 13, 1933), 4.

Le Temps du mépris. Paris: Gallimard, 1935. (*Days of Wrath*. Trans. Haakon Chevalier. New York: McGraw-Hill, 1964.)

L'Espoir. Paris: Gallimard, 1937. (*Days of Hope*. Trans. Stuart Gilbert and Alistair MacDonald. London: Hamish Hamilton, 1968.)

Les Noyers de l'Altenburg. Paris: Gallimard, 1948. (*The Walnut Trees of Altenburg*. Trans. A. W. Fielding. London: John Lehmann, 1952.)

B. *Essays*

La Tentation de l'Occident. Paris: Bernard Grasset, 1926. (*The Temptation of the West*. Trans. Robert Hollander. New York: Vintage Books, 1961.)

"D'une jeunesse européenne," *Ecrits*, ed. André Chamson. "Les Cahiers verts," pp. 129–33. Paris: Bernard Grasset, 1927.

Oeuvres Gothico-Bouddhiques du Pamir. Paris: Galerie de la NRF, [1932].

Esquisse d'une psychologie du cinéma. Paris: Gallimard, 1946. Reprinted in *Scènes choisies*, pp. 324–34. Paris: Gallimard, 1946.

Dessins de Goya au Musée du Prado. Geneva: Skira, 1947, pp. i–xli. Reprinted in Pierre de Boisdeffre, *André Malraux*, pp. 174–83. Paris: Editions Universitaires, 1960.

La Psychologie de l'art: Le Musée imaginaire, Geneva: Skira, 1947.

La Psychologie de l'art: La Création artistique. Geneva: Skira, 1948.

La Psychologie de l'art: La Monnaie de l'absolu. Geneva: Skira, 1949.

Léonard de Vinci. "La Galerie de la Pléiade." Paris: Gallimard, 1950.

Saturne. Paris: Gallimard, 1950. (*Saturn: An Essay on Goya*. Trans. C. W. Chilton. London, Phaidon Press, 1957.)

Les Voix du silence. Paris: Gallimard, 1951. (*The Voices of Silence*. Trans. Stuart Gilbert. New York: Doubleday, 1956.)

Le Musée imaginaire de la sculpture mondiale. Paris: Gallimard, 1952.

Van Gogh et les peintres d'Auvers chez le docteur Gachet. Paris: L'Amour de l'art, 1952.

Vermeer de Delft. "La Galerie de la Pléiade," pp. 15–24. Paris: Gallimard, 1952.

Le Musée imaginaire de la sculpture mondiale: Des bas-reliefs aux grottes sacrées. Paris: Gallimard, 1954.

Le Musée imaginaire de la sculpture mondiale: Le monde chrétien. Paris: Gallimard, 1954.

Du Musée. Paris: Editions Estienne, 1955.

Les Expositions de manuscrits à peintures à la Bibliothèque Nationale. Paris: Bibliothèque Nationale, 1955.

La Métamorphose des Dieux. Paris: Gallimard, 1957.

Antimémoires. Paris: Gallimard, 1967. (*Anti-Memoirs*. Trans. Terence Kilmartin. New York: Holt, Rinehart and Winston, 1968.)

Les Chênes qu'on abat. . . . Paris: Gallimard, 1971.

Oraisons funèbres. Paris: Gallimard, 1971.

C. Prefaces

"Préface." Charles Maurras, *Mademoiselle Monk*. Paris: Stock, 1923.

"Préface." D. H. Lawrence, *L'Amant de Lady Chatterley*. Trans. Roger Cornaz. Paris: Gallimard, 1932.

"Préface." William Faulkner, *Sanctuaire*. Trans. R. W. Raimbault and H. Delgare. Paris: Gallimard, 1933.

"Préface." Andrée Viollis, *Indochine S.O.S.* Paris: Gallimard, 1935.

"Préface." Louis Guilloux, *Sang Noir*. Paris: Le Club du Meilleur Livre, 1955. (Originally written in 1935.)

"Lettre-Préface." Bergeret and Herman Grégoire, *Messages Personnels*. Bordeaux: Editions Bière, 1945.

"Préface." Manès Sperber, *Qu'une larme dans l'océan*. Paris: Calmann-Lévy, 1952.

"Lettre-Préface." P. E. Jacquot, *Chimères ou réalités: Essai de stratégie occidentale*. Paris: Gallimard, 1953.

"Préface." Albert Ollivier, *Saint Just ou la force des choses*. Paris: Gallimard, 1954.

"Préface." Eddy du Perron, *Le Pays d'origine*. Rome: Botteghe Oscure, 1954.

"Texte liminaire." Nicolas Lazar and Izis, *Israel*. Lausanne: Editions Clairefontaine, 1955.

"Vorwort." *Jean Fautrier*. Leverkusen: Städtisches Museum, November–December, 1958.

"Préface." André Parrot, *Sumer*. Paris: Gallimard, 1960.

D. Articles and Speeches

"Des Origines de la poésie cubiste," *La Connaissance*, I, No. 1 (January, 1920), 38–43.

"Trois livres de Tailhade," *La Connaissance*, I, No. 2 (February, 1920), 196–97.

"Protestation," J. Valmy Baysse, "Mise au point," *Comoedia*, XIV, No. 2628 (February 26, 1920), 2.

"*L'Abbaye de Typhanes* par le comte de Gobineau," *NRF*, IX, No. 106 (July 1, 1922), 97–98.

"Art poétique par Max Jacob," *NRF*, IX, No. 107 (August, 1922), 227–28.

"Ménalque," *Le Disque vert*, 2d ser., I, No. 4–6 (February–April, 1923), 19–21.

"*Malice* par Pierre MacOrlan," *NRF*, X, No. 116 (May, 1923), 836–37.

"La Genèse des *Chants de Maldotor*," *Le Disque vert*, 4th ser., III, No. 4 (1925), 119–23.

"Seconde lettre à Monsieur de la Pommeraye," *L'Indochine*, I, No. 6 (June 23, 1925), 1–2.

"A Monsieur J. Menotte," *L'Indochine*, I, No. 8 (June 25, 1925), 1.

"Sur quelles réalités appuyer un effort annamite?" *L'Indochine*, I, No. 16 (July 4, 1925), 1.

"Grotesque," *L'Indochine*, I, No. 8 (July 6, 1925), 1.

"Première lettre à Monsieur Henry D'En-avant-pour l'arrière, moraliste sévère et journaliste sain," *L'Indochine*, I, No. 19 (July 8, 1925), 1.

"Petit éphéméride," *L'Indochine*, I, No. 20 (July 9, 1925), 1.

"Pris au piège," *L'Indochine*, I, No. 20 (July 9, 1925), 1.

"Le concours de l'Impartial," *L'Indochine*, I, No. 21 (July 10, 1925), 1.

"Les Boys quotiediens: Petit éphéméride," *L'Indochine*, I, No. 21 (July 10, 1925), 1–3.

"Revue de la presse locale," *L'Indochine*, I, No. 22 (July 11, 1925), 6.

"Revue de la presse locale," *L'Indochine*, I, No. 23 (July 15, 1925), 6.

"Sur la rôle de l'Administration," *L'Indochine*, I, No. 24 (July 16, 1925), 1.

"Comme ça c'est raté: Seconde lettre à M. Henry Chavigny d'En-avant pour l'arrière," *L'Indochine*, I, No. 26 (July 18, 1925), 8.

"Revue de la presse locale," *L'Indochine*, I, No. 27 (July 19, 1925), 6.

"Troisième lettre à M. Henry Chavigny d'En-avant pour l'arrière: Professor de délicatesse," *L'Indochine*, I, No. 29 (July 22, 1925), 1.

"Liberté de la presse," *L'Indochine*, I, No. 31 (July 24, 1925), 1.

"La presse locale: Toujours Chavigny ou un excès d'intelligence par jour," *L'Indochine*, I, No. 31 (July 24, 1925), 6.

"Les trente plaintes . . . ," *L'Indochine*, I, No. 32 (July 25, 1925), 1.

"Camau: Lettre de Jérome Coignard à Monsieur Cognacq Lieutenant-Gouverneur," *L'Indochine*, I, No. 35 (July 29, 1925), 1.

"Remarques sur la justification de M. Cognacq, parue dans *l'Opinion* d'hier," *L'Indochine*, I, No. 35 (July 29, 1925), 8.

"Revue de la presse locale: A Chavigny, vierge et martyr," *L'Indochine*, I, No. 37 (July 31, 1925), 6.

"Lettre ouverte à Monsieur Colonna, Procureur Général," *L'Indochine*, I, No. 39 (August 3, 1925), 1.

"Revue de la presse locale: Chavigny ou un excès d'intelligence par jour," *L'Indochine*, I, No. 42 (August 6, 1925), 3.

"Au très pur, très noble, très loyal gentilhomme Henry Chavigny d'En-avant pour l'arrière," *L'Indochine*, I, No. 46 (August 11, 1925), 1.

"M. Labaste, ex-Président de la Chambre d'Agriculture se cramponne," *L'Indochine*, I, No. 46 (August 11, 1925), 2.

"Encore Baclieu," *L'Indochine*, I, No. 48 (August 13, 1925), 1.

"Sélection d'énergies," *L'Indochine*, I, No. 49 (August 14, 1925), 1.

"Première lettre de Jacques Tournebroche à Jérome Coignard," *L'Indochine*, No. 2 (n.d.), p. 1.

"M. de la Pommeraye se pare l'une gloire immortelle," *L'Indochine*, No. 3 (n.d.), p. 1.

"Lettres d'un chinois," *NRF*, XIII, No. 151 (April, 1926), 409–20.

"André Malraux et l'Orient," *Les Nouvelles littéraires*, V, No. 198 (July 31, 1926), 2.

"*Histoire de la bienheureuse Raton, fille de joie* par Fernand Fleuret," *NRF*, XIV, No. 163 (April 1927), 550–51.

"Réponse à l'enquête sur *le Cuirassé Potemkine*," *La Revue Européene*, n.s., No. 5 (May, 1927), pp. 454–55.

"*Défense de l'Occident*, par Henri Massis," *NRF*, XIV, No. 164 (May, 1927), 813–18.

"*Bouddha Vivant*, par Paul Morand," *NRF*, XIV, No. 167 (August, 1927), 253–55.

"*Histoire comique de Francion*, par Ch. Sorel," *NRF*, XIV, No. 170 (November, 1927), 686–88.

"*Où le coeur se partage*, par Marcel Arland," *NRF*, XV, No. 173 (February, 1928), 250–52.

"A propos des illustrations de Galanis," *Arts et métiers graphiques*, No. 4 (April 1, 1928), pp. 225–31.

"*L'Imposture*, par Georges Bernanos," *NRF*, XV, No. 174 (March, 1928), 406–8.

"*Contes, historiettes et fabliaux: Dialogue d'un prêtre et d'un moribond (Stendhal et Cie)*, par le marquis de Sade," *NRF*, XV, No. 177 (June, 1928), 853–55.

"*L'Enfant et l'écuyère*, par Franz Hellens," *NRF*, XV, No. 179 (August, 1928), 291–92.

"Introduction à la lettre du Prestre Jehan à l'Empereur de Rome," *Commerce*, No. 17 (Autumn, 1928), p. 7.

"*Battling le Ténébreux*, par Alexandre Vialatte," *NRF*, XVI, No. 183 (December, 1928), 869–70.

"*Journal de voyage d'un philosophe*, par Hermann Keyserling," *NRF*, XVI, No. 189 (June, 1929), 884–86.

"Lettre à M. van Hecke," *Variétés*, II, No. 4 (August 15, 1929), 307.

"La Question des Conquérants," *Variétés*, II, No. 8 (October 15, 1929), 429–37.

"*Pont-Egaré*, par Pierre Véry," *NRF*, XVII, No. 195 (December, 1929), 838–39.

"Déclaration sur André Gide," *Cahiers de la quinzaine*, 20th ser., No. 6 (April 5, 1930), pp. 43, 49–51.

"Aprés *Les Conquérants: La Voie royale:* André Malraux nous parle de son oeuvre," *Monde*, III, No. 124 (October 18, 1930), 4.

"Un quart d'heure avec M. André Malraux," *Candide*, VII, No. 348 (November 13, 1930), 3.

"Lettre à André Rousseaux," *Candide*, VI, No. 349 (November 20, 1930), 3.

"Exposition Gothico-Bouddhique," *NRF*, XIX, No. 209 (February, 1931), 298–300.

"Réponse à Trotsky," *NRF*, XIX, No. 211 (April, 1931), 501–7.

"Galanis (Démétrius-Emmanuel)," *Dictionnaire Biographique des artistes contemporains* (Paris: Art et Edition), II (1931), 88–91.

"Jeune Chine," *NRF,* XX, No. 220 (January, 1932), 5–7.

"Exposition d'oeuvres de Semirami," *NRF,* XX, No. 223 (April, 1932), 771–73.

"*Documents secrets,* par Franz Hellens," *NRF,* XX, No. 224 (May, 1932), 915–16.

"En marge d'Hymenée," *Europe,* XXIX, No. 114 (June, 1932), 304–7.

"Exposition Fautrier," *NRF,* XXI, No. 233 (February, 1933), 345–46.

"Trotsky," *Marianne,* II, No. 79 (April 25, 1934), 3.

"A la découverte de la capitale mystérieuse de la reine de Saba: Porte de l'inconnu," *L'Intransigeant,* LV (May 3, 1934), 1–2.

"A la découverte de la capitale mystérieuse de la reine de Saba: Fantômes de sable," *L'Intransigeant,* LV (May 4, 1934), 1–2.

"A la découverte de la capitale mystérieuse de la reine de Saba: Mirages," *L'Intransigeant,* LV (May 6, 1934), 1–2.

"A la découverte de la capitale mystérieuse de la reine de Saba: Saba légendaire," *L'Intransigeant,* LV (May 8, 1934), 1.

"En survolant la capitale mystérieuse de la reine de Saba: Le prodigieux spectacle de la cité morte," *L'Intransigeant,* LV (May 9, 1934), 1–2.

"De la capitale mystérieuse de la reine de Saba à la Vallée de tombeaux: Quand le désert se brise aux arêtes steppes," *L'Intransigeant,* LV (May 10, 1934), 1, 3.

"Après la découverte de la ville mystérieuse: Le secret de Saba," *L'Intransigeant,* LV (May 13, 1934), 1–2.

"*Les Traqués,* par Michel Matveer," *NRF,* XXII, No. 249 (June, 1934), 1014–16.

"L'Art est une conquête," *Commune,* II, No. 13–14 (September–October, 1934), 68–71.

"Une politique de l'esprit: Le Premier Congrès des écrivains de l'URSS," *Cahiers du Sud,* XXI (November, 1934), 718–19.

"L'Attitude de l'artiste," *Commune,* No. 15 (November, 1934), pp. 166–74.

"*Journal d'un homme de quarante ans,* par Jean Guéhenno," *NRF,* XXIII, No. 256 (January, 1935), 148–51.

"Etre un homme c'est réduire sa part de comédie," *Monde,* VIII, No. 342 (June 27, 1935), 8.

"L'Oeuvre d'art," *Commune,* No. 23 (July, 1935), pp. 1264–66.

"*Sans reprendre haleine,* par Ilya Ehrenbourg," *NRF,* XXIII, No. 266 (November, 1935), 770–72.

"Réponse aux 64," *Commune,* No. 27 (December, 1935), pp. 410–16.

"*Les nouvelles norritures,* par André Gide," *NRF,* XXIV, No. 267 (December, 1935), 935–37.

"Discours," *Pour Thaelmann*, pp. 16–18. Paris: Editions Universelles, 1935.

"Sur l'héritage culturel," *Commune*, No. 37 (September, 1936), pp. 1–9.

"Forging Man's Fate in Spain," *Nation*, CXLIV, No. 12 (March 20, 1937), 315–16.

"Trotsky vs. Malraux," *Nation*, CXLIV, No. 13 (March 27, 1937), 351.

"La psychologie de l'art," *Verve*, I, No. 1 (December, 1937), 41–48.

"Psychologie des Renaissances," *Verve*, I, No. 2 (March–June, 1938), 21–25.

"De la Représentation en Occident et en Extrême-Orient," *Verve*, I, No. 3 (June, 1938), 69–72.

"Laclos," *Tableau de la Littérature francaise, XVII et XVIII siecles*, pp. 417–28. Paris: Gallimard, 1939. Reprinted in *Scènes Choisies*. Paris: Gallimard, 1946.

"L'Homme et la culture artistique," *Les Conférences de L'UNESCO*, pp. 75–89. Paris: Fontaine, 1947.

"Introduction à la psychologie de l'art," *Cahiers de la Pléiade*, No. 2 (April, 1947), pp. 9–26.

"La Féderation européenne autour de la France et non d'une Allemagne centralisée," *Le Rassemblement*, No. 44 (February 21, 1948), pp. 1–2.

"A des compagnons de la résistance," *Le Rassemblement*, No. 44 (February 21, 1948), pp. 1–2.

"L'Europe et la Russie," *Le Rassemblement*, No. 46 (March 6, 1948), pp. 1–2.

"La Technique du mensonge," *Le Rassemblement*, No. 47 (March 13, 1948), pp. 1–3.

"L'Européen s'éclairera au flambeau gu'il porte même si sa main brûle . . . ," *Le Rassemblement*, No. 48 (March 20, 1948), pp. 1, 3.

"André Malraux à James Burnham," *Le Rassemblement*, No. 51 (April 10, 1948), pp. 1–2.

"Salut," *Le Rassemblement*, No. 52 (April 17, 1948), pp. 1, 3.

"Les Intellectuels et le communisme," *Le Rassemblement*, No. 52 (April 17, 1948), p. 3.

"Liberté et volonté," *Le Rassemblement*, No. 53 (April 24, 1948), pp. 2, 3.

"18 Juin 1948," *Le Rassemblement*, No. 62 (June 26, 1948), p. 1.

"Entretien," in Bertrand de la Salle, "A la découverte du R.P.F.," *La Revue de Paris*, LV, No. 7 (July, 1948), 114–23.

"Les Figures de Paille," *Le Rassemblement*, No. 64 (July 10, 1948), p. 1.

"Leur fuite à Varennes," *Le Rassemblement*, No. 72 (September 4, 1948), pp. 1, 4.

"La Terre brûlée," *Le Rassemblement*, No. 76 (October 2, 1948), p. 1.

"Qui sommes-nous?" *Le Rassemblement*, No. 78 (October 16, 1948), p. 1.

"Grèves," *Le Rassemblement*, No. 81 (November 6, 1948), p. 1.

"Discours," *Le Rassemblement,* No. 84 (November 27, 1948), p. 4.

"Il faut que le langage de la France soit tenu," *Le Rassemblement,* No. 97 (February 26, 1949), p. 4.

"Culture," *Liberté de l'esprit,* No. 1 (February, 1949), pp. 1–2.

"N'Etait-ce donc que cela?" *Liberté de l'esprit,* No. 3 (April, 1949), pp. 49–51; No. 4 (May, 1949), pp. 86–87; No. 5 (June, 1949), pp. 117–18.

"Lettre aux intellectuels américains: Emporter l'Europe comme une victoire," *Carrefour,* VI, No. 274 (December 13, 1949), 1–2.

"Staline et son ombre," *Carrefour,* VI, No. 276 (December 27, 1949), 1, 3.

"Lawrence," in Gaëtan Picon, *Panorama de la nouvelle littérature francaise,* pp. 298–304. Paris: Gallimard, 1949.

"Hommage," in E. Raude and G. Prouteau, *Le méssage de Léo Lagrange,* pp. 179–83. Paris: La Compagnie du Livre, 1950.

"Lettre au Ministre de la Propaganda Goebbels," in André Gide, *Littérature Engagée,* ed. Yvonne Davet, pp. 41–42. Paris: Gallimard, 1950.

"Bretons de Sein que pensez-vous en écoutant la radio? . . . ," *Carrefour,* VIII, No. 278 (January 10, 1950), 1.

"Les entreteneurs de fantômes," *Carrefour,* VII, No. 282 (February 7, 1950), 1–2.

"Le Palais béant," *Carrefour,* VII, No. 285 (February 28, 1950), 1, 3.

"Le siècle de l'Espoir s'achève . . . ," *Carrefour,* VII, No. 288 (March 21, 1950), 1–2.

"Le Problème du siècle," *Carrefour,* VII, No. 296 (May 16, 1950), 1, 3.

"En marge de la Psychologie de l'Art," *Cahiers de la Pléiade,* No. 12 (Spring–Summer, 1951), pp. 9–10.

"La République," *Le Rassemblement,* No. 213 (June 1, 1951), p. 5.

"Discours prononcé l'occasion de la séance de clôture des Assises Nationales," *Rassemblement du Peuple Francais,* pp. 1–2. Paris: Assises Nationales, November, 1951.

"Malraux a dit," *Le Rassemblement,* No. 235 (November 30, 1951), p. 16.

"André Malraux nous dit: L'Art est l'une des défenses fondamentales de l'homme contre le destin," *Arts,* No. 335 (November 30, 1951), pp. 1, 10.

"Une leçon de fidelité," *Arts,* No. 338 (December 21, 1951), p. 1.

"La France ne s'achète pas au marché noir," *Le Rassemblement,* No. 238 (December 21, 1951), p. 3.

"Sur Barrès," in Pierre de Boisdeffre, *Barrès Parmi Nous,* pp. 189–90. Paris: Amiot-Dumont, 1952.

"Le Gaullisme sans de Gaulle et les Républicains sans République," *Carrefour,* VII, No. 384 (January 23, 1952), 1, 8.

"Les armes ne valent que par les mains qui les tiennent," *Le Rassemblement,* No. 248 (March 7, 1952), p. 12.

"L'Etat n'est pas fait pour diriger l'art mais pour le servir," *Carrefour*, VII, No. 393 (March 26, 1952), 1, 5.

"Rencontre avec Malraux," *Les Nouvelles littléraires*, No. 1283 (April 3, 1952), pp. 1, 4.

"Ce que nous avons à défendre," *Arts*, No. 362 (June 5, 1952), pp. 1, 6.

"Pour permettre à l'homme d'être moins esclave," *Le Rassemblement*, No. 262 (June 6, 1952), p. 12.

"Nous représentons la continuité historique de la France," *Le Rassemblement*, No. 267 (July 11, 1952), p. 3.

"Malraux Salle Gaveau," *Liberté de l'esprit*, IV, No. 33 (July–September, 1952), 214–15.

"Le Premier Musée imaginaire de la sculpture mondiale," *Carrefour*, IX, No. 429 (December 3, 1952), 20.

"Marginal Notes," in Gaëtan Picon, *Malraux par lui-même*. Paris: Editions du Seuil, 1953.

"Lettre à M. André Parinaud," *La Parisienne* (March, 1954), p. 359.

"Le Problème fondamental du Musée," *La Revue des Arts*, IV, No. 1 (March, 1954), 3–12.

"La Métamorphose des Dieux," *NRF*, XXII, No. 17 (May, 1954), 769–92; No. 18 (June, 1954), 961–92.

"Premier entretien avec André Malraux," *L'Express*, II, No. 83 (December 25, 1954), 10–11.

"Entretien du 3 et 4 février 1945," in Roger Stéphane, *Fin d'une jeunesse*, pp. 40–69. Paris: La Table ronde, 1954.

"L'Entretien avec André Malraux," *L'Express*, III, No. 88 (January 29, 1955), 8–10.

"Dialogue entre Montherlant et Malraux autour de Racine," *L'Express*, III, No. 92 (February 26, 1955), 12–13.

"Lignes de force," *Preuves*, V, No. 49 (March, 1955), 5–15.

"L'Homme et le fantôme," *L'Express*, III, No. 104 (May 21, 1955), 15.

"André Malraux parle de Rembrandt," *L'Express*, IV, No. 252 (April 20, 1956), 18–19.

"Le Portrait," *April in Paris Ball*. Paris: Femina Illustration, 1956.

"Discours," *Discours prononcés à l'occasion des manifestations patriotiques du 14 juillet 1959 sur de l'Hotel-de-Ville à Paris*, pp. 33–36. Paris: Imprimerie Municipale, 1958.

"L'Acte par lequel l'homme arrache quelque chose à la mort," *Le Courrier*, XIII, No. 5 (May, 1960), 9–11.

"Le Discours d'Athènes," in Pierre de Boisdeffre, *André Malraux*, pp. 146–49. Paris: Editions Universitaires, 1960.

"Le Discours de Brasilia," in Pierre de Boisdeffre, *André Malraux*, pp. 149–53. Paris: Editions Universitaires, 1960.

"M Malraux inaugure la fondation Maeght," *Le Monde,* XXI, No. 6078 (July 31, 1964), 9.
"Allocution," *Lectures Choisies d'André Malraux,* ed. Anne Jones, pp. 189–95. New York: Macmillan, 1965.
"Malraux parle avec Michel Droit," *Le Figaro littéraire,* No. 1120 (October 2–8, 1967), pp. 6–9.
"Douze jeunes francais . . . faces à André Malraux," Emission Spéciale au Journal Parlé. Paris, Europe No. 1, October 24, 1967.
"Tôt ou tard la culture doit être gratuite," *Le Monde,* XXV, No. 7174 (February 5, 1968), 13.

II. WORKS ON MALRAUX

Albérès, René-Marill. "André Malraux and the 'Abridged Abyss,'" *Yale French Studies,* No. 18 (Winter, 1957), pp. 45–54.
Ball, Bertrand L., Jr. "Nature, Symbol of Death in *La Voie royale,*" *French Review,* XXV, No. 4 (February, 1962), 390–95.
Baumgartner, Paul. "Solitude and Involvement: Two Aspects of Tragedy in Malraux's Novels," *French Review,* XXXVIII, No. 6 (May, 1965), 766–76.
Blend, Charles D. *André Malraux: Tragic Humanist.* Columbus: Ohio State University Press, 1963.
Blumenthal, Gerda. *André Malraux: The Conquest of Dread.* Baltimore: Johns Hopkins Press, 1960.
Boak, Denis. "Malraux's *La Voie royale,*" *French Studies,* XIX, No. 1 (January, 1965), 42–50.
Boisdeffre, Pierre de. *André Malraux.* Paris: Editions Universitaires, 1960.
—— "André Malraux," *Les Nouvelles littéraires,* XL, No. 1795 (January 25, 1962), 6–7.
Brincourt, André. *André Malraux ou le temps du silence.* Paris: La Table ronde, 1966.
Brombert, Victor. "Malraux: Passion and Intellect," *Yale French Studies,* No. 18 (Winter, 1957), pp. 63–76.
Chavalier, Haakon M. "André Malraux: The Return of the Hero," *Kenyon Review,* II, No. 1 (Winter, 1940), 35–46.
Cordle, Thomas. "The Royal Way," *Yale French Studies,* No. 18 (Winter, 1957), pp. 20–26.
Delhomme, Jean. *Temps et Destin: Essai sur André Malraux.* Paris: Gallimard, 1955.
Douthat, Blossom. "Nietzschean Motifs in *Temptation of the Occident,*" *Yale French Studies,* No. 18 (Winter, 1957), pp. 77–86.
Fitch, Brian T. "André Malraux," in *Le Sentiment d'étrangeté chez Malraux, Sartre, Camus et S. de Beauvoir.* Paris: Minard, 1964.

—— *Les Deux univers romanesques d'André Malraux.* "Archives des Lettres Modernes." Paris: Minard, 1964.

—— "Le Monde des objets chez Malraux et chez Sartre," *Bulletin des Jeunes Romanistes,* No. 1 (June, 1960), pp. 22–25.

Flanner, Janet. "The Human Condition," in *Men and Monuments,* pp. 1–70. New York: Harper & Brothers, 1957.

Frank, Joseph. "André Malraux: The Image of Man," in *Malraux,* ed. R.W.B. Lewis, pp. 71–85. Englewood Cliffs: Prentice-Hall, 1964.

Frohock, Wilbur M. *André Malraux and the Tragic Imagination.* Stanford: Stanford University Press, 1952.

—— "Malraux and the Poem of the Walnuts," in *Style and Temper,* pp. 62–77. Cambridge, Mass.: Harvard University Press, 1967.

—— "Notes on Malraux's Symbols," *Romanic Review,* XLII, No. 4 (December, 1959), 274–81.

—— "*Le Temps du mépris:* A Note on Malraux as a Man of Letters," *Romanic Review,* XXXIX, No. 2 (April, 1948), 130–39.

Gannon, Edward, S.J. *The Honor of Being a Man: The World of André Malraux.* Chicago: Loyola University Press, 1957.

Girard, René. "L'Homme et le cosmos dans *L'Espoir* et *Les Noyers de l'Altenburg* d'André Malraux," *PMLA,* LXVIII, No. 1 (March, 1953), 49–55.

—— "Man, Myth and Malraux," *Yale French Studies,* No. 18 (Winter, 1957), pp. 55–62.

—— "Les Réflections sur l'art dans les romans d'André Malraux," *Modern Language Notes,* LXVIII, No. 8 (December, 1953), 544–46.

—— "Le Régne animal dans les romans d'André Malraux," *French Review,* XXCI, No. 4 (February, 1953), 261–67.

—— "The Role of Eroticism in Malraux's Fiction," *Yale French Studies,* No. 11 (n.d.), pp. 49–54.

Goldmann, Lucien. *Pour une sociologie du roman.* "Collection idées nrf." Paris: Gallimard, 1964.

Hartman, Geoffrey H. *André Malraux.* London: Bowes and Bowes, 1960.

Hoffman, Joseph. *L'Humanisme de Malraux.* Paris: Libraire Klincksieck, 1963.

Holoch, George. "Discovery and Conquest." Unpublished thesis, Columbia College, 1960.

Hoog, Armand. "André Malraux et la validité du monde," *La Nef,* IV, No. 28 (March, 1947), 121–26.

—— "Malraux, Möllberg and Frobenius," *Yale French Studies,* No. 18 (Winter, 1957), pp. 87–96.

Horvath, Violet M. "André Malraux: The Human Adventure." Unpublished dissertation, Columbia University, 1967.

Knight, Everett W. "Malraux," in *Literature Considered as Philosophy: The*

French Example, pp. 128–59. London: Routledge & Kegan Paul, 1957.

Langlois, Walter G. *André Malraux: The Indo-China Adventure.* New York: Praeger, 1966.

Leefmans, Bert M-P. "Malraux and Tragedy: The Structure of *La Condition humaine,*" *Romanic Review,* XLIV, No. 3 (October, 1953), 208–14.

Lewis, R. W. B. "Introduction: Malraux and His Critics," in *Malraux,* pp. 1–11. Englewood Cliffs: Prentice-Hall, 1964.

Magny, Claude-Emmanuel. "Malraux le fascinateur," *Esprit,* XVI, No. 149 (October, 1948), 513–34.

Matthews, J. H. "André Malraux," *Contemporary Review,* No. 1099 (July, 1957), pp. 24–28.

Mauriac, Claude. "Malraux contre la littérature avilie," *La Nef,* III, No. 14 (January, 1946), 24–34.

——— *Malraux ou le mal du héros.* Paris: Bernard Grasset, 1946.

Merleau-Ponty, Maurice. "Le Langage indirect et *Les Voix du Silence,*" *Les Temps modernes,* VII, No. 80 (June, 1952), 2113–44; VIII, No. 81 (July, 1952), 70–94.

Moser, Yvonne. *L'Essai de la constitution d'un monde dans l'oeuvre d'André Malraux.* Aarau, Switzerland: H.R. Sauerländer, 1959.

Mounier, Emmanuel. "André Malraux: Le conquérant aveugle," in *L'Espoir des désespérés,* pp. 11–81. Paris: Editions du Seuil, 1953.

Nizan, Paul. "*Le Temps du mépris* par André Malraux," *Monde,* VIII, No. 339 (June 6, 1935), 8.

Oxenhandler, Neal. "Malraux and the Inference to Despair," *Chicago Review,* XV, No. 3 (Winter–Spring, 1962), 72–74.

Patry, André. *Visages d'André Malraux.* Montreal: Editions de l'Hexagone, 1956.

Pia, Pascal. "André Malraux: *Lunes en papier,*" *Le Disque vert,* I, No. 3 (July, 1922), 78.

Picon, Gaëtan. *André Malraux.* Paris: Gallimard, 1945.

——— *Malraux par lui-même.* "Collection Ecrivains de Toujours." Paris: Editions du Seuil, 1953.

——— "Man's Hope," *Yale French Studies,* No. 18 (Winter, 1957), pp. 3–6.

——— "Notes sur *La Lutte avec l'ange,*" *Cahiers du sud,* XXI, No. 266 (June–July, 1944), 405–16.

Reck, Rima Dell. "Malraux's Transitional Novel: *Les Noyers de l'Altenburg,*" *French Review,* XXXIV, No. 6 (May, 1961), 537–44.

Rees, G. O. "Animal Imagery in Novels of André Malraux," *French Studies,* IX, No. 2 (April, 1955), 129–42.

——— "Sound and Silence in Malraux's Novels," *French Review,* XXXII, No. 3 (January, 1959), 223–30.

——— "Types of Recurring Similes in Malraux's Novels," *Modern Language Notes,* LXVIII, No. 6 (June, 1953), 373–77.

Riffaterre, Michael. "Malraux's *Antimémoires*," *Columbia Forum*, XI, No. 4 (Winter, 1968), 31–35.

Righter, William. *The Rhetorical Hero*. New York: Chilmark Press, 1964.

Roudiez, Léon. "Schème et vocabulaire chez Malraux," *French Review*, XLI, No. 3 (December, 1967), 304–18.

Sartre, Jean-Paul. "Préface," in Roger Stéphane, *Portrait de l'aventurier*, pp. 11–30. Paris: Bernard Grasset, 1965.

Savane, Marcel. *André Malraux*. Paris: Richard-Masse, 1946.

Simon, Pierre-Henri. "André Malraux ou le défi de la mort," in *L'Homme en procès. pp. 27–50. Paris: Petite Bibliothèque Payot, 1965.*

—— "L'Esthétique d'André Malraux," *Les Etudes classiques*, XVIII, No. 4 (October, 1950), 449–51.

—— "Valeurs et ambiguités de l'esthétique d'André Malraux," *Terre humaine*, No. 5 (May, 1951), pp. 7–19.

Sonnenfeld, Albert. "Malraux and the Tyranny of Time: The Circle and the Gesture," *Romanic Review*, LIV, No. 3 (October, 1963), 198–212.

Stéphane, Roger. "André Malraux," in *Portrait de l'aventurier: T. E. Lawrence, Malraux, von Salomon*. Paris: Bernard Grasset, 1965.

—— "Malraux et la révolution," *Esprit*, XVI, No. 149 (October, 1948), 461–68.

Stokes, Samuel E. "Malraux and Pascal," *Wisconsin Studies in Contemporary Literature*, VI, No. 3 (Autumn, 1965), 286–92.

Tarica, Ralph. "Imagery in the Novels of André Malraux: An Index with Commentary." Unpublished dissertation, Harvard University, 1966.

Vandegans, André. *La Jeunesse littéraire d'André Malraux*. Paris: Jean-Jacques Pauvert, 1964.

Wilkinson, David. *Malraux: An Essay in Political Criticism*. Cambridge, Mass.: Harvard University Press, 1967.

Wilson, Edmund. "André Malraux," in *Malraux*, ed. R. W. B. Lewis, pp. 25–30. Englewood Cliffs: Prentice-Hall, 1964.

III. WORKS ON METAPHOR

Brown, Stephen J., S.J. *The World of Imagery: Metaphor and Kindred Imagery*. London: Kegan Paul, Trench, Trubner & Co., 1927.

Day Lewis, C. *The Poetic Image*. London: Jonathan Cape, 1947.

Friedman, Norman. "Imagery," in *Encyclopedia of Poetry and Poetics*, ed. Alex Preminger, pp. 363–70. Princeton: Princeton University Press, 1965.

Hornstein, Lillian Herlands. "Analysis of Imagery: A Critique of Literary Method," *PMLA*, LVII, No. 3 (September, 1942), 638–53.

Jung, C. G. "Archetypes of the Collective Unconscious," in *The Basic Writings of C. G. Jung*, ed. Violet S. de Laszlo, pp. 286–326. New York: The Modern Library, 1959.

—— *Man and His Symbols.* New York: Doubleday & Co., 1964.

Richards, I. A. *The Philosophy of Rhetoric.* New York: Oxford University Press, 1936.

Spurgeon, Caroline F. E. *Shakespeare's Imagery and What It Tells Us.* New York: Macmillan, 1935.

Ullmann, Stephen. *The Image in the Modern French Novel.* New York: Barnes & Noble, 1963.

—— *Language and Style.* New York: Barnes & Noble, 1964.

—— *Style in the French Novel.* Cambridge: The University Press, 1957.

Wheelwright, Philip. *Metaphor and Reality.* Bloomington: Indiana University Press, 1968.

IV. GENERAL WORKS

Howe, Irving. *Politics and the Novel.* New York: Horizon Press, 1957.

Laing, R. D. *The Divided Self.* Baltimore: Penguin, 1966.

Lawrence, T. E. *Seven Pillars of Wisdom.* New York: Doubleday, 1966.

Lukács, Georg. *Théorie du roman.* Trans. J. Clairevoye. Paris: Gonthier, 1963.

Malraux, Clara. *Le Bruit de nos pas: Apprendre àvivre.* Paris: Bernard Grasset, 1966.

—— *Le Bruit de nos pas: Nos vingt ans.* Paris: Bernard Grasset, 1966.

—— *Portrait de Grisélidis.* Paris: Editions Colbert, 1945.

Nietzsche, Friedrich. *Thus Spoke Zarathustra.* Trans. R. J. Hollingdale. Baltimore: Penguin, 1964.

Pascal, Blaise. *Pensées.* Baltimore: Penguin, 1966.

INDEX

Trotsky, Leon: quoted on *C*, 11

Ullmann, Stephen: quoted, 4

Voix du silence: cited on subconscious in art, 6-8; on control in art, 7, 9; on reduction in art, 9; on schema in art, 10; on consciousness of self, 118, 170; on theory vs. practice in art, 161; on destiny, 176; on artist's domination of model, 179

Wager, theme of: in *C*, 18-21; in *VR*, 52-54, 168-69; in *CH*, 68-71, 170; in *NA*, 130; in *E*, 175

Water, theme of: in *TM*, 91-96, 173; in *E*, 102-5, 174-75; in *NA*, 122-23, 137, 140, 144, 149-50, 154